UNIVERSITY OF CALIFORNIA PUBLICATIONS IN HISTORY

VOLUME XLII

EDITORS
ENGEL SLUITER
W. N. DAVIS
GORDON GRIFFITHS

Tsarevna Sophia Alekseevna

RUSSIA UNDER TWO TSARS
1682-1689
THE REGENCY OF SOPHIA ALEKSEEVNA

BY

C. BICKFORD O'BRIEN

UNIVERSITY OF CALIFORNIA PRESS
BERKELEY AND LOS ANGELES
1952

UNIVERSITY OF CALIFORNIA PUBLICATIONS IN HISTORY
EDITORS (BERKELEY): ENGEL SLUITER, W. N. DAVIS, GORDON GRIFFITHS

Volume 42, pp. xiv + 1–178, frontispiece, 2 maps

Submitted by editors August 31, 1951
Issued June 18, 1952
Price, Paper, $2.50; cloth, $3.50

UNIVERSITY OF CALIFORNIA PRESS
BERKELEY AND LOS ANGELES
CALIFORNIA

◆

CAMBRIDGE UNIVERSITY PRESS
LONDON, ENGLAND

TO
M. I. O'B.

PREFACE

THE LATE seventeenth century, like the early eighteenth in Russian history, has been dominated largely by the figure of Peter the Great. Other arresting personalities have crossed the political scene, but the towering figure of the Great Tsar has thus far successfully subordinated them and given them importance only in relation to the events and developments of his spectacular career. Although it has generally been admitted that the generation before 1689 saw notable changes in national culture and important developments in Russian foreign relations, the dozen years between the reigns of Tsars Alexis and Peter have been slighted by most historians. An impression has long prevailed that these years represented a twilight period in Russian history, an interim between the Muscovite Russia of the early Romanovs and the "new" Russia of Peter the Great. It was recognized that individual Russians showed remarkable intellectual energies and interests during this period, and that the government, under Ukrainian and Polish influences, attempted a series of moderate reforms. But in general, the feeling has been that this was a time of ineffective government and military failures. After the feeble rule of Tsar Feodor (1676–1682), a quarrel over the succession developed, which, after a military uprising, culminated in a palace revolution and the quasi exile of young Tsar Peter. Although the crown was nominally shared by Peter and his elder brother Ivan, actual power rested thereafter in the hands of their ambitious sister, the Tsarevna Sophia Alekseevna. The failures of Sophia's regency, in turn, and her designs to remove Peter from the throne finally precipitated a coup d'état in which Peter, goaded to action through fear for his life, seized power and inaugurated the epoch which has brought him lasting fame.

These are over-all impressions formed from reading many accounts of Russian history of the late seventeenth century. Such impressions are misleading if not incorrect. The years 1682–1689 were of unusual interest in Russian history. In the realm of foreign affairs, a number of vital questions arose in connection with national boundaries and the advancement of Russian interests in both the eastern and western hemispheres. New trade and diplomatic relations were established with the nations of the East and the West. Internally, a number of reforms were effected. A strong impulse was given to education. The national propensity toward cultural isolation was attacked. Efforts were made to bring better order into internal trade and to landed property, and to free the state from an excessive dependence on foreign industry. Not only the events themselves but their relation to the reforms of Peter's epoch, gave extraordinary significance to the regency of Sophia.

A number of nineteenth-century historians gave attention to Sophia's regency but few attempted to show it as a comprehensive political segment. In 1856, P. K. Shchebal'skii published a short monograph, *The Regency of Tsarevna Sophia,* which dealt imaginatively with the political events of the regime but largely omitted the cultural and economic changes of the period and neglected the Far Eastern issue entirely. In "Moscow Rebellions at the end of the 17th Century," published in 1887 in the *Journal of the Ministry of National Instruction,* A. E. Belov gave attention to the Strel'tsy Revolt of 1682 and to the relation of the Tsarevna's party to that event but proceeded no further. E. F. Shmurlo in an article published in the same journal a year later examined in great detail the events leading to the fall of the regent's government in 1689. Solov'ev, Ustrialov, Stählin, and Brückner also have dwelt at length upon the political aspects of the period, and recent historians like Rozhkov and Bogoslovskii have analyzed it from the standpoint of particular phases of later seventeenth-century history. But the tendency to minimize the importance of Sophia's regency by merging it with the history of the preceding or succeeding period has continued. The regime has thus been portrayed as a prelude to Peter's reign, a time of reaction and political bungling that chiefly served to make the achievements of the succeeding generation appear more brilliant.

In this study, an attempt will be made to eliminate some of the false notions about Sophia's regime and to show it for what it was—a government of unusual distinction and promise, which pursued with intelligence and imagination the interests of Russia abroad and introduced reforms at home that are usually believed to have originated in succeeding generations.

This monograph is an outgrowth of graduate work at the University of California, Berkeley, with Professor Robert J. Kerner, who many years ago first inspired my interest in Russian history. To him I am indebted for suggesting the topic of this investigation and for many favors in connection with its composition.

I would like also to express my sincere thanks to Professor George V. Lantzeff, of the University of California, for his critical reading of the manuscript and for his helpful suggestions in the organization of materials. My gratitude also goes to Professor Oleg Maslenikov and to Mrs. Ludmilla Patrick of the Slavic Department at Berkeley, and to many other friends for suggestions and for aid in preparating the manuscript.

C. B. O'B.

University of California, Davis

CONTENTS
PART I: THE REGENCY BEGINS

CHAPTER   PAGE

I. The Setting   3

    The geographic outlines of Russia in the second half of the seventeenth century—Territorial deficiencies of the state—Muscovite social structure—Central administration—National economy—Social unrest—Problems of government in 1682

II. The Rise of the Tsarevna Sophia to Power   14

    The question of the succession—Political factions at court—The emergence of Tsarevna Sophia—The accession of Peter Alekseevich—The Strel'tsy revolt—Sophia's encounter with the Old Believers—The Khovanskii affair—The Strel'tsy subdued—The political retirement of Tsar Peter—Sophia's regency begins

PART II: INTERNAL DEVELOPMENTS

III. Seventeenth-Century Moscow and the West   43

    General character of the intellectual ferment in Russia—Principal schools of the late seventeenth century—Silvester Medvedev—Sophia's interest in learning—Prince Vasily V. Golitsyn—The growth of the schism—The clash between Medvedev and the Graecophiles—Founding of the Moscow Academy—The regency and the reform movement

IV. Changes in National Economy   62

    The gradual shift from domestic economy to trade capitalism—The predominance of agriculture—The government's need for greater income—Principal sources of national revenue—Obstacles to domestic and foreign trade—The interest of all classes in trade—Prices—Coinage—Main categories of traders—Centers of trade—Communal production—Internal trade policy—Foreign trade policy—Fugitive peasants—The regency's effort to bring order into land tenure—Completing the national census

PART III: FOREIGN AFFAIRS

V. The "Eternal Peace" with Poland   85

    Limited character of Russian foreign relations—European tensions of the early eighties—The Turkish advance—The basis of Russian foreign policy in Europe—Russia as a potential ally of the West against the Turk—The Polish and Austrian missions to Moscow, 1684—Problems of an agreement with Poland—The Polish embassy of 1686—The Treaty of "Eternal Peace"—The Dolgorukii mission to France and Spain, 1687—Moscow's failure to enlarge the anti-Turkish coalition—The Sheremetev mission to Vienna—Significance of the peace with Poland

Contents

CHAPTER	PAGE
VI. The Treaty of Nerchinsk	105

The pattern of Russian advance in Asia—Russian expansion along the Amur—Moscow's early failures to establish relations with China—The difficult position of the eastern ostrogs, 1682—The Chinese ultimatum of 1683—Golitsyn's cautious policy toward China—The undeclared war, 1685–1686—End of the siege of Albazin—The Golovin mission—Terms of the Treaty of Nerchinsk—Importance of the treaty in Russian history

PART IV: THE LAST YEARS

VII. The Fall of the Tsarevna Sophia's Government	125

Preparations for the Crimean war, 1686–1687—Physical and political obstacles of campaigning against the Crimea—Failure of the Russians to engage the Tatars—End of the first campaign—Growing political tensions in Moscow—Political necessity for a second campaign—Vienna's desire to end the war with Turkey—Preparations for a second campaign, 1688–1689—Golitsyn's indecisive encounters with the Tatars—Negotiations before Perekop—Failure of the second campaign—Golitsyn's return to Moscow—Sophia's efforts to glorify the campaign—Growing opposition of the Naryshkins to the regency—Peter's "flight" to Troitsa-Sergeiev monastery—Sophia's loss of followers—End of the regency

VIII. The Regency of the Tsarevna Sophia Alekseevna: An Appraisal	147

Sophia's regency in Russian cultural history—Economic trends of the late seventeenth century—Their relation to the regency—Growth of foreign relations under Sophia—Conclusion

BIBLIOGRAPHICAL ESSAY	155
BIBLIOGRAPHY	159
INDEX	173

ILLUSTRATIONS

Portrait of the Regent Sophia Alekseevna, from Charles Gavard, *Galeries historiques de Versailles*, 1838 . . . . . . *frontispiece*

Genealogical Chart of the House of Romanov, 1613–1762 . . . 16

Map 1. Russian settlements in the Amur River Area in the Late Seventeenth Century 108

Map 2. The Ukraine and the Crimea in the Late Seventeenth Century 126

"Sophia enjoyed all the honors of a sovereign; she was possessed of good understanding, and some wit; made verses in the Russian language, and both spoke and wrote extremely well. These talents were set off by an agreeable person, . . ."—Voltaire

" . . . never had there been such wise government in the Russian State; and during the seven years of her rule the whole state did come to a flower of great wealth, . . ."—Prince Boris I. Kurakin

Part I
THE REGENCY BEGINS

ABBREVIATIONS

A.A.E.	*Akty arkheograficheskoi ekspeditsii*
A.I.	*Akty istoricheskie*
A.R.I.	*Akty Rossiiskoi Imperii*
Chteniia	*Chteniia v imperatorskom obshchestve istorii i drevnostei rossiiskikh pri moskovskom universitete*
D.A.I.	*Dopolneniia k aktam istoricheskim*
D.R.V.	*Drevniaia rossiiskaia vivliofika*
P.S.Z.	*Polnoe sobranie zakonov rossiiskoi imperii s 1649 goda*
R.I.B.	*Russkaia istoricheskaia biblioteka*
S.G.G.D.	*Sobranie gosudarstvennykh gramot i dogovorov*
Vremennik	*Vremennik imperatorskago moskovskago obshchestva istorii i drevnostei rossiiskikh*
Zh.M.N.P.	*Zhurnal ministerstva narodnago prosveshcheniia*

CHAPTER I
THE SETTING

RUSSIA in the period immediately preceding the reign of Peter the Great was in a state of flux. Changes in such vital spheres of national life as education, taxation, trade, and defense, as well as the foreign relations of Russia had been in progress throughout the seventeenth century. But the shifting areas of emphasis in domestic reform and the rapidity of change in foreign relations gave special interest and importance to the third quarter of the century. Mild reforms in domestic affairs and foreign relations had been undertaken by Peter's two predecessors, Tsar Alexis (1645–1676) and Tsar Feodor (1676–1682). The regency of Tsarevna Sophia Alekseevna (1682–1689) brought the nature of reform into sharper focus and provided an immediate base for the more spectacular changes of the epoch of Peter's personal rule (1689–1725). Russia's deep-rooted problems and the changes associated with Sophia's regency bore a special relationship to Peter's reforms. Indeed, the reforms of Peter take on an evolutionary rather than a revolutionary character as the changes effected during Sophia's regime are examined closely. Peter increased the tempo of change in Russia but, contrary to the popular belief long held, created no abyss between the old Russia and the new. In almost every direction—as will be shown by the accomplishments of Sophia's regency—he accelerated rather than inaugurated changes in the reform of Russian national institutions and policies.

By mid-seventeenth century Russia had already acquired the dimensions of a world power. In size, geography, and natural resources it was a land of superlatives—giant rivers and inland lakes, vast forests, majestic steppes and mountain ranges, rich untapped mineral deposits. In Europe the national frontiers stretched from the Barents Sea in the Northwest to the mouths of the Don and Volga rivers in the Southwest. In Asia, the Siberian segment of the country extended roughly from the Arctic Circle in the Northwest to the Kirghiz Steppe in the south and in the Far East from the Bering and Okhotsk seas to the Shilka River and Lake Baikal. Russia's expanse across Eurasia, aside from trade, however, gave it no great immediate advantage. Much of the total land mass was tundra, taiga, and steppe and remained sparsely populated. The heterogeneous population included many non-European peoples whose political ties with Moscow were loose and unreliable. In the temperate region of European Russia the boundaries remained vulnerable to attack from hostile neighbors. A Baltic or Black Sea littoral had not yet been won. Russia had no direct round-the-year access to the great western seas and oceans. In Asia, Russian boundaries extended either into the frigid zones or into areas so poorly defined as to discourage stability and peaceful settlement. In short, the country had distinct physical and political-geographical handicaps in spite of its gigantic size and abundant natural resources.

Because of these deficiencies Russia's desire for territorial adjustments remained strong in the seventeenth century. Long-range plans had sought to promote such adjustments. Russian designs in the west centered on the acquisition of outlets to the Baltic Sea and the stabilization of the Ukrainian frontier, the latter ostensibly to accommodate the Cossacks in their long-standing quarrels with the Tatars. Progress toward the Baltic, however, had been slow. The advance southward toward the Crimea was more promising. The eastern Ukraine and the Smolensk region had been a part of Poland until 1667, when they were incorporated into Russia under terms of an armistice, the Truce of Andrusovo. A peace settlement was needed to confirm the territorial cession. The extension of Russia's control over the western Ukraine and that part of the southeast Ukraine known as the Zaporozh'e remained to be accomplished. These developments increased the opportunities for Russian conflicts, whether with the Poles, the Tatars of the Crimea, or the Ottoman Turks (the overlords of the Tatars).

Russian ambitions in the east pointed toward the Amur River. A treaty was needed with the Chinese empire to settle the issue of the boundary between the two states. Sweeping Russian advances between 1607 and 1648 along the Enisei and Lena river basins matched the earlier similar strides along the Ob' and Irtysh rivers between 1585 and 1604. Penetration eastward to the Irtysh, Ob', Enisei, and Amur rivers brought the Russians into contact with the Mongols over a wide area and with the Chinese empire. This penetration precipitated serious conflicts, especially in the area of disputed ownership between the Shilka and Argun rivers.

The centrifugal expansion of Moscow and the incorporation of many non-Russian peoples into the Russian realm coincided in time with the emergence, on a national scale, of grave social-economic stresses. The explanation of these disturbances cannot easily be deduced, but they largely stemmed from the corrosive social inequalities that grew worse in the seventeenth century, and from the costly and inefficient national administration so characteristic of the bureaucracies of that century.

While masses of the people suffered very distressing social-economic restrictions, the government sustained acute shortages of revenue which periodically encouraged it to adopt questionable financial expedients.

Russian society in the seventeenth century consisted of three main categories, each of which had a larger or smaller number of subdivisions. At the top stood the ruling class—the nobility and the higher clergy. The nobility was subdivided into almost a dozen ranks.[1] The highest nobles were the descendants of the boyars and of the old princely families who held patrimonial landed estates (*votchinas*). Below them were the various classes of lesser gentry who held landed estates (*pomesties*) in return for public service. The clergy had representatives in all groups. The princes of the church belonged to the ruling class; the clergy of the towns to the small middle class; the parish priests and monks to the great mass of underprivileged.

Below the ruling class were the underprivileged or nonprivileged classes. The merchants, the artisans, and special categories of the town population comprised a small middle class. These had certain privileges and many obligations. The mass of the people were the peasants and serfs of whom there were several divisions. In the first half of the seventeenth century, however, there had been a general leveling of distinctions among the peasantry whereby most of the peasants became the serfs of private landowners whose control over them was extended to replace the several forms of dependency that had existed earlier.[2] Various classifications of peasants still existed, but the serf was the most numerous. In general, peasants on crown lands and those belonging to religious foundations continued to live under less harsh circumstances than the serfs on private estates. The non-Russian peoples, in turn, formed many distinctive minority groups, some of which enjoyed great freedom. These were subordinate to the central government yet had virtual autonomy. The Cossacks, for example, had personal freedom as well as political influence. At the base of the social structure stood the bondsmen and retainers (*kholopi*) who were virtually slaves without rights or obligations and who were the personal property of their owners. Their number in the seventeenth century was small and steadily declined.[3] In general, the bounds between neighboring groups of the population, though marked, were neither rigid nor insurmountable. The turbulent social-economic conditions of the times enabled changes in personal status to be made without too great difficulty.

---
[1] George V. Lantzeff, *Siberia in the Seventeenth Century*, pp. 6–7 n.
[2] B. D. Grekov ed., et al., *Istoriia SSSR*, I, 424.
[3] James Mavor, *An Economic History of Russia*, I, 92, 109.

Much of the widespread unrest during the seventeenth century came from the nature and policies of Russian administration and economy. In theory the government was still a patriarchal absolutism, though not in the sense of the tsarist votchina of the sixteenth century. Under the cautious leadership of the early Romanovs, administrative practices that had long proved inefficient and costly, were maintained.[4]

The tsar, in theory, acted as the complete and sole master of the realm. Tradition and convention had given his office an exalted character. The Russian people from the highest state official down to the kitchen menial occupied an almost servile position in relation to the crown. The obsequious attitude shown by the nobility toward the tsar, on occasion, resembled that observed toward the emperor of the medieval Byzantine empire. When performing the ceremony of obeisance to the tsar, the Russian boyars touched the ground with their foreheads. When addressing him, they not infrequently referred to themselves in the diminutive form as a symbol of inferiority.[5]

The tsar was not only the head of the state but in theory the chief coördinator of all departments of the government. In theory he controlled all appointments to office and was the final arbiter in matters of domestic and foreign policy. In practice he relied on his advisors, on the Boyar Duma, and on the central government offices (*prikazes*) to carry out the administrative functions. His chief advisors were often selected from his own family circle or from that of the tsaritsa. At times they exercised great influence in political affairs. On ordinary matters the tsar took their counsel and reached decisions without further advice. But on larger questions of national import he relied on the Boyar Duma and on the Raspravnaia Palata (Chamber of Settlement or Adjustment), a standing committee of the Duma, for recommendations in coming to decisions. From the Duma, executive officers also were selected to serve as military governors (*voevodas*) of the towns and as heads of the offices of the central government. The Raspravnaia Palata exerted a growing influence in administrative affairs in the late seventeenth century and served to unify the work of the prikazes and to control the appointment of voevodas to office.[6]

---

[4] P. Shchebal'skii, *Pravlenie Tsarevny Sofii*, p. 71.
[5] "Ivashka" or "Artemoshka," for example, was used. Matveev, a prominent minister of Tsar Alexis, in appealing to Tsar Feodor for clemency after his exile from the court, slavishly addressed his sovereign in these words: "We humbly beseech you, we your slave, Artemoshka Matveev, with the lowly worm, my small son, Andriushka, before the high throne of your royal Majesty, bowing our faces to the face of the earth ... beg you not to destroy our hope...." A. S. Matveev, *Istoriia o veninnom zatochenii blizhniago boiarina Artemona Sergievicha Matveeva*, pp. 146 ff.
[6] Lantzeff, *op. cit.*, pp. 16–17.

The role of the prikazes in government was most important. The bulk of administrative labors fell upon them. These central offices, of which there were between thirty and forty in number, roughly corresponded to the departments or ministries of a later time.[7] They had originally attended to the affairs of the princely household and even in the late seventeenth century continued to perform many such duties.[8] But their primary function was to perform special types of government business throughout the state and to administer the affairs of certain territories such as Kazan and Novgorod. Their responsibilities were not always clearly delimited. The prikazes, having grown spontaneously rather than by thoughtful planning, had duties that often overlapped. Often their secondary duties had come to overshadow their original functions. The government by prikazes was a costly one. It developed into a vast bureaucracy which was not easily controlled and which was subject to corrupt influences.

Russia felt the impact of mercantilist principles on its national economy and to a limited extent adopted them. Here again the reaction was similar to that of most European states of the seventeenth century. Although the country was predominately agricultural, the importance of trade and industry to the state had become steadily more apparent. The country was still regarded, in the last analysis, as the heritable property of the tsar. The right to possess and cultivate land and to engage in trade came from the sovereign. Production, trade, and such industry as existed, developed almost entirely within the controls exercised by a small, privileged group of merchants and members of the trade associations known as "hundreds." All these and others bore a servile relationship to the tsar.

Russian trade and industrial enterprise suffered from many restrictions in the seventeenth century. The government's growing need for revenue encouraged a more systematic collection of customs and excise duties in the seventeenth than in the sixteenth century, a factor that weighed heavily on the small urban trader and artisan.[9] The wealthier

---

[7] G. Kotoshikhin, *O Rossii v tsarstvovanie Aleksiia Mikhailovicha*, p. 131; Lantzeff, *op. cit.*, p. 3.

[8] The *Khlebnoi Prikaz* or Grain Court, for example, prepared bread and pastries for the imperial household. The Office of Secret Affairs (*Prikaz Tainnykh Del*) administered the tsar's private landholdings and performed such extraordinary functions as administering his extensive falconry establishment. A. I. Zaozerskii, "Tsar Aleksei Mikhailovich v svoiem khoziaistve," in A. M. Bol'shakov, *Istoriia khoziaistva Rossii*, I, 194.

[9] P. Miliukov, *Gosudarstvennoe khoziaistvo Rossii v pervoi chetverti XVIII Stoletiia i reforma Petra Velikago*, p. 77.

merchants enjoyed special privileges.[10] Taxes on trade were heavy.[11] The artisan had to meet the trade competition of the peasant craftsmen who worked on the estates of private landowners and had to accept a smaller reward for his skilled labor or his finished product than was just. The mounting costs of production and an unstable currency further handicapped the small trader and craftsman.

The unredressed grievances of these categories of the urban population came to the front in the disturbances of the late 1640's and early 1660's.[12] In June, 1648, Tsar Alexis, en route to Moscow from a religious pilgrimage, was confronted by a group of urban petitioners. They vehemently complained against the extortions of one of his principal favorites, the entrepreneur Morozov. Instead of redressing their grievances, Tsar Alexis ordered them dispersed with knouts. Thereupon they proceeded to the capital and vented their wrath by attacking the homes of several prominent officials of the government. This event touched off a chain of outbreaks in Kursk, Ustiug, and other towns. The spirit of disorder abated slowly, and subsequent outbreaks in Pskov and Novgorod had to be more vigorously suppressed.[13] In July, 1662, outbreaks known as the "copper riots" occurred in Moscow and Kolomenskoe Village. A mob representing segments of the lower urban population demanded that certain unpopular boyars be delivered into their hands, that taxes be reduced, and that copper coinage be abolished. The intimidated tsar momentarily yielded and promised a number of concessions to the insurgents, but later reversed himself and successfully quelled the disturbance with the aid of Strel'tsy regiments. Copper money, nevertheless, was abolished.[14]

As in most parts of Western Europe, the governing classes in Russia still held the mass of the people in serf bondage. But whereas serfdom in the West was declining, in Russia it had not yet attained its peak. The Law Code of 1649, in fact, had legalized the institution, sanctioning new restrictions that extended the control of the landowner over the serf. The policies of the government further strengthened serf landholding by transforming thousands of small free landholders (tiaglo-paying households of the sixteenth century) into serfs.

The lot of the privately owned serf was especially onerous. The amount of land assigned him for the support of his household was in-

---
[10] G. Kotoshikhin, *op. cit.*, p. 157.
[11] P. I. Lyashchenko, *History of the National Economy of Russia*, p. 266.
[12] S. F. Platonov, *Moskva i Zapad*, p. 111.
[13] V. O. Kliuchevsky, *A History of Russia*, III, 133–138.
[14] A. Brückner, "Das Kupfergeld in Russland 1656–1663," *Finanzgeschichtliche Studien*, pp. 62–70.

adequate; the labor required by the landlord tended to increase; and the taxes imposed upon him in kind and in money as rent and as household tax were heavier in the seventeenth than in the previous century. The amount of ploughland given the serf for his personal use toward the end of the seventeenth century was from 20 to 25 per cent less per individual than it had been in the census of 1646. The demands of the master's household became increasingly burdensome. The sum total of taxes, particularly the hearth-money tax (*podvornaia povinnost*) collected from the peasant also increased. Unable to cope with such handicaps the serf found expression for his anguish in the support of local uprisings, in flight to frontier regions, and in sympathy for religious extremism. To escape the resurgence of feudal oppression, many peasants fled to the frontier, joined the Cossacks, and participated in local uprisings against landowners.[15]

The most striking example of peasant unrest was the uprising (1667–1671) led by Stenka Razin. Razin, an ataman of the Don Cossacks and a combination of freebooter and popular agitator, became the leader of a vast Cossack and peasant uprising in the late sixties. His championship of the interests of the poor and oppressed against the landowner and tsarist official won him many followers. Masses of peasants, malcontents, and many non-Russians joined his Cossack supporters. During 1667–1668, detachments of Razin's Cossacks raided the Volga, the Don, the Urals, and the Caspian Sea. By 1670, the movement had acquired the character of a peasant war, covering a wide area of the Volga region and spreading north to the Oka River. Many towns, including Tsaritsyn and Astrakhan, were captured by the insurgents and others were besieged. Tsarist forces gradually overcame Razin, however, and recaptured many of his strongholds along the right bank of the Volga. The leader himself was taken captive in April, 1671, and executed the following June in Moscow. Soon afterward the movement collapsed.[16] It was the most formidable peasant uprising of the century and clearly demonstrated the wide scope of peasant unrest.

In addition to the hardships imposed upon its laborers, Russian agriculture in general suffered handicaps. The primitive methods of land cultivation, the inequalities in the distribution of land, and the growing use of serf labor in manufacturing combined to produce lower returns from agriculture than would be expected of a country with the population, area, and resources of Russia. Even on the crown lands, which were cultivated with the best equipment available and occasionally under the

---
[15] Grekov, *op. cit.*, I, 421–424.
[16] Grekov, *op. cit.*, pp. 463–468; Lyashchenko, *op. cit.*, p. 199.

guidance of foreign technicians, agricultural production was disappointing.[17]

Closely related to the unhappy position of the peasantry and the urban trading population was the decline in status of the Strel'tsy. Numbering some fifty thousand men in 1676, the Strel'tsy[18] were a permanent hereditary branch of the army, introduced into Russia during the reign of Ivan IV. The government had granted them certain privileges including the right to dwell in private homes rather than in barracks, to engage in petty trade, and to make alcoholic beverages for their own use. During the first half of the seventeenth century they had performed their various duties creditably. In wartime they served in the field as infantrymen and took part in the defense of towns. In time of peace they served as guards, gatekeepers, policemen, and firemen. Their privileged position continued in the later seventeenth century but was slowly undermined by a combination of circumstances.

The attitude of the government toward the Strel'tsy gradually changed. As war and the preparation for war were the order of the day throughout Europe, the need for a better trained, more modern soldiery than the Strel'tsy was felt in Russia. The morale of the organization also began to decline. Certain regiments, particularly in Moscow, took a casual attitude toward their responsibilities. Discipline in the service became lax. The government's insistence that the Strel'tsy perform their military duties more faithfully, giving greater attention to training and conduct, was unheeded by particular regiments. At the same time the administration of the Strel'tsy fell into neglect. Gross corruption and cruelty in discipline embittered relations between the higher ranking officers and their command. Disorders and even mutinies sometimes occurred.

During the reign of Tsar Feodor, Strel'tsy regiments frequently petitioned the government to punish officers found guilty of irregularities. The government failed to respond properly to these requests or to check a repetition of the abuses. Punishments were sometimes meted out to the petitioners rather than to the officers concerned, and in other cases officers found guilty were chastised in a perfunctory manner. The rank and file Strel'tsy thus became another disgruntled element of the population. If given an opportunity they too could become a source of internal danger.

---

[17] Zaozerskii, *op. cit.*, pp. 194–195.
[18] Singular *strelets* (shooter); Lantzeff, *op. cit.*, p. 66, "named because their chief weapons were muskets, although they were armed also with swords, pikes, and battle-axes. Some of them were mounted, but the majority were infantrymen"; N. A. Rozhkov, *Russkaia istoriia i sravnitel'no-istoricheskom osveshchenii*, V, 59–61.

In the religious sphere storm clouds also darkened the horizon. The great religious controversy which stemmed from the church reforms initiated by Patriarch Nikon in the 1650's remained unsettled. The differences between the Church and the government had been settled by a compromise in 1666–1667 which condemned Nikon for attempting to subordinate the royal power to that of the Church, but which retained the revisions in the service books and rituals that he had sponsored. The latter decision offended a large group of earnest believers within the Church who regarded the religious revisions as erroneous and sinful. These dissenters (*raskol'niki*) became known as the Old Believers (*starovery*). The Nikonian changes, it appeared, persuaded them that the state was seeking to advance its control over every phase of Russian life including religion. They believed that the tsar and the patriarch, forgetting the true Christian faith, had succumbed to the false theological influences of Byzantium, which already had suffered divine displeasure for its sins by the Turkish conquest of 1453.[19]

So strong was this conviction that rather than accept the religious changes they separated themselves from the Church. This action constituted a schism which, despite a vigorous governmental policy of extirpation, grew into a large-scale revolt. The Old Believers were more than mere obscurantists who struggled against the minor corrections of liturgical practices. Their opposition was as much against the power of the government to compel changes in religious convictions as in their disagreement over the spelling of the Savior's name and the use of two or three fingers when giving a blessing. Like the Strel'tsy, they too formed a nucleus around whom those who struggled for economic prosperity, social equality, and political liberty might gather.[20]

As often occurs in opposition movements the principal force behind the schism was a negative one; there was zeal in opposing changes and little else. The Old Believers lacked organization, unity of purpose, adequate restraint, and leadership. Its martyrs were many and its effective leaders were few. Strong factions within the general group appeared, such as those who regarded themselves as prophets (*khlysty*), those who

---

[19] S. Melgunov, "Les mouvements religieux et sociaux en Russie aux XVIIe–XVIIIe siècles," *Le Monde Slave*, XII (Dec., 1926), p. 392: "The reforms of Nikon in all domains of religious life were only the servile copy of the patterns of Byzantium, the transfer to Moscow of Byzantine practice of that time. Considering this character, the reforms of the Patriarch Nikon were not convincing to the great majority of the representatives of Muscovite society."

[20] Melgunov, *op. cit.*, p. 384: "All that is old becomes a synonym for liberty and emancipation from the social yoke."

repudiated the priesthood entirely (*bezpopovshchina*), and those who sought a compromise between orthodoxy and complete anticlericism (*popovshchina*).[21]

The fervor of these religious sects won many sympathizers and adherents. There were wholesale movements of Old Believers to frontier districts along the Viatka, Tura, Volga, and Don rivers, where the old beliefs were openly practiced. Some of the schismatics adopted extreme ascetic practices—self-flagellation, ordeal by fire, mass suicide. Such actions repelled some persons who had earlier sympathized with the general ideas of the Old Believers. To others, they appeared as pathetic protests against the unpopular changes that the government was ruthlessly effecting in religion no less than in other spheres of Russian life.

Thus Russia faced many problems in the third quarter of the seventeenth century. The pattern of its eastward expansion, its unfulfilled territorial designs, and the numerous social tensions existing throughout the state called for bold decisions in both foreign and domestic policy. The social disorders of the mid-century testified to the existence of some feeling among the people that the authority above them might be fallible. By the late seventeenth century this viewpoint left its mark in an altered relationship between the tsar and his people. In theory, the tsar remained free of all legal and moral limitations on his authority. In practice, he ceased to direct the entire life of the realm, or to speak alone for the interest of his subjects. His government came to be increasingly influenced from outside, particularly from the landholding nobility and the trading-industrial elements of the population. Petitioning the government for changes in policy and for the alleviation of particular distresses had become a common political practice.[22]

Tsars Alexis Mikhailovich and Feodor Alekseevich had felt the urgency for changes and had attempted to institute moderate reforms in trade, religion, and education. But their efforts were principally designed to placate small segments of the population rather than to dispose of the larger problems that adversely affected the mass of the people. During the reign of Tsar Alexis great strides had been made in Russia's eastward advance and in extending the Russo-Polish frontier westward. It remained for succeeding regimes to consolidate these changes and to follow up Russia's territorial designs.

To summarize—the most critical social turmoils the government faced

---

[21] P. Miliukov, *Ocherki po istorii russkoi kultury*, II, 70–74, discusses the various religious sects; F. A. Brokhaus, I. A. Efron, *Entsiklopedicheskii slovar*, XXVI, 291, and XXXVII, 402, summarize the origin of each in the seventeenth century.

[22] Platonov, *op. cit.*, pp. 110–113.

in the 1680's concerned the serf, the Strel'tsy, and the Old Believers. Of these the runaway serf posed the gravest problem. The serf had resisted the further decline in his social status in various ways but perhaps in no way more effectively than in fleeing the estate of the landlord for a new life in frontier lands. Because the serf was essential to agriculture and to many types of industrial enterprise, this evacuation of labor from the land threatened the national economy with serious new dislocations. The unrest among the peasantry was paralleled by disturbances among the lower urban population and the Strel'tsy. The government's need for revenue encouraged taxes to be collected more zealously in the second half of the seventeenth century than in the first. This worked to the disadvantage of the small trader whose margin of profit was less than that of his competitor, the wealthy merchant. The artisan in turn felt the competition of the peasant craftsman whose labor and skill were exploited by the landlord on private estates. Among the Strel'tsy a problem had arisen involving discipline and morale, and the relations between the government and the Strel'tsy had steadily declined. Because it was now the principal law-enforcing agency of the state as well as the main branch of the standing army, the disaffection of the Strel'tsy, particularly in Moscow, represented a dangerous national development. In the religious sphere a storm of controversy had broken in the fifties which was still unresolved in the eighties. The Old Believers, convinced that the state was advancing its control over the Church as over every other phase of life, constituted a formidable religious minority which threatened to subvert political as well as spiritual authority. The religious controversy and the issues stemming from it affected all classes. Among the nobility and clergy it renewed agitation over the orientation of national culture and education. Among the lower urban population and the peasantry it added a spiritual element to the already smoldering unrest felt in other spheres of national life. How the government that entered power in 1682 would deal with these long-standing issues will be discussed in the following chapters.

CHAPTER II

THE RISE OF THE TSAREVNA SOPHIA TO POWER

THE RUSSIAN sovereigns of the seventeenth century followed an unusual practice for monarchs of the time—selecting their consorts from within, rather than from without, the state. Whether because of loose diplomatic ties with foreign powers and fear of establishing family connections with hostile dynasties abroad, or such factors as insurmountable religious differences and false pride in making alliances with lesser powers, the rulers of Moscow invariably selected their tsaritsas from the Russian nobility. They did not exploit marriage, as was customary in Western Europe, to further dynastic or national ambitions. This spared Russia from dynastic warfare and the costly intrigues common to the pursuit of family interests at that time, but it perpetuated Moscow's isolation from Western Europe and periodically created political tensions at home difficult to resolve.[1]

Marriages between the tsars and the daughters of prominent boyar families more often than not projected various members of the tsaritsa's families into public life. The government frequently became embroiled

---

[1] The printed sources published by various agencies of the tsarist government have yielded only a small amount of material for this chapter. Volume X of *Dopolneniia k aktam istoricheskim* (Supplements to Historical Acts) and volume IV of *Akty sobrannye v bibliotekakh i arkhivakh rossiiskoi imperii, arkheograficheskoiu ekspeditsieiu imperatorskoi akademii nauk* (Acts collected in the libraries and archives of the Russian Empire by the Archeographic Expedition of the Imperial Academy of Sciences) have much material on the Strel'tsy uprising but little else for the year 1682. *Polnoe sobranie zakonov rossiiskoi imperii*, II (Full collection of laws of the Russian Empire), has a number of decrees relating to Prince Ivan Khovanskii and the pacification of the city of Moscow after the Strel'tsy rebellion of 1682 but throws little light on the larger events of that year.

For a fuller picture of the immediate background of the rise of Tsarevna Sophia to power, reliance must, therefore, be placed on secondary materials. Of a number of works published before 1917, those of Aristov, Belov, Shchebal'skii, and Solov'ev, cited in the footnotes below and in the bibliographical essay at the end of this work, deal most fully with the subject. Little in fact has been added to their description of the political events of 1682 nor is there any indication that serious alterations will occur in their combined analyses of the principal developments of that year. Of the recent historians who deal with the seventeenth century, N. A. Rozhkov, K. Stählin, and M. M. Bogoslovskii give greater attention to the years 1682-1689 than most. Both Rozhkov and Stählin in their histories of Russia devote much space to a reëxamination of the political intrigues and leaders of Sophia's regency. Rozhkov deals more sympathetically with Sophia's government than does Stählin. M. M. Bogoslovskii in the first volume of his biography of Peter the Great has a short chapter discussing the Strel'tsy uprising of 1682. His references to source materials are scanty. V. I. Lebedev in volume I of *Istoriia SSSR* (History of the USSR), edited by B. D. Grekov (1948), has a chapter on the growth of the Russian Empire. This also deals briefly with the government of Tsarevna Sophia.

[14]

in petty family quarrels. At the accession and marriage of a tsar, office and revenues were customarily provided not only for the tsaritsa's immediate relatives but for her friends and family retainers. The abuses inherent in this practice became aggravated at the close of the seventeenth century because of the dual marriages of the tsars. Both Tsars Alexis (1645–1676) and Feodor (1676–1682) were twice married. The political repercussions of Alexis' two marriages were still resounding at his death in 1676 and continued to plague the country throughout the reign of his successor, Tsar Feodor.

The immediate difficulty in 1682 was the matter of succession to the throne. All the elements of a troublesome dispute had arisen between two branches of the Romanov family—the Miloslavskiis and the Naryshkins. Tsar Alexis' first wife, Maria Il'inishna, belonged to the prominent Miloslavskii family. This marriage had given the tsar thirteen children—five sons and eight daughters. Of the five sons, three died in early childhood and the remaining two, Feodor and Ivan, had physical handicaps. Feodor, the more promising, ascended the throne in 1676— a gentle, temperate youth of fourteen, intellectually inclined, but a semi-invalid. His brother Ivan, in addition to several minor physical handicaps, was mentally deficient. Of the eight daughters little is known except for Sophia Alekseevna, as in the seventeenth century only the birth and death of tsarevnas evoked interest.

Upon the first marriage of Alexis the brother of Tsaritsa Maria, Prince Ivan Miloslavskii, appeared at court. Ivan proved to be an accomplished courtier and an able promoter of the Miloslavskii interests. For at least a dozen years (1659–1671) he had a preëminent political influence, as testified by the names of the various Miloslavskii relatives which so frequently appear in rosters of high public office. Alexander Miloslavskii became a court dapifer; Prince I. B. Miloslavskii served as voevoda of Kazan; and Ivan himself held numerous titles and positions.

Tsaritsa Maria died in 1669. Shortly after the tsar married Natalia Naryshkina, member of a noble but less illustrious family, regarded by many of the boyars as parvenus. This marriage created regrettable but understandable resentments on the part of the Miloslavskiis. Tsaritsa Natalia was a protégé of Artemon Matveev, a confidante of Tsar Alexis in his later years. Matveev had gradually displaced Ivan Miloslavskii as the principal figure at court. The position of the Naryshkins grew stronger in 1672 when Tsaritsa Natalia presented the tsar with a son, Peter. The obvious delight the tsar took in his healthy new offspring contrasted strongly with the concern he undoubtedly felt for the health

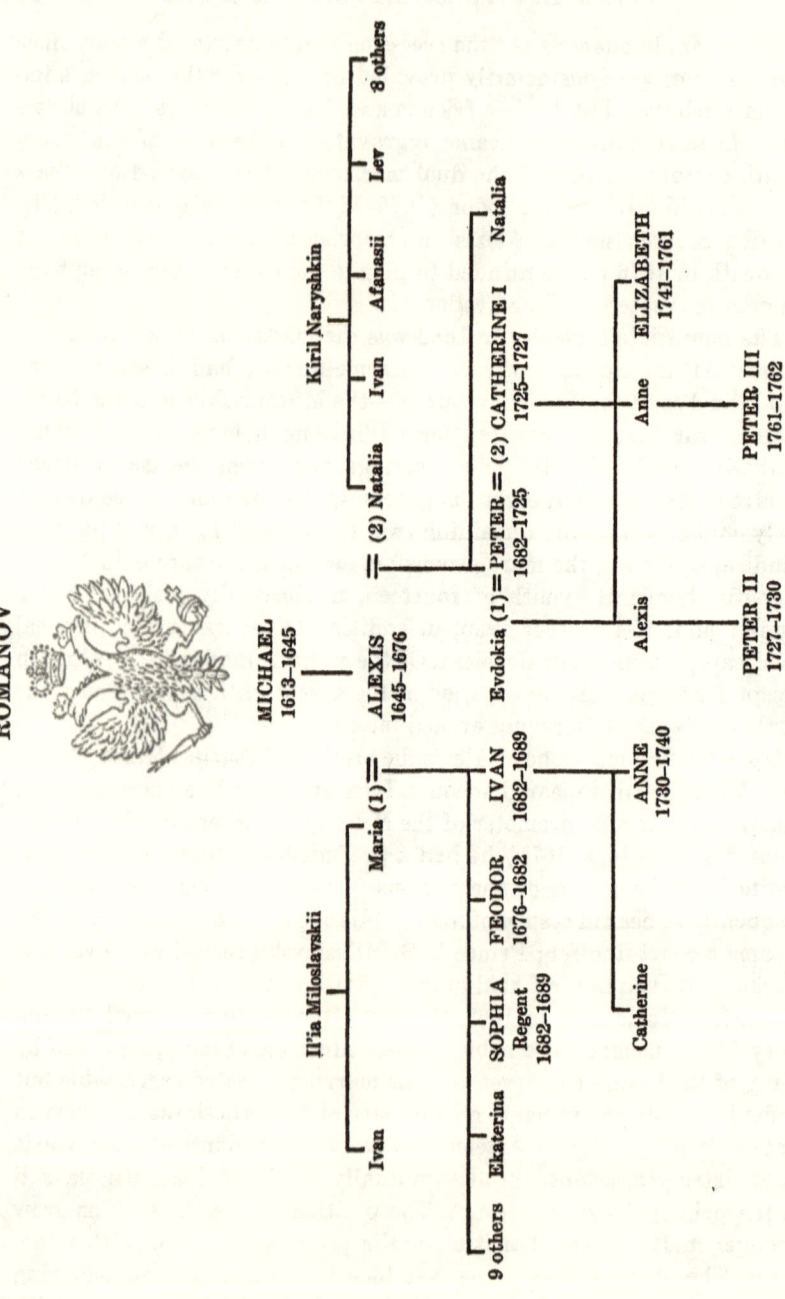

Genealogical Chart of the House of Romanov, 1613–1762

of the elder tsareviches by his former marriage.[2] A second child was born to Natalia and Alexis in 1674, Natalia Alekseevna. The influence of Matveev and the Naryshkins was now in the ascendant.

But their influence was short lived. Tsar Alexis died in 1676 and with the accession of his oldest living son, Feodor, the Miloslavskiis regained power. Feodor reinstated his uncle Ivan Miloslavskii at court and exiled Matveev, together with members of his family, to remote Pustozersk on the Mezen' River. Ivan Miloslavskii's second tenure of power, however, had a different character from the first. The young tsar divided his favors between his uncle, Ivan Miloslavskii, and a new group of courtiers led by Ivan Maksimovich Iazykov. He also failed to show the degree of bitterness toward the Naryshkins that other members of his family manifested. As Feodor's health declined and he produced no heirs, he even considered the advantage of naming his promising half brother Peter, rather than his full brother Ivan, as his successor. Such a suggestion, at least, appears to have been made shortly before the tsar's death in 1682, but it was not acted upon. In the last year of Feodor's reign, the Naryshkins enjoyed further advantage from the tsar's marriage to Martha Matveevna Apraksina, goddaughter of Matveev and relative of Ivan Iazykov. The new tsaritsa almost immediately arranged for the removal of Matveev from bleak Pustozersk to a gentler exile in Lukh, southeast of Kostroma. During the last months of Feodor's life the position of the Naryshkins was thus definitely improving.

By the spring of 1682, three political groups had emerged at court. Ivan Iazykov and his supporters, the Likhachevs, constituted the party in power. Iazykov was of humble, obscure origin but had skillfully advanced himself until he reached a position of great influence in 1681 upon the marriage of his relative, Martha Matveevna Apraksina and Tsar Feodor. His principal subordinate in power was the cupbearer, Semion Likhachev.

The second party at court was that of the Naryshkins. Seriously weakened by the exile of its able leader, Matveev, it was nevertheless strong in having the most popular candidate for the succession. During Matveev's exile, the Tsaritsa Natalia had assumed leadership of the party. She was an attractive, womanly figure, strong in her attachments and easily swayed by bolder spirits around her. The Naryshkins had meanwhile gathered support among the boyar families and counted

---

[2] Numerous stories and legends attended the birth of the Tsarevich Peter. One circulating among foreigners and the Moscow populace asserted that the somewhat ailing tsar was not the father of the vigorous infant, Peter. K. Stählin, *Geschichte Russlands von den Anfängen bis zur Gegenwart*, II, 1; N. Ustrialov, *Istoriia tsarstvovaniia Petra Velikago*, I, 1.

members of such prominent families as the Cherkasskiis, Troekurovs, Lykhovs, Urusovs, and Streshnevs among their adherents. In addition, the higher members of the clergy—including the Patriarch of Moscow, Joachim, the Metropolitan of Rostov, Ioann, and the leaders of the Troitsa-Sergeiev Monastery—inclined toward them.

Third of the political groups were the Miloslavskiis. Small in size and led by the aging Ivan Miloslavskii, warmly supported by numerous maiden sisters and aunts of the late tsar and by a few of the nobility—Prince B. M. Khitrovo, Prince V. V. Golitsyn, and Peter and Ivan Tolstoi—the hope of the party was the legal claim to the succession of the incompetent Tsarevich Ivan, full brother of Tsar Feodor, by right of seniority. A regency would inevitably be established for sixteen-year-old Ivan, under his uncle Ivan Miloslavskii or some other member of the Miloslavskii family.

In line with the secluded existence led by Russian women of gentility, the daughters of the tsar attracted little attention. Their rare appearance at court ceremonies, the infrequent references to them in official documents and registers and in the writings of Russian and foreign observers of the time, indicated their general inaccessibility as well as the public disinterest in them. Relegated to a part of the royal palace known as the *terem,* they led an almost cloistered existence. Unmarried, dedicated to time-consuming embroidery projects, making occasional religious pilgrimages, and indulging in petty gossip, they learned little of the larger events around them. When they went driving, their conveyance was shrouded with draw curtains. When attending church service, they moved along private galleries to that part of the edifice affording them maximum privacy. For a greater part of their lives, no male glance fell upon them.[3] Few, in fact, among the multitude of court officials ever caught sight of a daughter of the tsar. Even the tsar saw them infrequently—perhaps during an occasional feast day celebration or brief visit paid them in the terem.

In this intellectually stifling atmosphere of the Belvedere Palace terem, the third daughter of Alexis, the Tsarevna Sophia Alekseevna, was born September 17, 1657. The Court Record Book of that year announced her birth in simple terms, stating that "it was to be celebrated according to her rank."[4] The great Patriarch Nikon baptized her, and her name day provided an occasion for feasting and celebration in the capital.

---

[3] Peter K. Shchelbal'skii, *Pravlenie Tsarevny Sofii,* p. 9; "... passing their gloomy days in a monotonous succession, ... they were born, lived, and died knowing nothing of what occurred around them, and themselves unknown to anyone...."

[4] M. Pomialovskii, "Sofia Alekseevna," *Russkii Biograficheski Slovar',* XIX, 126.

The pattern of Sophia's childhood and youth varied only slightly from that of her sisters. She enjoyed good health, had a lively imagination, and early evidenced a keen grasp of things around her. Her father's appreciation of Western learning and culture caused him to permit a marked departure in the education usually provided for daughters of the royal family. For the first time, male instructors entered the terem. They came to instruct Sophia and her sisters in the humanities and arts. The famous scholar and monk, Simeon Polotskii, taught her languages. Karion Istomin and Silvester Medvedev taught her theology and were impressed by her serious effort to acquire knowledge, her rapid grasp of essential information, and her power of assimilation. Sophia's association with these men sharpened her desire for learning and for greater personal freedom.[5] During the reign of her brother Tsar Feodor, Sophia saw her uncle Ivan Miloslavskii more frequently, met Prince Vasilii V. Golitsyn and other nobles interested in Western learning. Conversations with them quickened Sophia's interest in political affairs and apparently awakened in her a desire to play a prominent role in impending events. At the age of twenty Sophia was among the best-informed women in Russia, with a growing concern for the political interests of her immediate family and a tendency to dramatize issues. In appearance she was short, her head somewhat large for her stature, her body inclined toward corpulence. Majesty of bearing, self-assurance, and a certain winsome, forthright manner were her greatest attractions.

The physical condition of Tsar Feodor, meanwhile, gave the Miloslavskiis grave concern throughout the winter of 1682. By April his sufferings had increased, and the remedies applied by his German physicians furnished him no relief. That his death was imminent could not be denied. With this development the efforts of the Miloslavskiis centered in more vigorously urging Feodor to name the Tsarevich Ivan as his successor. But Feodor could not decide. Tsarevich Peter, in contrast to Ivan, was extremely popular among all classes. Tsar Feodor made no attempt to curb this popularity. Under pressure from all sides to take action, he took none.

During the final weeks of Tsar Feodor's illness, the figure of Tsarevna Sophia—moving about the palace, entering and leaving her brother's bedchamber, consulting with the doctors, and exchanging ideas with dignitaries lingering in antechambers—became a familiar sight at court. It was Sophia to whom Feodor turned for support in his last hours of

---

[5] I. Zabelin, *Domashnii byt russkikh tsarits v XVI i XVII st.*, p. 174, "the terem had come into independent contact with scholars and bookmen even during the time of Tsar Feodor."

life. It was she who manifested the greatest tenderness toward him, sympathizing with his suffering and seeking to minister personally to all his needs. When not actually with him, she showed the greatest solicitude for his welfare. Her direct and practical ministrations were obviously more welcome to the suffering tsar than the tearful outbursts of his recent bride, Tsaritsa Martha. Sophia gradually assumed principal direction of her brother's welfare. She permitted few people to see him and succeeded in gaining the respect if not the affection of those nearest him. Moreover, it appeared that Sophia rather than her uncle Ivan was to become the leading figure in the Miloslavskii cause. The activities of the elder Miloslavskii had suddenly shown less energy than formerly. Whether through physical inertia, discouragement at events, or some unknown circumstance, his agitations on behalf of Tsarevich Ivan became more perfunctory than real.

On the afternoon of April 27, 1682, solemn strokes of the bell from the Ivan Velikii bell tower in the Kremlin proclaimed the death of Tsar Feodor. Less surprise was evinced among the Moscow populace than apprehension as to what the event might produce. For weeks, the declining condition of the tsar had been freely discussed in various quarters of the capital. Speculation, as always, arose as to the ultimate cause and manner of the death of the tsar, but there was even greater curiosity about the selection of his successor. Men and women of all ranks and parties quickly congregated in the palace square to hear some pronouncement. As custom demanded, the tsar's corpse was placed in state so that all might officially acknowledge his death and those of proper rank and distinction pay formal respect to the deceased. A queue formed of boyars, courtiers (*pridvornye chiny*), and nobles of lesser rank slowly filed past the bier.

Within a matter of hours Patriarch Joachim summoned a secret council of the higher clergy and such members of the Boyar Duma as could be located to determine how the matter of the succession might be resolved. It was agreed that the decision be referred to a National Assembly (*Zemskii Sobor*). A so-called session of the Sobor duly convened, though its composition has been a subject of much debate. At best it represented a rump rather than a true Sobor since its membership was largely limited to the nobility present in Moscow at the time.[6] The patriarch's predilection for the Naryshkins' candidate was obvious. He reminded those in attendance of the Tsarevich Ivan's affliction and

---

[6] Nikolai Kostomarov, *Ocherk domashnei zhizni i nravov velilorusskago naroda v XVI i XVII stoletiakh (izdanie tret'e) i starinnye zemskie sobory*, pp. 392–394.

poor health. In posing the question as to which of the tsareviches should be tsar, he asked his listeners to decide according to conscience. "Shall one or both rule? I ask and demand that you state the truth according to conscience."⁷

The will of the assembly came rapidly. Cries for Peter arose on all sides. "Let Peter be Tsar! Let Tsar Peter be sole autocrat of all Russia!"⁸ There were a few cries for Ivan from Miloslavskii partisans like Maxim Sambulov and the Tolstois, but they could scarcely be heard.⁹ The patriarch then proceeded to the palace and asked Peter to receive the scepter of his predecessors. The nine-year-old tsarevich, perhaps in confusion, at first questioned or protested his right to rule. But Joachim and his retinue reminded him of the will of the people and of his half brother's handicaps and concluded with an appeal, "Sovereign, don't scorn the prayers of your subjects!" Without awaiting a further reply from Peter, he blessed him and proclaimed him tsar. A council secretary then went out onto the Red Balcony and announced Peter's accession.¹⁰

The ease with which the Naryshkins had come to power might well have bewildered a less courageous spirit than that of the Tsarevna Sophia. She had anticipated that Tsarevich Ivan's seniority might carry sufficient weight to delay at least immediate action and cause the ultimate decision to be arrived at after careful deliberation. Such was not the case. The swift decision of the issue profoundly moved the tsarevna. Sophia asked the patriarch to explain the sudden turn of events. "This election is unjust," she declared, "Peter is young and impetuous. Ivan has reached his majority. He must be the tsar!" Joachim sought to explain how the matter had been determined, stating that there could be no alteration of the decision. "But let both rule at least!" pleaded Sophia. Joachim protested. "Joint rule is ruinous. Let there be one tsar! It is thus pleasing to God!"¹¹ Sophia, sensing that the occasion was unsuitable for the pursuit of her idea, appeared to let the matter rest. Outwardly resigning herself to developments, she and her sisters went sorrowfully to the new tsar to proffer their congratulations.

On the day of the late tsar's funeral, Sophia showed her readiness to break with tradition by participating actively in the religious ceremony. Ignoring an established custom which forbade daughters of the tsar from taking part in public processions, Sophia insisted on following her

---
⁷ M. M. Bogoslovskii, *Petr I*, I, 37.
⁸ Shchebal'skii, *op. cit.*, p. 17.
⁹ N. Aristov, *Moskovskiia smuty v pravlenie tsarevny Sofii Alekseevny*, p. 66.
¹⁰ Shchebal'skii, *op. cit.*, p. 18.
¹¹ Shchebal'skii, *op. cit.*, p. 19.

brother's casket through the streets into the cathedral, attracting wide attention by her cries of grief before and during the service. Moreover, during a pause in the ceremony she took occasion to launch an extreme charge against her enemies and to enlist aid against them. Her brother, she charged, had not died, but has been "poisoned by evil-wishing enemies."[12] The rift between the Miloslavskiis and Naryshkins had been brought to public attention. The Tsaritsa Natalia responded by departing early from the service with Tsar Peter. Her demand, issued somewhat later, that Sophia explain her conduct and the affront to the late tsar's memory, received only a casual reply which in no way eased the situation.

The accession of Tsar Peter was accompanied by the usual dismissal of the favorites of the previous regime. Those who had stood closest to the late tsar—I. M. Iazykov, the Likhachevs, and their relatives—soon lost office and influence.[13] The Naryshkins, in fact, showed unusual energy in exploiting the advantages of their newly won position. On the very day of Feodor's death, six Naryshkins were advanced to the rank of *spal'nik* (courtiers of the bedchamber). Ivan Naryshkin, the twenty-three-year-old brother of Tsaritsa Natalia, became a boyar; Afanasii Naryshkin, a privy chamberlain; Kiril Naryshkin, father of Tsarita Natalia, a cupbearer. Such honors assumed by recent "country gentry" astonished Moscow—accustomed though it was to rapid changes in personal fortune—and created speculation as to what glories might next be coveted. Artemon Matveev had been summoned to Moscow from exile. Many hoped that he would become the guiding influence in the new regime, but whether he could hold the ambitions of the younger Naryshkins in bounds remained questionable.

An additional element of concern meanwhile came from another source, the Strel'tsy. The chronic restlessness of the Strel'tsy had steadily mounted during the last months of Tsar Feodor's reign. The accession of the youthful Tsar Peter, and the unstable character of some of his immediate advisors, had encouraged the Strel'tsy to put forward bolder demands for relief from oppressions. On April 29, a petition from sixteen regiments regarding the abuses by nine Strel'tsy regimental commanders had been sent to the new tsar. Unless certain officers were brought to trial for cruelties and extortions, it was

---

[12] E. Belov, "Moskovskiia smuty v kontse XVII veka" in the *Zh.M.N.P.*, CCXLIX, 112. "Take pity on us poor orphans. We have neither father, mother, nor brother. Our elder brother, Ivan, was not elected to the throne, and if we have committed ill against you or against the boyars, let us go abroad with our lives to the lands of some Christian Prince."

[13] Aristov, *op. cit.*, p. 67.

threatened, the Strel'tsy would take direct action against them, killing them and pillaging their homes.[14] Tsaritsa Natalia, fearing a rebellion, acquiesced, ordering that the accused colonels be given over to them for punishment, and that the Strel'tsy be reimbursed for their losses by the treasury. This open bribe only led the Strel'tsy to make more serious demands. During the following days their morale rapidly declined. Meetings were held within regiments, where the regimental commanders and the commander in chief of the order, Prince Dolgorukii, were openly denounced.

The possibility of exploiting this unrest among the principal military force in Moscow did not long escape the attention of the Miloslavskiis. If the chronic grievances of the order could be turned against the Naryshkins, the latter might yet be removed from power. Justification for such action might be argued on the basis of national as well as party interests. The distinction between the merits of the two parties and their candidates was subordinate to the immediate question of the country's need for an able regent. No matter which of the tsareviches came to rule, for at least a decade actual power would be exercised for them. In personal promise, Peter had every advantage over Ivan, though his later attributes could hardly be foreseen in 1682. Years would elapse before his personal influence would be felt. To Sophia, a government dominated by the Naryshkins must clearly have appeared lamentable for both national and personal reasons. Tsaritsa Natalia from all indications would be as much influenced by her impulsive brother Ivan as by her able but aging advisor Matveev. The retention of power by the Naryshkins would inevitably involve the virtual exile of political figures like her uncle Ivan Miloslavskii, and others whose political experience and knowledge made them in Sophia's mind the superiors of any of the Naryshkins. Finally, from a personal standpoint a regency under Natalia would quite probably mean further social restrictions for Sophia, either in the terem or a convent, separated perhaps from beloved sisters and aunts and cut off from even the occasional meetings with men of learning whom she had come to revere. Against such a fate the tsarevna might well have chosen to rebel.

An intensive intrigue to undermine the Naryshkin government began almost immediately. From among the motley crowd—mendicant friars, petty craftsmen, beggars—which could always be found lingering near the imperial palace, additional supporters and agents were recruited. Liaisons were established with the more dissatisfied Strel'tsy regimental

---

[14] Aristov, *op. cit.*, p. 68.

commanders, such as Lieutenant Colonel Ivan Tsykler and Lieutenant Colonel Ivan Ozerov. Nightly rendezvous were held at the home of Ivan Miloslavskii to discuss means of promoting anti-Naryshkin sentiment. Miloslavskii agents wandered among the Strel'tsy suburbs in the evenings, inflaming the malcontents by forecasting even greater oppressions under Tsar Peter than under Tsar Feodor. What was to be expected, it was asked, from the reign of a child surrounded by enemies of the Strel'tsy, when in the reign of Tsar Feodor—a benevolent ruler and in his majority—such grave oppressions were perpetrated against the Strel'tsy? Extravagant stories were circulated among them and among the Moscow populace, that the Naryshkins had poisoned the late tsar, that Ivan Naryshkin himself aspired to the throne, and that the life of Tsarevich Ivan was endangered by the party in power. The plan of the Miloslavskiis, it appears, was (1) to incite a revolt of the Strel'tsy; (2) to turn the revolt against the Naryshkins and any prominent boyars opposing the Miloslavskiis; and (3) to elevate Tsarevich Ivan to the throne by deposing Peter altogether or by arranging a joint rule. A death list of forty-six names was drawn up, headed by the Naryshkins and Matveev and including many prominent officials. These were to be destroyed by the Strel'tsy.

The Naryshkin government failed to sense how strong the opposition had become. Their mentor, Matveev, journeyed pleasantly from his exile in Lukh to Moscow, arriving at the capital May 12, after visiting old friends like Iurii Dolgorukii, the hated oppressor of the Strel'tsy, and receiving flattering honors and attentions.[15] It was known that unrest existed among particular Strel'tsy regiments, but no precautions were taken against a possible outbreak.

On the morning of May 15—a day recalled somewhat ominously in Moscow[16]—alarm signals sounded throughout the capital. As principal guardians of the Kremlin, the Strel'tsy quickly rallied to arms. While aligning themselves in formation, certain Miloslavskii emissaries, Alexander Miloslavskii, Peter Tolstoi and others, appeared at the regimental courtyards with the information that the Tsarevich Ivan had been murdered—"strangled!" As if to confirm the announcement, great bells throughout the city tolled mournfully. The Strel'tsy, still disgruntled at many of their officers because of the treatment received at their hands, and contemptuous of a government which had already yielded to their demands, apparently decided that the moment for more drastic action

---

[15] Belov, *op. cit.*, p. 121.
[16] It was the day on which Tsarevich Dmitri, son of Ivan Groznyi, had been murdered.

had arrived. Many of the lesser leaders had been subsidized and indoctrinated with ideas inimical to the Naryshkins. The sudden announcement of Tsarevich Ivan's death, therefore, was readily accepted. Seeking no confirmation of their darkest suspicions, the Strel'tsy regiments hastened to the Kremlin, armed with lances, muskets, and various small arms. The Naryshkin leaders had passed the early morning hours at Granovitaia Palace in council with Matveev and had just ended their discussion. Matveev himself was on his way home when he learned that several Strel'tsy regiments had entered Belyi Gorod. Orders were immediately given to close all gates to the Kremlin. But they came too late. The Strel'tsy had already moved into the Kremlin and were veering toward the Great Palace.

The next few hours saw the beginning of one of Moscow's ugliest blood baths. The pillage and carnage that gripped the city lasted for a week. At least seventy prominent leaders in the new government were literally butchered—twelve boyars and well-known courtiers, three secretaries (*diaks*), many lesser nobles, as well as military and civil officials. Churches were desecrated, victims tortured, their corpses outraged, and their property seized. Most of the individuals named on the death list met a violent end—Matveev, three Naryshkins, Iurii Dolgorukii (commander of the Strel'tsy), Ivan Iazykov—to name only the most prominent. Those who remained were driven into hiding.

Entering the Kremlin, the Strel'tsy had proceeded to the Red Staircase (*Krasnoe Kryl'tso*) opposite the Cathedral of the Annunciation.[17] Upon reaching their destination, cries had arisen from the regiments demanding that the traitors—Artemon Matveev, Ivan Naryshkin, and others who had "destroyed" Tsar Feodor and the Tsarevich Ivan—be turned over to them. After a short delay, Tsaritsa Natalia appeared on the porch above the stairway leading young Tsar Peter and the Tsarevich Ivan. The shouting subsided. Several Strel'tsy clamored up the stairway and demanded of Tsarevich Ivan if he were the true Ivan Alekseevich and, if so, to name those who had molested him. Ivan's reply, if indeed he gave any, provided them no satisfaction. Many of the Strel'tsy accepted him as the true tsarevich and realized they had been deceived; others did not, but among the majority the spirit of revolt had proceeded too far to be halted by a vague answer. The ringleaders refused to let the matter rest. Cries ensued that certain boyars be delivered over for

---

[17] It was here that Ivan Groznyi had received Vasilii Shibanov, a messenger of Prince Kurbskii, who had taken refuge with the Poles. Ivan, thrusting the iron point of his staff through Shibanov's foot, listened to his message while leaning on the staff. There too, the false Dmitry had received petitioners during the Time of Troubles.

judgment, whereupon Iurii Dolgorukii and his son Mikhail summarily ordered the Strel'tsy to leave the Kremlin and return to their barracks. Within a matter of moments, young Dolgorukii was seized and hurled from the porch onto the pikes of Strel'tsy standing below, where he was promptly dispatched by vigorous halberd strokes. A wholesale massacre ensued. Artemon Matveev rushed to Tsar Peter but was quickly torn from him and cut down, meeting a fate similar to that of young Mikhail Dolgorukii. These moments undoubtedly jarred the mind of the youthful tsar and may in part explain his morbid will to mete out justice to the Strel'tsy in person after their second revolt a decade later.

While one group of Strel'tsy remained at the palace to search for various members of the Naryshkin family, a second roamed the city seeking other victims. Feodor Saltykov was murdered upon the mistaken assumption that he was Ivan Naryshkin. Prince Grigorii Romodanovskii, commander of the Russian forces at Chigirin, and Prince Iurii Dolgorukii were slain in their homes. The search for the Naryshkins proved less fruitful. Kiril Naryshkin succeeded in fleeing the city. Ivan Naryshkin found temporary sanctuary in a hidden chamber of the great palace between feather beds.[18] Young Afanasii Naryshkin alone was discovered and promptly slain. During the remainder of the day terror filled all Moscow as the Strel'tsy combed the various quarters for their enemies.

Convinced that the Tsaritsa Natalia knew the whereabouts of its principal intended victim, Ivan Naryshkin, the Strel'tsy demanded of her the following day that he be delivered to them for judgment, or reprisals would be taken against other members of the family. The court was in an uproar. Tsarevna Sophia, supported by several prominent boyars, urged Natalia to yield as the only means of curbing the Strel'tsy. Natalia refused, insisting that an alternative be found to handing her brother over for slaughter. Since none could be advanced, she at length yielded. Ivan Naryshkin was sorrowfully brought out of hiding, and after receiving communion and extreme unction in the church, Blessed Behind Golden Bars, was delivered over to the Strel'tsy. Lengthy artful torture soon ended his youthful career.

During the next several days, the Tsarevna Sophia assumed a more active political role. Administrative orders were given at her command, decisions were made upon her advice, and a liaison was established between her and the supporters of the Miloslavskiis.[19] On May 18, repre-

---
[18] Shchebal'skii, op. cit., p. 49.
[19] Aristov, op. cit., p. 76.

sentatives of the Strel'tsy appeared at the palace demanding that Kiril Naryshkin be ordered to take monastic vows. The government again yielded. Communications established between Natalia and her father Kiril ended with the elder Naryshkin agreeing to enter Kirilov Monastery. On May 20, a petition from the Strel'tsy called for the exile of all remaining Naryshkins along with their supporters, the Likhachevs and Iazykovs. Arrears in pay were to be given the Strel'tsy and their right to possess the confiscated properties of their victims recognized.[20] A spokesman for the order, Prince Ivan Khovanskii, had meanwhile approached Sophia with a report that the Strel'tsy and "many other men of the Muscovite State" desired that Ivan Alekseevich and Peter Alekseevich reign jointly in Russia in line with ancient Byzantine precedent. The suggestion had probably come originally from Sophia, since it conformed with one she had made a fortnight before to Patriarch Joachim. Nevertheless the tsarevna, acting upon the idea, requested the boyars at court to look into the matter. They, in turn, referred it to Joachim and the higher clergy.

Within three days (May 26) a new meeting of the rump Sobor assembled. After hearing the proposal and deliberating upon it, they agreed that because of "the unrest among the people created by the sole rule of Tsar Peter," the Tsarevich Ivan should be elevated to the throne and a joint rule be established with Ivan as "first tsar" and Peter as "second." Actual control of affairs would rest with a regent to be appointed—Sophia Alekseevna. No opposition having showed itself, the change in government was accomplished. The Miloslavskii forces overturned their rivals in power, and the political career of Tsarevna Sophia began.

The imperium granted the new government was accompanied by a realization of the need for removing a dangerous obstacle to its exercise of genuine power—the Strel'tsy. The element that had brought the Miloslavskiis to power might also undermine or overturn them by insisting upon further favors. Their new spokesman Prince Ivan Khovanskii, Chief of the Strel'tsy Prikaz, had taken no pains to curb their rebellious instincts but, on the contrary, had abetted them. Khovanskii's influence and designs were difficult to determine. He was of Lithuanian ancestry and claimed descent from the Lithuanian royal house of Gedemin. It was early rumored that he aspired to the office of tsar himself and was taking steps in that direction by seeking marriage with a member of the Romanov family—Tsarevna Ekaterina Alekseevna.

---

[20] S. M. Solov'ev, *Istoriia Rossii s drevneishikh vremen*, XIII, 903–904.

An immediate necessity facing the new regime was to restore respect for the Romanov name. The split between the two factions of the royal family had gravely undermined its prestige and had suggested the possibility of a dynastic overturn. At least outward coöperation between both tsars and their immediate household would be required if the political stability of the royal office was to be assured and its prerogatives and authority maintained.

Throughout June the high pitch of unrest among the Strel'tsy continued. Collaboration between the Miloslavskiis and Khovanskii had ceased the day Sophia became regent. Minor clashes between the Strel'tsy and various prominent boyars and lesser nobles occurred, and alarm bells, warning of local disturbances, were frequently heard in the capital. On June 5, an alarm had sounded in all government offices, and "during that alarm there was shooting the whole night long."[21] The Strel'tsy petitioned the following day that a pillar be erected in Red Square to commemorate their patriotic deeds of May 15.[22] The pillar was to be inscribed with the names of those killed during the uprising, but the Strel'tsy were not to be referred to as rebels. Guilt and fear began to infiltrate the order, and a need was felt to justify its recent actions. A second petition followed, asking the government to explain to the people why certain prominent figures at court had been killed by the Strel'tsy during the revolt. It was to be stated in the declaration that Prince Iurii Dolgorukii and his son Mikhail had been put to death for their long-standing oppressions of the Strel'tsy; Prince Romodanovskii, for his treason "in surrendering the Russian fortress of Chigirin to the Turks"; Ivan M. Iazykov, for his political corruption; and Ivan and Afanasii Naryshkin, because of their political intrigues and iniquities against Tsar Ivan.[23] At the same time loyalty for the office of tsar was reaffirmed and a reminder given that the Strel'tsy had served the tsars "from time immemorial with all kinds of faithfulness and without treason."[24] The government, upon the insistence of the Strel'tsy, ordered that they henceforth be called Court Infantry (*nadvornaia pekhota*). After June 14 the disturbances grew more frequent, and "there were few nights without shooting."[25]

As the connection between the new government and the Strel'tsy

---
[21] *D.A.I.*, X (Sept. 17, 1682), 31; *Excerpts from the Notes of the Hall of Records Concerning the Moscow Uprisings and its Surroundings*; Solov'ev, op. cit., XIII, 921.
[22] *A.E.I.*, IV (June 6, 1682), 358, *Royal Charter Providing That a Pillar be Erected on the Red Square Bearing the Names of Those Killed During the Rebellion.* . . .
[23] *Ibid.*, pp. 358–361.
[24] *Ibid.*, p. 363.
[25] *D.A.I.*, X, 30–31.

weakened, the order sought support from other directions—from the merchants, craftsmen, the Old Believers, the serfs. A dramatic incident of the May outbreak had been the sacking and partial destruction of the Serf Office (*Kholopii Prikaz*) by the Strel'tsy, with the loss of many contracts of bondage. On that occasion the liberation of all serfs in the capital had been proclaimed. Contrary to expectations, little reaction had followed among the serf population. The bondsmen in the capital enjoyed a somewhat better status than those in the provinces. Some had even entered bondage to escape the growing obligations imposed upon them as freemen and had little desire to regain their former liberties.[26] Others probably sensed that the Strel'tsy had acted without authority and that, lacking consent from their masters and the government, a liberation effort would be futile. The bid for the support of the serfs thus failed, as did that tendered the merchants. The interests of the latter were too closely bound up with those of the government. Support was, however, enlisted from the Old Believers, the element which promised to provide them the greatest additional strength.

That a connection existed between the Moscow Strel'tsy and the Old Believers had been manifest since May. Many Strel'tsy had become Old Believers whereas the Naryshkins were orthodox. During the peak of the outbreak, various schismatic monks had surged through the crowd openly lauding the action of the Strel'tsy forces and condemning the evil Naryshkins. Prince Ivan Khovanskii openly adhered to the schismatic doctrines—a factor which made him a potential leader of the schism as well as of the Strel'tsy. Avvakum, the former leader of the Old Believers, had been burned at the stake after long internment in a subterranean prison at Pustozersk, April 14, 1682.[27] No successor to this shrewd, colorful figure had yet appeared nor, in probability, would appear. Khovanskii, however, sympathetic to both the Old Believers and the Strel'tsy, might provide a substitute leadership to that of Avvakum—a leadership which might in the end promote the Old Believers more effectively than the fiery exhortations of the older leader. Be that as it may, Khovanskii's opportunism became clear and unmistakable by July. Fomenting revolutionary sentiment among the populace and the Old Believers on the one hand, he deplored the violence and unrest of the mob to the government on the other, exaggerating the confusion, depicting the people as restive and eager for a clarification of the religious question. At the same time, his recommendations for action by the

---
[26] Solov'ev, *op. cit.*, XIII, 904.
[27] G. P. Fedotov, *A Treasury of Russian Spirituality*, p. 135.

government pointed toward creating greater confusion rather than in aiding the government to promote stability. A proposal that received his particular endorsement called for a public debate between the higher clergy and the schismatics to resolve the outstanding religious differences. This coincided with a petition received simultaneously by Patriarch Joachim from the schismatic monk, Nikita, demanding a public airing of the outstanding theological issues. That such an event might engender further bitterness and end in violence instead of settling the dispute was fully indicated, yet the new regent accepted the challenge and utilized it as an occasion to strengthen her own position.

The interest of Sophia in theology, and her facility in its terminology and doctrinal premises emanated from an early association with churchmen. Attracted as she had been to the teachings of Polotskii and Medvedev, one might have expected relations between the patriarch with his Graeco-Byzantinism and the regent to have remained strained. But recent events in Moscow had drawn the two together. The patriarch felt the need of continued support from the government in parrying the attack upon the Church by critics. The regent, in turn, felt inclined to align herself firmly on the side of orthodoxy: first, in the hope of winning more enthusiastic support from the patriarch to dignify her position; and second, in case of a later collision with him, to safeguard herself from reproaches of faithlessness or heresy.[28]

The outcome of the debate between eminent theologians of the Church and a group of incendiary Old Believers with little or no formal education was by no means conclusive. The advantage held by the Church in learning, prestige, and government support was offset to a substantial degree by the fervor of the Old Believers, the popular appeal of many of their doctrines, and the immediate support given them by the Strel'tsy. Khovanskii put less faith in the persuasive powers of his religious adherents than in the presence of a substantial Strel'tsy force to influence the outcome of the debate. If necessary he hoped that the Strel'tsy, already tinged with schismatic sentiments, might be present at the meeting, rally behind the schismatic leaders, and sustain their arguments by force. In this he was disappointed. Divining his scheme, the government agreed to a debate on condition that it be held in Granovitaia Palace in the presence of the court and representatives of all ranks and classes. Failing in this first plan, Khovanskii sought to persuade the patriarch to go to the meeting by way of the Red Porch—the scene of the May uprising—foreseeing that he might be molested

---

[28] Pomialovskii, *op. cit.*, XIX, 135.

as he passed through the crowd of Old Believers. Once more the government frustrated his design by ordering Joachim to proceed to the palace at the last moment by way of a secret passageway.

The conclave opened July 5, 1682. A large number of dignitaries gathered in the low-vaulted audience chamber of the palace—both tsars, the regent Sophia, the patriarch, eight metropolitans, five archbishops, two bishops, and the Tsarevnas Tatiana Mikhailovna and Maria Alekseevna. Taking the places assigned them, they gave orders to admit the schismatics. Led by Nikita and accompanied by Khovanskii and a few representatives of the Strel'tsy, the dissidents entered in somewhat disorderly fashion, laden with candles, crosses, benches, pulpits, ikons, and the Gospels. Several appeared intoxicated. Without awaiting recognition, Nikita proclaimed that the schismatics had come "to affirm the old faith without which no man can save his soul." He then read a petition denouncing the Nikonian changes in the text and wording of the Gospels. Having heard this through, the patriarch answered the charges, opening his reply with a firm rebuke to the Old Believers for their arrogance and disobedience, saying the texts to which they referred had long been corrected by learned scholars from ancient authoritative documents. "We have not come here to discuss grammar, but dogma,"[29] Nikita retorted and asked the patriarch to justify his use of certain rituals. Athanasius, Bishop of Kholmogory, rose to reply for the patriarch, only to be silenced abruptly by Nikita under threat of being struck.[30] "Do you the foot, exalt yourself above the head?" Nikita asked. "I spoke to the patriarch, not to you." Tsarevna Sophia halted the discussion. "What! Would you strike a holy bishop before our eyes? You are unfit to stand or speak in our presence. Take away his petition and let another read it!" This was done. The reading of the petition resumed until a statement was read referring to Nikon as a "heretic." Sophia interrupted:

I have heard enough. If Patriarch Nikon were a heretic, then so were my father, Tsar Alexis, and my brother, Tsar Feodor, and the reigning tsars are no tsars, and the reigning patriarch is no patriarch, and we have no right to rule this realm. Exposed to these affronts, it were better for the tsars to leave Moscow and go elsewhere and relate how they have been treated here.

The patriarch now took over the discussion. He described the changes introduced at the last synod and presented documentary evidence to justify the alteration of certain critical passages. But his appeals to scholarship failed. The adherence of the schismatics to ancient forms

---
[29] William Palmer, *The Patriarch and the Tsar*, V, 870.
[30] Shchebal'skii, *op. cit.*, p. 59.

and their deep-seated grievances could not be overturned by the pleas and explanations of their hated opponent, the patriarch. All during his discourse there were repeated interruptions from the schismatics, denying and ridiculing his statements. "Let us cross ourselves this way, believe thus!" they insisted.

Convinced that the discussion had reached an impasse, the royal family prepared to depart. The commanding presence of the regent had its effect. The Strel'tsy present, impressed by her forceful attitude, gave no signs of actively upholding the schismatics. No settlement of the religious issue had been reached, nor had any progress in that direction been made, but the hand of the government had shown unexpected strength. Khovanskii's purported design to use the occasion for promoting an alliance between two forces which would undermine the government and elevate him in power had been thwarted. The government had localized the conflict, had bound the interests of the Church more closely to its own, and had enhanced its prestige substantially. A vigorous suppression of the schism was renewed. Nikita, having incurred the disfavor of the Strel'tsy for his criticisms of their failure to support him, was soon after seized and beheaded.[31]

In spite of the setback to Khovanskii's ambitions, his position in the capital remained strong. The schismatics still regarded him as their intermediary and the Strel'tsy as their indulgent "father" (*batiushka*). Khovanskii encouraged such sentiment, particularly among the Strel'tsy, by catering to their whims and showing sympathetic concern for their well-being. The removal of unpopular Strel'tsy regimental commanders and lesser officers continued. A complaint had only to be lodged against a leader, and he was in danger of dismissal or corporal punishment or both. The grievances and complaints of the order against the government received solicitous attention. The properties of boyars and other nobles killed in the May uprising were to be turned over to the order, and steps taken to gather arrears in pay for Strel'tsy in the provinces.[32]

The government viewed these disorders with growing apprehension. A sense of dismay pervaded Moscow. Houses appeared uninhabited, their windows and doors were barricaded, and few people showed themselves on the streets. Ivan Miloslavskii retired to an estate outside the capital, warning the regent of the danger from Khovanskii:

Khovanskii fosters dangerous projects. He flatters the Strel'tsy for a purpose, at-

---

[31] Belov, *op. cit.*, p. 139. "On this day Sophia showed the brilliant side of her character—firmness, persistence, resourcefulness; perhaps on this day the house of Romanov owed its salvation to her."

[32] Shchebal'skii, *op. cit.*, p. 61.

taches them to himself by every possible indulgence, and at the same time arouses them against the government.... He plots to exterminate the most important boyars, the clergy, and the royal house itself, and to make himself the Russian tsar.[33]

Without support equivalent to that of the Strel'tsy the government could take no strong action. Appraising the situation carefully, the regent decided on a lesser move. For weeks Sophia had threatened to remove the government from Moscow. She now resolved to carry the plan forward. In mid-August a report circulated—perhaps it had been planted—that the Strel'tsy plotted to destroy the tsars.[34] Capitalizing upon it, the government, including both tsars, the regent, and the entire court, left Moscow August 20 for Kolomenskoe Village about seven miles from the capital. There in the summer palace, once a favorite residence of Ivan Groznyi, the court took refuge.

The flight from the capital precipitated a wholesale evacuation of the propertied classes from the city. By September it was estimated that only one courtier (*okol'nichii*) of the immediate entourage of the tsar remained in Moscow.[35] The fear and unpopularity of the Strel'tsy increased daily after the government, the only element regarded as capable of curbing their excesses, and the nobility, the class upon whom the economy of the city largely rested, had removed themselves. At Kolomenskoe the government enjoyed greater rein either to arrange terms with the Strel'tsy, bargaining for their loyalty on the basis of a return to the capital and removal of the odium now resting upon them for having driven the tsars from the capital, or to appeal to the country at large for support against them and their leader Khovanskii.

Communications between the government and the Strel'tsy opened almost immediately. Khovanskii found himself in the awkward role of having to justify his actions and to dispel the fears of the populace about his intentions. Protestations soon came to the regent from various Strel'tsy regiments lamenting the departure of the government and avowing the loyalty and faithfulness of the order to the sovereigns. Khovanskii sought to force a return by suggesting that the nobility of Novogorod had gone over to the Strel'tsy cause and planned a march on Moscow to inaugurate a new reign of terror. The tsars, he recommended, should come back to the capital if only to forestall such an event.[36]

---

[33] Shchebal'skii, *op. cit.*, p. 62.
[34] Solov'ev, *op. cit.*, XIII, 921.
[35] Shchebal'skii, *op. cit.*, p. 63.
[36] Solov'ev, *op. cit.*, XIII, 921.

Early in September the government took further steps to isolate Khovanskii. A mysterious letter reached Sophia at Kolomenskoe purporting to have been written by two trading men and a member of the Moscow Strel'tsy, charging Khovanskii with "treasonable acts against the sovereigns."[37] The authorship of the letter was not established. It may well have been a forgery by the Miloslavskiis. Without deciding the point, the government considered the charges against the prince sufficiently strong to justify prompt action. According to the information contained in the letter, Khovanskii and his son, Andrei, had plotted "all sorts of evils to the Great Sovereigns."[38] They sought to rule Russia, to eliminate important boyars, voevodas, and high religious leaders, and to incite the country to rebellion.[39] Upon attaining the crown, the message explained, Khovanskii would have a new patriarch elected from among the Old Believers. That the message had been prepared by Miloslavskii partisans appears highly probable, since the charges against Khovanskii closely coincided with rumors circulated by them in Moscow in August. But the charges were regarded seriously by many at Kolomenskoe and momentarily transformed some of the government's passive supporters into active sympathizers. Representing the charges as a plot against the whole Romanov family and the country at large, Sophia used it to call upon all classes to rally to her support.

The intrigue developed with remarkable success. Armed men of all ranks began assembling at Vozdvizhenskoe. On September 9 the government took further precautions by removing itself to Troitsa-Sergeiev Monastery, some forty-four miles from Moscow. There behind the heavy walls and towers of the monastery which had successfully resisted three Polish attacks in the past, the sovereigns felt greater security. So long as Khovanskii remained in Moscow, there was little hope of overturning him quickly. An effort would therefore have to be made to force him or to lure him from the capital. This was accomplished with an ease that almost denied the dangers inherent in the prince's position in the state. By the simple ruse of a forged letter, the prince was persuaded to meet the son of an ataman of the Ukrainian Cossacks at an appointed rendezvous near Moscow. With his son Andrei, a force of thirty-seven Strel'tsy impressively armed and attired, and numerous servants and acquaintances, Khovanskii set forth from Moscow in mid-September.

At Pushkino Village, the Khovanskii entourage halted for rest. Splen-

---
[37] *A.R.I.*, IV, 368–369.
[38] *Ibid.*
[39] *D.A.I.*, X, 31.

did tents for the prince and his retinue were set up on the peasant threshing floors near the main road. Meanwhile, upon order from Sophia, Prince Lykov with a large force of cavalrymen had ridden against him. Surrounded by surprise, Khovanskii and his Strel'tsy supporters were seized without resistance. On the same day Prince Andrei Khovanskii, who had become momentarily separated from his father, was also captured. Procedure against them moved swiftly. Within a matter of hours they were brought to Vozdvizhenskoe and charged with high crimes against the state. The elder Khovanskii demanded a trial and asked to be confronted with the witnesses against him. He offered to name the real instigators of the revolt. All his requests were denied and such testimony as he offered apparently only hastened final judgment. Declared guilty of all the charges, Khovanskii, his son Andrei, and the thirty-seven Strel'tsy in his retinue were executed. Judgment of the offenders moved so rapidly that the arrival of state executioners from Moscow was not awaited; the decapitations were carried out by members of the Strel'tsy regiment which had remained loyal to the tsars.

A younger son of Khovanskii, Prince Ivan, eluded capture for several weeks by fleeing to Moscow to bring the Strel'tsy there news of the death of their *batiushka*. Momentarily they flared with rage, beat their drums, seized weapons, and demanded that they be led against the court.[40] But in the end anger gave way to fear and anguish. The decisive action of the court in removing their leader and his Strel'tsy retinue filled the order with foreboding about its own fate. An atmosphere of near panic prevailed in the capital.[41] Strel'tsy forces roamed the city, seized government munitions, confiscated property, and constructed defenses in the Zemlianoi Gorod. The younger Ivan Khovanskii's warning that the boyars were organizing a powerful force to take over the capital only augmented fear and confusion among the Strel'tsy rather than increased their sense of resistance.[42]

By the end of September, the mutinous spirit of the Strel'tsy had run its course. A deputation of representatives of all the Moscow regiments approached Patriarch Joachim September 24 to ask his intercession on their behalf with the government.[43] Joachim agreed and on the following day sent Illarion, Metropolitan of Suzdal, to the tsars with a petition asking forgiveness. The petition reviewed the faithful service the Strel'tsy

---

[40] Shchebal'skii, *op. cit.*, p. 67.
[41] *A.I.*, V, 147–148.
[42] *A.R.I.*, IV, 378–379.
[43] *Ibid.*, p. 371.

had rendered Russia in the past and stated that the various regiments in Moscow were then performing their duties without treason.

> ... we shall serve the great Sovereigns and work for them faithfully and unswervingly. Should we hear of any dastards plotting against their Royal Highnesses, we shall seize them and bring them to our regiments, to our meeting houses, and shall hold them there until the sovereigns come to Moscow."

Sophia heard the petition and ordered the Strel'tsy to send representatives to her at Troitsa Monastery for a discussion. A large army of nobles which had assembled at the monastery greatly strengthened her bargaining powers. On October 2 Strel'tsy representatives duly appeared at the monastery "in all humility." Further protestations of their faithfulness to the government followed, with an admission of their guilt in the recent outbreak. The Khovanskiis were assigned the major blame for many of their acts, such as the seizure of arms in Moscow.

Sophia's terms were stringent but effective. The Strel'tsy were to plot no more rebellions, to form no secret agreements or hold secret meetings with anyone, and even to "think no evil." They were to join no schismatic movements, to bring seditionists promptly to justice, and to cease wandering in noisy bands through Moscow, acting brazenly and meddling in affairs "that were of no concern to them." All arms and supplies removed from the state armory were to be returned. No recruits were to be gathered from among the peasantry or among vagrants without the express permission of the government. Those recruited from such groups since the May outbreak were to be returned to their former dwelling places. The Strel'tsy were under no circumstances to question the government's action against the Khovanskiis. Anyone who was found glorifying the recent outbreak was to be apprehended, tried, and executed.[45] These terms the Strel'tsy accepted. Their submission appeared to be complete. At the end of the month the pillar commemorating the revolt of May 15 was removed from the capital.[46] The government returned to Moscow the first week in November.

The reconciliation between the regent and the Strel'tsy, however, failed to restore the political liaison which had existed before the May outbreak. The Strel'tsy found themselves replaced as Kremlin guards by regiments of nobles. Feodor Shaklovityi, an adherent of the regent, was named the new Strel'tsy commander. Faint rumblings of discontent at these changes and at the government's failure to remove unpopular

---

[44] *Ibid.*, p. 372.
[45] *Ibid.*, pp. 383–387.
[46] *Ibid.*, p. 391.

regimental colonels reappeared briefly. A few cases of desertion even occurred. Shaklovityi took strong action. The ringleaders were rounded up and summarily executed.[47] Close watch was established over all regiments to forestall further disorders.[48] Twelve of the nineteen regiments in Moscow were reassigned to Ukrainian, Polish, and Swedish border patrol, and only the most trustworthy regiments were retained in the capital.[49] As a further precaution the heavily populated Belyi Gorod section was closed to all traffic at night, and during certain hours of the day no one could enter the city. The decree which arranged these measures also provided for such details as the itineraries of columns arriving at or departing from Moscow, the transport of Strel'tsy families to border patrol stations, and the levying of food for the migrants.[50]

After the removal of Khovanskii and the pacification of the Strel'tsy, Sophia gave her attention to another immediate problem—that of securing her position against the remaining claimants to power in the royal family. The Naryshkins had been subdued, but the popularity of Tsar Peter and the Tsaritsa Natalia had not diminished. Soon after the return of the court to Moscow in November, the younger tsar and his mother retired to an estate outside Moscow on the left bank of the Yauza River at Preobrazhenskoe. Both the Tsaritsa Natalia and the regent undoubtedly welcomed the arrangement. Their relations had inevitably become strained since the death of Natalia's brothers in May and the part played by the Miloslavskiis in the Strel'tsy revolt. The simplicity and quiet of the suburbs must have appealed strongly to Alexis' young widow in contrast to residence in the capital under the surveillance of her stepdaughter.

Tsar Peter's role during the next nine years has created great sentimental interest and speculation. An inference might almost be drawn, from the sketchy treatment accorded the political events of these years, that the most noteworthy development between the death of Feodor and Peter's reassertion of power in 1689 was Peter's association with foreigners, his interest in their technical skills, and his preoccupation with war games. From a personal standpoint, these were formative years for the young tsar, but they have tended to obscure the larger events of the years 1682–1689. Peter's sojourn at Preobrazhenskoe cannot justifiably be portrayed as an exile. During the first two years of Sophia's regency, Peter and his mother passed a large part of each year in the

[47] Belov, *op. cit.*, p. 322.
[48] *D.A.I.*, X, 202–203.
[49] *A.R.I.*, IV, 409.
[50] *P.S.Z.*, II, 490.

capital.⁵¹ During 1683, they made frequent trips to Moscow to attend diplomatic and religious functions; in 1684, Peter spent less than six months at Preobrazhenskoe. The fact was that the younger tsar and his mother preferred living in the crown villages of suburban Moscow, and only upon necessity came to the capital. It was only after 1684 that Natalia and her son, still probably through choice, passed longer periods of time away from Moscow. The belief that Sophia compelled them to remain there seems to have no foundation.⁵²

The primary obstacles to power surmounted, Sophia could now devote her energies to the more normal demands of government. An immediate need was for the appointment of officials to leading government offices. For her principal minister the regent selected the boyar, Prince V. V. Golitsyn. Golitsyn had long been admired by the tsarevna for his learning and abilities. That he had become her favorite and lover was now generally accepted. Golitsyn was named head of the Foreign Office (*Posol'skii Prikaz*). Within the year he was given the titles "Guardian of the Great Royal Seal and of the Office of Foreign Affairs" (*Tsarstvennyia bol'shiia pechati i gosudarstvennykh velikikh posol'skikh del oberegatelia*), honors which in the past only Ordyn-Nashchokin and Matveev had borne. Further responsibilities were put upon him later.⁵³ Appointments to other posts were as follows: Chamber of Settlement or Adjustment (*Raspravnaia Palata*)—Prince Nikita Odoevskii; Treasury Office (*Prikaz Bol'shoi Kazny*)—Aleksei Rzhevskii; Office of Estates (*Pomestnyi Prikaz*)—Prince Ivan Troekurov; Office of Kazan (*Kazanskii Dvorets*)—Prince Boris Golitsyn; Office of the Large Palace (*Prikaz Bol'shogo Dvortsa*)—Semion Tolochanov; Siberian Office (*Sibirskoi Prikaz*)—Prince Ivan Repnin; Police Office (*Razboinichii Prikaz*)—Vikula Izvol'skii. As head of the Strel'tsy Office (*Streletskii Prikaz*) Sophia named Feodor Shaklovityi whose firm discipline of the Moscow regiments had commanded wide respect.⁵⁴ For counsel in educational and religious matters, Sophia turned to Silvester Medvedev, the theologian whose learning and theological views she had admired while in the terem.

In this chapter attention has been directed to the principal events leading to Tsarevna Sophia's seizure of power in May, 1682. The accession of Tsar Peter to the throne in April of that year had precipitated

---

⁵¹ Bogoslovskii, *op. cit.*, I, 48.
⁵² S. F. Platonov, *Moskva i Zapad*, p. 148.
⁵³ F. A. Brokhaus and I. A. Efron, *Entsiklopedicheskii slovar*, IX, 47; Pomialovskii, *op. cit.*, p. 137.
⁵⁴ Papers of Prince Boris Ivanovich Kurakin [1676–1727], *Arkhiv Kniazia F. A. Kurakina*, I, 49.

a palace revolution which culminated in a change of leadership and in a dyarchy, with power nominally divided between Peter and his half brother Ivan. Actual power rested with the regent and her followers. Sophia, by directing the Strel'tsy revolt against her enemies and then renouncing and curbing it, had won the acquiescence, if not the genuine support, of the ruling classes—the nobility and the clergy. The factional strife within the Romanov family deeply affected political alignments in Moscow. Having restored the political stability of the state to a degree at least, the regency could now turn to the broader tasks of government.

Part II
INTERNAL DEVELOPMENTS

CHAPTER III

SEVENTEENTH-CENTURY MOSCOW AND THE WEST

THE STRUGGLE that brought the Tsarevna Sophia into power might never have acquired historical significance had it not been for the larger issues with which her government became identified. The seventeenth century was an age of far-reaching intellectual ferment in Europe. Religion, learning, and political authority—to mention only the more important fields—felt the challenge of the renewed interest in science and philosophy. In Russia, the ferment assumed various forms but was chiefly manifested in the struggle to defend Russian orthodoxy and learning from the subversive influences of Western theology and scholarship and to assure the loyalty of the literate elements of the population by placing church doctrines and educational activity on a sounder intellectual basis.[1]

The principal arena of Russia's intellectual conflict in the late seven-

---

[1] The larger collections of printed sources have provided some excellent materials for this chapter. *P.S.Z.*, II, contains the decrees for judicial and other reforms sponsored by Tsarevna Sophia's government. *A.I.*, V, and *D.A.I.*, X, have numerous decrees and instructions pertaining to the Old Believers, especially for methods of apprehending and punishing them. The journals *Chteniia* and *Russkaia Starina* have reproduced several important memoirs of the period which are of particular interest for cultural history. The works of Silvester Medvedev, for example, have been carefully edited by A. Prozorovskii in *Chteniia* (1896): parts iii-iv. De la Neuville's *Zapiski ... o Moskovii* (Notes About Muscovy) appears in *Russkaia Starina* (Russian Antiquity) (Sept.–Nov., 1891). Volume I of *Arkhiv Kurakina* (The Kurakin Archives) contains the colorful account of Prince B. I. Kurakin on the accession of Tsarevna Sophia. Of the secondary sources those published before 1917 are still the most important. V. O. Kliuchevsky's *Kurs russkoi istorii*, III (Course of Russian history), has devoted the greater part of the last seven chapters to a discussion of the principal problems facing Russian scholarship and theology in the seventeenth century. Two of the chapters deal with western influences on Russian society, and the concluding chapter with Prince V. V. Golitsyn and the background of the reform movement. S. F. Platonov's *Moskva i Zapad* also includes a remarkable analysis of western influences in Muscovite society in the later seventeenth century and an appraisal of the principal promoters and critics of westernism. A. E. Belov's article in *Zh.M.N.P.* (1887), "Moskovskiia smuty v kontse XVII veka" (Moscow rebellions at the end of the seventeenth century), describes the fluctuations in Greek influence on Russian education of the time. A. Brükner in *Beiträge zur Kulturgeschichte Russlands in XVII Jahrhundert* has a chapter on Prince V. V. Golitsyn and his interests in education and reform. P. Miliukov's *Ocherki po istorii russkoi kultury*, which has been translated in part into English as *Outlines of Russian Culture*, has several excellent chapters on the secularization of literature, the origin of the Great Schism, and the various sects of Old Believers. N. A. Rozhkov's *Russkaia istoriia*, V (Russian history), has an interesting chapter entitled "Spiritual Culture in the Second Half of the Seventeenth Century," which critically reappraises the outstanding intellectual leaders of the time. N. K. Gudzy's *History of Early Russian Literature*, a translation of the second Russian edition of his *Istoriia drevnei russkoi literatury*, has important chapters on Russian literature of the seventeenth century, the Russian theater, and dramaturgy.

[43]

teenth century was the Church. There a controversy raged over the direction to be given education, both spiritual and secular. The higher clergy gravitated toward the Graeco-Christian culture of the Byzantine East, but certain groups among the nobility and among church scholars felt strongly attracted to the culture and learning of Western Europe. The Church in Muscovite Russia was still the principal agency of learning. It controlled the few schools that existed. Some private schools had appeared to which laymen were occasionally admitted as pupils. But these for the most part were short lived; and in almost every case, churchmen determined the scope and goals of education. In the Ukraine, which had lately been a part of Poland, a more impressive system of parochial, secondary, and even higher schools had developed. Although they, too, were controlled by the orthodox clergy, the fact that they had long been exposed to Latin-Polish influences tended to make them more liberal. The Ukrainian schools, in an effort to preserve the orthodox faith from Roman Catholic domination, had opened their doors more freely than Muscovite schools not only to churchmen but to nobles, Cossacks, and other laymen.[2]

To understand the attitude of the Russian Orthodox Church toward education certain historical factors should be recalled. Although Greek in tradition and form the Russian Church in the seventeenth century was a national church. Moscow had become both the religious and political capital of the state since the establishment of the patriarchate in 1589. Thereafter the subordination of the Russian Church to the Patriarch of Constantinople ceased.[3] But despite the administrative break between Moscow and Constantinople, the cultural tie with Byzantium endured. Greek Christians of the seventeenth century looked hopefully toward Russia for support in winning freedom from the Turkish yoke.[4] During the second half of the century Byzantine influence was strengthened through Patriarch Nikon's religious reforms. At the

---

[2] Hans Nicolas, *History of Russian Educational Policy*, pp. 9–10.

[3] Paul Miliukov, *Outlines of Russian Culture, Part I, Religion and the Church*, p. 27.

[4] N. F. Kapterev, *Kharakter otnoshenii Rossii k pravoslavnomu vostoku v XVI i XVII stoletiiakh*, pp. 369–371. In September, 1688, the archimandrite Isaiah of the Athos Paulian Monastery came to Moscow bearing letters from the former Patriarch of Constantinople, Dionysius, from the voevoda of Wallachia, and from a Serbian archbishop. Dionysius wrote: "Our churches are becoming empty, our monasteries going bankrupt, our crosses defiled, our ikons defamed ... and who can save us except ... your sovereign majesty, who is preëminent both in riches, in power and in the strength of his armies?" Dionysius also wrote Tsarevna Sophia that in the past God had saved his people through Deborah, Judith, and Esther. "Lend a hand of aid in word and in deed.... Come, then, like Deborah and Judith, and Esther ... in word and in deed.... Your holy name will then be preached from generation to generation and you will be remembered forever."

Church Council of 1656, Nikon had declared that "although I am a Russian and the son of a Russian, my faith and convictions are Greek."[5] His patronage of Greek scholars and the authority he allowed them to exert in the correction of the church books made it appear for a time that Moscow was again to be subjected to Greek influence.

A combination of circumstances unexpectedly undermined Greek prestige. The Greek scholars either made little effort or did not know how to exploit the advantages they had acquired. Their uncompromising attitude on theological questions, their haughtiness and venality gave them the reputation of being "narrow, proud, and avaricious." They were prepared, it was frequently said, "to sell the truth and to sacrifice the sacred cause for liberal 'favors,' that is, subsidies and bribes."[6] Many Russians openly questioned their intellectual superiority over the Kievan and native academicians. Even though the Greeks were well educated, it was argued, much of their higher learning had been acquired in the Latin West—in Italy. Why, therefore, should one be taught by a Greek, when one could be taught more readily by a Russian? And why should one apply himself to Greek when, in any case, it was necessary to study Latin for greatest advantage in scientific studies?[7]

The curricula in Russian schools of the seventeenth century was still medieval. The trivium, part of the quadrivium, the Slavic, Greek, and Latin languages were the principal subjects taught. All instruction was liberally saturated with theology. A better understanding of theology was often the pretext for explorations into new fields of study. For many Russians, such learning proved intellectually sterile and amounted to little more than a familiarity with the Gospels, the writings of the church fathers, and some of the intricacies of theological doctrine. Students specializing in theology might graduate from the most advanced schools and still have no critical understanding of church doctrine and symbolism, since few of the instructors themselves—to say nothing of the higher clergy—could provide logical answers to many questions posed by Western polemicists and theologians. Arsenius, an elder of the Church and corrector of the liturgy under Nikon, ascribed the condition to the clergy's primary concern for the letter rather than the spirit of the scriptures.[8] Almost everyone agreed that the situation needed correction. Greek and Kievan scholars were imported to Moscow to improve the quality of instruction. But improvement was slow.

[5] Miliukov, *op. cit.*, p. 35.
[6] S. F. Platonov, *Moskva i Zapad*, p. 143.
[7] Platonov, *op. cit.*, p. 144.
[8] Miliukov, *op. cit.*, Part I, 28.

Among the advanced schools in Russia in the late seventeenth century the Academy of Kiev enjoyed highest respect. Founded in 1631 by Peter Mogila when under Polish rule, the academy had continued to thrive as a Russian Orthodox Church school after the incorporation of the Ukraine into Russia during the reign of Tsar Alexis. Kievan graduates brought new luster to the intellectual life of Moscow and performed valuable state service in the correction of the church books. Kiev produced a galaxy of eminent theologians—Epiphany Slavinetskii, Dmitri of Rostov, Simeon Polotskii—to mention only a few. These had found influential positions in the administration of the Ukraine and in government service in Moscow. As Russia's hold on the Ukraine became established the flow of Kievans to the capital steadily increased. In monasteries, in the government printing office, and at court, more and more high positions fell to them. The trend became so marked that certain eastern patriarchs became alarmed. In 1686, for example, Dosifei, Patriarch of Jesusalem, urged that "the ancient rule in Moscow be preserved, which provided that there be no abbots or archimandrites of Cossack descent, but of Muscovite birth."[9]

Outside the Church as well, the number of Kievans entering professions steadily increased. Among the official engravers, distillers, ikon painters, and horticulturalists of Tsar Alexis' time, Ukrainian names frequently appeared. The tsar chose Ukrainians as his principal viticulturists and apiarists. In private homes as in church schools, Kievans entered as tutors and instructors. Many Kievans found employment as professional speakers at court levees, private receptions, and other gatherings.[10]

Despite the fame of Kiev in the late seventeenth century, the vogue for things Ukrainian began to wane in the reign of Tsar Feodor. Tsar Feodor, like his father before him, had befriended the Ukrainians. But during the intermittent struggle with Poland for control of the Dnieper towns, the loyalty of the Ukrainians to the tsar had proved disappointing. The government found them politically untrustworthy. One prominent Kievan, Simeon Polotskii, noted the change in the early seventies and stated that though he personally had not suffered any discrimination because "he sat quietly in his cell, not flying forth like a bee into

---

[9] Platonov, *op. cit.*, p. 139; N. K. Gudzy, *History of Early Russian Literature*, p. 373.

[10] The custom of giving speeches on holidays and namedays in praise of some hero or benefactor or beloved member of the family had become popular in Moscow. The Ukrainians had developed a particular panegyrical style which was in great demand. Their poetry, folk tales, and songs had also become popular. See Platonov, *op. cit.* p. 139.

the frosty atmosphere," in general things had gone badly for his countrymen in Moscow. He assigned the cause in part to the mercenary attitude of many Ukrainians and to their indiscretions which had lost them "the last vestiges of Muscovite good-will."[11]

But ideological differences, as well as resentment over Kievan disloyalty and infiltration into high office, explained this sudden loss of favor. In the late seventies, theological controversies had developed between Muscovite and Ukrainian church dignitaries. These for the most part had discredited the Ukrainians and created doubt in the minds of many Muscovite theologians about the fidelity of Kievans to the Orthodox Church. Only those Little Russians with an impeccable record of loyalty to orthodoxy were permitted to remain in public office.

In contrast to the declining popularity of Kiev in the late seventies and early eighties, four schools appeared in Moscow which gradually attained high intellectual stature. These were the Chudov Monastery School. the Graeco-Latin School, the Zaikonospasskii Monastery School, and the Andreev Monastery School. "Even if," as Professor N. K. Gudzy has written, "these schools were not all fully organized educational institutions and did not command any very impressive number of students, nonetheless they undeniably gave a serious impetus to the further development of intellectual and, indirectly, of literary culture in Muscovite society."[12] In these four schools the clash between the advocates of Graecophile orthodoxy and Kievan learning was joined. The Chudov Monastery School, under the guidance of the scholarly Epifany Slavinetskii, and the Graeco-Latin School, founded by Nikon (1653), vigorously opposed the western tendencies of the Andreev Monastery School, founded by the nobleman Feodor Rtishchev, and the Zaikonospasskii Monastery School, founded by Simeon Polotskii in 1644. Slavinetskii in various sermons, treatises, and biographies woefully lamented the growing infiltration of "Latinism" into Russia and denounced the indifference of such scholars as Polotskii toward Greek learning and culture. Of Polotskii, he wrote: "He knows something of Latin, that is true, but knows not even a modicum of Greek."[13]

The Zaikonospasskii Monastery School was primarily a training school for government clerks and lesser officials. It enjoyed a reputation for high scholarship and able instruction. It stressed the study of Latin and Polish literature. The great prestige of Polotskii at the court of Tsar Alexis at first enabled the school to withstand the strong criticism leveled

---
[11] Platonov, *op. cit.*, p. 139.
[12] Gudzy, *op. cit.*, p. 374.
[13] Platonov, *op. cit.*, p. 142.

against it by the Graecophiles, but during the reign of Tsar Feodor such violent disputes developed that shortly before his death in 1680 the school was closed. It was, nevertheless, to a graduate of that school, Silvester Medvedev, that Tsarevna Sophia turned in 1682 for counsel and guidance in the administration of religious and educational matters.

Silvester Medvedev (1641–1691) was a promising young clerk (*pod'iachii*) from Kursk. He had come to Moscow in 1665 to enter the Zaikonospasskii School for the completion of his training in public service. His intelligence and energy soon recommended him to the boyar Ordin-Nashchokin, and in 1674 he accompanied the famous Nashchokin to Andrusovo for the conclusion of the treaty with Poland. Three years later, after entering a monastic order, he returned to Moscow to participate in the correction of the church books. When his great teacher Polotskii died in 1680, he was generally recognized as the most brilliant pupil in the school and the principal protagonist of Kievan learning in Moscow. He was soon after named Archpriest of Zaikonospasskii Monastery, and while in that office won the friendship of young Tsar Feodor. The tsar "frequently visited Medvedev in the monastery, chatted with him in the palace and even personally corresponded with him."[14]

It was Medvedev's dream to see founded in Moscow an academy which would carry on the tradition of the Zaikonospasskii School more ambitiously and would one day rival the earlier prestige of Kiev. Polotskii had once developed such a plan, but when it was shown to Patriarch Joachim, the primate had insisted upon so many modifications of the proposed charter that Polotskii had abandoned the idea.[15] During the reign of Tsar Feodor, Medvedev renewed the suggestion more emphatically. Joachim again thwarted the plan. But Medvedev gained a small victory in that direction when he was allowed to reopen the Zaikonospasskii School in January, 1682. Tsar Feodor might even have yielded further had it not been for the concerted influence of the anti-Latin party.

With Sophia's regency established in the spring of 1682, Medvedev's hopes for the academy grew more sanguine. He had known the tsarevna since youth and regarded her as a maid of "marvelous understanding and judgment" (*chudnyi smysl i suzhdenie*).[16] He might appeal more successfully to her interest in learning than he had to her brother. The patriarch still strongly opposed the plan. His support of Graecophilism

---
[14] A. Prozorovskii, "Sil'vestr Medvedev," *Chteniia* (1896): no. III, 190.
[15] V. Nechaev, *Tri Veka*, p. 85.
[16] Prozorovskii, *op. cit.*, Part III, p. 207.

was not so much one of conviction as an outgrowth of fear of Roman Catholicism and of relinquishing a position that he had inherited.[17] Joachim was naturally conservative. Originally trained for a military career he had abandoned it in favor of a more promising one in the Church. He was not deeply informed on any subject, theology included, and felt keenly disturbed by the numerous signs of restiveness in Russia. These he assigned to "foreign" influence. Joseph, Archimandrite of Kolomna, wrote that "the patriarch does not even know how to read and write well. At the conclaves only the Metropolitan of Nizhni-Novgorod and I do the talking, while the patriarch merely sits and looks into his beard."[18] Medvedev added that he was a kindly man but "has studied little and does not know theology."[19] In his attack on the Latin party, as Nechaev has suggested, "he primarily wanted to hold liberal arts down to the minimum."[20] Protestantism, Catholicism, Mohammedanism alike were anathemas to Joachim, and he would have chosen to see all foreign churches in Russia removed and never rebuilt. In a word, Joachim, finding intellectual pursuits of any kind unattractive, was not an enthusiastic supporter of the expansion of knowledge and sought to eliminate all elements which promoted discord, challenged orthodoxy, and advocated changes in the traditional educational curriculum.

Besides the adherents of the Western educational trend among the clergy, the Graecophiles had to cope with the less open opposition of those devotees of Western culture within the government. Among them the regent herself must be numbered. The exceptional education acquired by Tsarevna Sophia has already been noted. Of the eight daughters of Tsar Alexis and Maria Miloslavskaia, undoubtedly she was the most talented and the one to avail herself most fully of the new freedom and educational opportunities permitted the daughters of the tsar. Simeon Polotskii, the eminent Kievan scholar, had taught her Latin and Polish and awakened in her a love of literature, Polish as well as Russian. Her association with him had greatly extended her mental horizon, for he had observed the course of political events closely over many years and could not avoid touching upon controversial subjects with his capable and inquisitive pupil. He found her to be "a maid of great intelligence and of the most delicate penetration, with more of an accom-

[17] A. E. Belov, "Moskovskiia smuty v kontse XVII veka, *Zh.M.N.P.*, pt. I, pp. 102–104: "The representative of Greek education at the height of the struggle was Patriarch Joachim.... Patriarch Joachim was very much afraid of the pressure of Roman Catholicism."
[18] Nechaev, *op. cit.*, II, 83.
[19] *Ibid.*
[20] *Ibid.*, p. 84.

plished masculine mind."[21] Through Karion Istomin and Silvester Medvedev, the tsarevna became acquainted with theology and rhetoric. Like Polotskii, Istomin and Medvedev were scholarly monks who were regarded among the most learned men of the late seventeenth century.[22] Medvedev was an adherent of the Latin trend in education, whereas Istomin supported the Greek. Istomin was a prolific versifier and writer of homilectic and pedagogical works. Medvedev was a persuasive polemicist.[23] Both were employed in the Moscow Printing Office as editors and had a wide knowledge of Western as well as Russian literature. They further encouraged Sophia's appreciation of Russian and Polish literature. The tsarevna acquired an unusual familiarity with poetry, sermons, saints' lives, and folk songs. It was not surprising that she undertook to write verse and inscriptions and developed a taste for theatricals. Polotskii had staged some of his mystery plays in the terem in which it was said Sophia had performed. Other plays, such as Molière's *Malade Imaginaire,* were also presented there.[24] To her uncle Ivan Miloslavskii and to Prince V. V. Golitsyn, Sophia was indebted for the completion of her education. In her long conversations with these accomplished courtiers, her own political views matured, and she became convinced that politics was the field most worthy of her efforts. An important element in her decision was the fact that all who surrounded Sophia, Golitsyn included, were people of less energy than herself. In fact, not until Tsar Peter successfully challenged her position in 1689 did the tsarevna encounter anyone who could overawe her in strength of character. The realization of her own capabilities—her intellectual attainments and personal magnetism—encouraged her political ambitions and tended to place her in the camp of those who thought most independently, the adherents of Western learning. It was no coincidence that the man to whom Sophia turned for chief support in bearing the responsibilities of government should be accounted one of the most active supporters of closer ties with the West.[25]

Prince Vasilii V. Golitsyn belonged to the tradition of "new men of the seventeenth century." Like his prototypes—Ordin-Nashchokin, Rtishchev, Matveev—he had acquired an education beyond the custom for men of his class. As a youth he had studied Latin, Greek, and German and had mastered them sufficiently to dispense with the services of interpreters in ordinary conversations with foreigners using those

---

[21] M. Pomialovskii, *Russkii Biograficheskii Slovar'*, p. 127.
[22] Gudzy, op. cit., pp. 511–512.
[23] *Ibid.*, pp. 511–513.
[24] A. Rambaud, *Receuil des instructions* ... VIII, 75; Nechaev, op. cit., II, 139.
[25] N. A. Rozhkov, *Russkaia istoriia*, V, 91.

languages. He had read widely in history, theology, and the classics and in later life became something of a bibliophile. His tastes also ran strongly toward political theory and ideas of social reform. He was interested in the advancement of education, particularly technical training, had explored the problem of the emancipation of the serfs, improvements in military and fiscal administration, and changes in the Law Code. The most tangible result of his interests along such lines was the part he had played in the abolition of the order of social precedence (*mestnichestvo*) in 1681.[26]

The system of family precedence or mestnichestvo arose from the patrimonial system. The member of an "older" family would refuse to sit at the tsar's table below the member of a "younger" family. Whoever through negligence or lack of insistence yielded his place to the representative of a younger family not only suffered a loss to his own position but degraded that of his family as well. These ideas extended into the civil and military service. During Tsar Feodor's reign Golitsyn had served as chairman of a commission for the reorganization of the Russian military service. Toward that end the commission recommended, among other changes, that the system of mestnichestvo be abolished. The recommendation was acted upon and by a decree of January 12, 1682, mestnichestvo was abandoned.[27]

During Sophia's regime, Golitsyn brought about a number of humanitarian changes in legal procedure. In March, 1683, punishment for sedition was modified from the death penalty to corporal punishment and exile.[28] Punishment by mutilation was curtailed. Methods of court procedure were improved. Attendance at court proceedings had been difficult for litigants, owing to lengthy trials and numerous delays in obtaining judgment. In 1685, the government decreed that justice must henceforth be more rapid. Plaintiffs and defendants were to appear in court within a fixed period of time, and once a trial opened it could not be subject to inconclusive delays and postponements.[29]

Like many enlightened Russians of his time, Golitsyn found stimulus in the company of foreigners. He held frequent conversations with the Scot, Patrick Gordon, who had entered Russian service in the sixties. During leisurely dinner discussions reported in Gordon's diary, the

---

[26] De la Neuville, "Zapiski de-la Nevillia o Moskovii," *Russkaia starina*, LXXI (1891), 441; A. Brückner, *Beiträge zur Kulturgeschichte Russlands im XVII Jahrhundert*, pp. 289–290.
[27] Brückner, *op. cit.*, pp. 288–289; V. O. Kliuchevsky, *A History of Russia*, III, 366; P. K. Shchebal'skii, *Pravlenie Tsarevny Sofii*, pp. 101–102.
[28] *P.S.Z.*, II, 515.
[29] *Ibid.*, pp. 689–699.

topics ran from appraisals of the latest projectiles and firearms to English politics and the problems arising from the decline of the Ottoman empire. Golitsyn leaned toward the constitutional party of William III of England, whereas Gordon was an avowed Jacobite. From Gordon's writings one gains the impression that Golitsyn was thoroughly class conscious, impatient of breaches in etiquette, and possessive in his attitude toward talented foreign residents like Gordon.

Other foreigners—the Swiss LeFort, the German Hartmann, the Dutchman Tarbet, the Frenchman de la Neuville—adjudged him something of a dreamer, "filled with all kinds of good intents," but at the same time a man of critical tastes and judgments.[30]

Throughout his tenure of office, Golitsyn's friendly interest in foreigners endured. When Gordon went to England in 1686, Golitsyn corresponded with him, urging him to seek out English recruits for service in Russia as engineers, miners, army officers, and so on.[31] Golitsyn's home in Moscow became a gathering place for educated foreigners—merchants, diplomats, travelers. There they received a cordial welcome and might freely exchange ideas. Even Jesuits, whom most Russians profoundly mistrusted and discriminated against, found in Golitsyn's home a social haven to which they might retreat.[32]

Golitsyn had a lively interest in the physical appearance of Moscow and particularly in the erection of stone buildings. Moscow in the eighties was still a wooden city, picturesque and impressive in parts, but in many respects an overgrown town, with unpaved streets, low-ceilinged, roughly hewn lumber buildings, vegetable gardens, open-air markets. Foreigners sometimes described it as the burning city because of the frequent fires that swept the various quarters. Two great fires had occurred in Moscow in 1611 and 1671 and, according to contemporary accounts, had destroyed the greater part of the city.[33] A decree of 1681 ordered every building roofed with planks, and the planks covered with earth and stamped with turf to insure against fire, but the fire hazard remained a grave one.[34]

---

[30] Platonov, *op. cit.*, p. 126: "If I had a mind to write down everything I have learned about this prince, I would never finish; it is enough to say that he wished to populate the desert places, enrich the beggars, transform the savages into men, the cowards into brave men, the shepherd huts into stone palaces."—De la Neuville as quoted by Platonov.
[31] Brückner, *op. cit.*, p. 294.
[32] Platonov, *op. cit.*, p. 127.
[33] I. M. Kulischer, *Russische Wirtschaftsgeschichte*, I, 294.
[34] De la Neuville noted that fires in Moscow were often not brought under control until several hundred homes had burned. "In 1689 I saw three fires, each of which destroyed from 500–600 houses...." De la Neuville, *op. cit.*, LXXII, 269.

To combat the danger Golitsyn ordered the erection of many new stone buildings and bridges. A palace for foreign ambassadors erected in stone and Golitsyn's own palace built of stone with heavy brass sheet roofing served as models for the wealthy nobility. According to contemporary accounts, the Golitsyn palace was "one of the most magnificent in Europe" and more like "the palace of an Italian prince." Its interior was ornamented with wood carvings and murals. Costly mirrors filled the space between windows, and in the larger rooms portraits of Russian and foreign nobles enlivened the walls, interspersed with German maps in heavy gilt frames. During Sophia's regency some 3,000 stone buildings reportedly were erected in Moscow, a change, according to de la Neuville, "directly attributable to Golitsyn."[35]

Throughout the eighties, the religious question remained a thorny one and posed a particular problem for a regime that felt strong attractions for the Latin West. In its attitude toward the Old Believers, the regency adopted the same uncompromising position as its predecessors. Tsarevna Sophia, like her brother Feodor, regarded them as heretics and rebels, dishonoring the Holy Church and subverting the very foundations of the state. Their movement had political as well as religious overtones which made its destruction even more necessary for the stability of the government. Thousands of heretics had perished on the gallows or at the stake, but their ideas lived on and their ranks were rapidly filled with new converts. Patriarch Joachim, temperate though he was as compared to Nikon, vigorously supported the extirpation of the schism. The tsarevna, even had she chosen otherwise, could do no less than give him support, since at a time when her government was already charged with sanctioning many innovations, she could ill afford the further reproach of religious inconstancy.[36]

Following the regent's return to Moscow after the Strel'tsy disorder of 1682 a decree had been issued November 14 to Kornilius, Metropolitan of Novgorod, to search out all Old Believers in his city and its environs and to turn them over to the courts. The voevoda of Novgorod was simultaneously instructed to provide troops to carry out the decree.[37] In the Tobolsk area, converts to the movement were prohibited from leaving their towns for schismatic camps along the Berezovka River between Berezov and Verkhoturie.[38] Detailed instructions for the apprehension of local schismatic leaders soon followed to many cities and

---
[35] De la Neuville, *op. cit.*, Part II, p. 266; Brückner, *op. cit.*, p. 299.
[36] Pomialovskii, *op. cit.*, p. 135.
[37] *A.I.*, V, 161–162.
[38] *Ibid.*, pp. 162–163.

towns. Periodic reports were to be furnished the government by metropolitans and archbishops, in districts where schismatic sentiment was known to be strong, about the measures that had been adopted to carry out the government order. Gelasius, Archimandrite of Ustiug, for example, reported to the government in November, 1683, that he had received instructions from Patriarch Joachim about the methods of protecting the orthodox from the false teachings of the Old Believers and had succeeded in winning back many to the fold.[39] In some respects the government's undertaking suggested that of the Counter Reformation in Western Europe, so successfully waged during the course of the same century.

In 1684 a series of regulations established more stringent measures for the seizure and punishment of heretics.[40] Anyone who failed to attend church services was to be questioned, and those who fell under suspicion of heresy were to be tortured until their guilt or innocence was established. Those who admitted heretical beliefs and who refused to recant were to be burned at the stake. At the same time the population in various districts where schism was rife were warned against giving them shelter. Those who did so willfully were to have their property confiscated and were to be exiled. Those who unwittingly failed to observe this regulation were to be fined. Those in turn who had persuaded others to accept heretical teachings and then later recanted were to be put to death without mercy. Anyone who did not acknowledge the Orthodox Church as the only true church was to suffer death. The latter regulation, of course, did not apply to those minority groups who had never been Orthodox Christians, such as the Tatars, Kalmyks, and foreign residents in Moscow.[41] But it did apply to all Orthodox Christians without exception. During the following three years, other decrees were promulgated concerning the suppression of the Old Believers, but the movement showed few signs of abating. In certain districts, it was true, the movement went underground, but in others it flourished openly and was even flaunted before the Orthodox Church in the community. Flagellations, imprisonment, the gallows, burning at the stake could not stamp it out; nor did less drastic measures—fines, segregation, and property confiscation—root out the sympathy felt by many orthodox Russians for its adherents.[42]

---

[39] *D.A.I.*, X, 445–446.
[40] *P.S.Z.*, II, 647–650.
[41] *Ibid.*, pp. 662–663: "Concerning the christening of the Non-Orthodox only in accordance with their own free desire and without any compulsion. Concerning the observance of decorum toward non-baptized Tatars and other non-orthodox peoples."
[42] Miliukov, *op. cit.*, Part I, pp. 59–60.

In the Olonetsk district, to cite one example, a band of one hundred and fifty Old Believers had appeared before the Paleostrovskii Monastery in the fall of 1688 and taken the orthodox brethren captive. From there they launched an active campaign in the vicinity to win converts, which met with considerable success. The threats and entreaties of the local archpriest to get them to abandon their activities proved unavailing, only resulting in reprisals against his parishioners and the conversion of the local monastery into a citadel. For nine weeks the neighboring districts were proselytized while the monastery was sacked of its churchbooks, charters, certificates of enserfment of its peasants, vestments, relics, and vessels. The services of a Strel'tsy regiment were finally required to dislodge the invaders, but they forestalled capture by setting the monastery afire and perished to a man in the flames, forcing, at the same time, the captive orthodox brethren into martyrdom with them.[43]

As the struggle between the Church and the schismatics wore on, the conflict between the advocates of Greek and Latin learning in Russian education was renewed. The Zaikonospasskii Monastery School, under Medvedev's guidance, had reopened in 1682, and like Polotskii's before it, soon became noted for its Latin tendencies. Its enrollment remained small, never exceeding twenty-three students, but it enjoyed the quiet encouragement of the government. Medvedev, like Polotskii, stressed Russian grammar, Latin, and rhetoric. His approach to education, like most instruction at that time, had a strong moral-religious character. Medvedev deplored the unconditional faith of Russian grammarians in the Greeks, from whom they accepted all knowledge "like babes."[44]

On religious holidays and other occasions, pupils of the Zaikonospasskii School often gave orations before Patriarch Joachim and other religious dignitaries. Their intellectual attainments and familiarity with Latin theological literature were impressive but disturbing to Joachim as well as to some other high churchmen. To offset the influence of the school, the patriarch redoubled his support of the Graecophile school of the monk Timothy, founded in 1679 at the Moscow Printing Office. Timothy had sojourned for many years in the Near East, was a master of Greek, and taught only those subjects approved by the Church. In 1684, there were 191 students enrolled in his school, of whom 168 specialized in Slavic and 23 in Greek studies. Within two years, enrollment increased to nearly 250 students.[45]

---

[43] *A.I.*, V, 255–257.
[44] Prozorovskii, *op. cit.*, p. 196; Belov, *op. cit.*, p. 101.
[45] Nechaev, *op. cit.*, III, 86–87.

Medvedev was gradually drawn into further conflict with his rivals. In 1681 he had been assigned to refute the heretical teachings of a certain reformist-preacher, Jan Belobodsky. Belobodsky had come to Moscow from Lithuania to offer his services as an instructor. He held no definite faith, and for a professorship was ready to make intellectual concessions. Upon instruction from Patriarch Joachim, Medvedev exposed him. Medvedev's reply to Belobodsky's *Confession of Faith* appeared in 1685 as *Khleb Zhivotnyi* (The Book of the Life-Giving Bread). In his reply Medvedev tended to ignore some of the basic questions posed by Belobodsky and became involved in controversial matters regarding transubstantiation, particularly the time when the wine and wafer used in the sacrament were transformed into the blood and body of Christ. In attacking the problem, Medvedev perhaps thought to weaken the teachings of the Graecophiles on that subject, but instead only succeeded in providing his enemies with material for charges against his quasi-Roman Catholic views.[46]

The *Khleb Zhivotnyi* of Silvester Medvedev was written in Socratic form—thirty questions and answers were posed between a pupil and teacher. The pupil, suffering from doubt and confusion about certain passages in the Scriptures—a condition presumably representative of many in the Russian Church—sought a solution for his religious quandaries from his teacher, a native Russian authority, who led him out of his torment. Medvedev's approach was calm and without the religious fervor common to so many theological treatises of that time. He cleverly developed a position on the Eucharist which suggested that of the Roman Church on the moment of transubstantiation. His views were more clearly defined in a later work entitled *Manna* (1687), but, with the appearance of *Khleb Zhivotnyi*, a long debate began between Medvedev and his enemies which ended in his downfall.

In the same year in which the controversy began, 1685, Medvedev intensified the issue by formally requesting Tsarevna Sophia to establish an academy in Moscow. The request took the form of a petition in verse for a Charter of Privileges (*Privilegiia*). This lengthy encomium, written in the high-flown panegyric style of the Kievans, extolled the virtues of the regent in extravagant fashion. Her wisdom, piety, kindliness, nobility of character, and other attributes were dwelt upon at length, and repeated to the point of monotony—all toward the end of

---

[46] Prozorovskii, *op. cit.*, pp. 416–417.

encouraging her to fulfill the hope so long entertained by Medvedev of founding an academy that would bring the light of learning to Russia.

> As the sun is reflected in the mirror
> So in your soul we behold the Holy Ghost...
> O gracious Grand Tsarevna, the very wise Sophia Alekseevna,
> Beloved by the Holy Trinity
> Who had endowed her with holy gifts...
> Just like Olga who showed the light of faith
> For which she gained eternal heaven,
> So the same do you wish to bring to Russia the light of learning,
> And for this you are to live in Heaven forever.[47]

Medvedev's flattering entreaties were not without effect. The Privilegiia received favorable attention from Sophia, and a commission was appointed, made up of Graecophiles and Western sympathizers, to look into the matter and make recommendations. The curriculum suggested by Medvedev included grammar, philosophy, ethics, dialectics, physics, law, and theology in addition to Greek, Latin, Polish, and Slavic. No restrictions in rank were to be imposed on students seeking admission to the academy, but all must be of the orthodox faith. The academy was to be administered by a government-appointed corporation under the direction of a rector. The corporation was to control all academy funds which were to be derived principally from the income of eight monasteries and one crown patrimony. The academy was to have jurisdiction over its students in all matters except criminal cases. And even then "crimes of a religious nature" were to be punished by the staff. Any heretical beliefs entertained by faculty members and students were to be dealt with by the academy. All books in the Polish, Latin, and German languages, as well as those dealing with the Lutheran and Calvinistic faith, were to be placed in custody of the corporation, and certain books belonging to the government were to be given to the academy.[48]

The Graecophile party became alarmed at these proposals. It determined that if such an academy were to be instituted, the interests of orthodoxy must be preserved. So long as Sophia was in power, Medvedev had a sponsor and could not be easily removed, but the Graecophiles insisted that an institution which was to become the highest center of learning in the state must be adequately protected from "Latinism." However greatly the regent may have sympathized with Medvedev, she was in no position to see herself charged with failure to protect the

[47] Prozorovskii, *op. cit.*, pp. 385–386.
[48] Nechaev, *op. cit.*, pp. 85–86.

Orthodox Church, nor could she afford to permit a key institution like the Church, which supported the autocratic order, suffer further embarassment and weakening at a time when its struggle with the Old Believers was in full force. Medvedev's leadership in the new institution could not be assured by the regent, nor could his stand against the Graecophiles be openly supported.

The hand of Medvedev's opponents was greatly strengthened in March, 1685, by the appearance in Moscow of two learned Greeks, the Likhudy brothers. They had arrived in response to a request from Patriarch Joachim to the Patriarch of Jerusalem for two theologians who might successfully combat the growing prestige of the Latin party. The pro-Greek loyalties of the Likhudy brothers and their wide acquaintance with Latin scholarship made them the most formidable foes yet encountered by Medvedev. The patriarch rapidly thrust them forward as the principal spokesmen for orthodoxy and as potential leaders for the academy. Joachim simultaneously supported a measure to insure further that the academy would never fall under the influence of Kievan scholarship. This measure provided that no White Russians or Ukrainians were to be admitted to the faculty without first furnishing proof of their loyalty to orthodoxy. Each candidate for an official position in the academy would have to produce recommendations from loyal orthodox churchmen for his religious faithfulness and reliability. Medvedev's efforts to remove this restriction from the final draft of the charter failed. Thus instructors who were properly qualified according to Kievan standards were barred from the academy. Medvedev parried the blow of his opponents somewhat by insisting that similar restrictions be imposed against the Greeks. After much argument this was agreed to.

Having successfully assured themselves about the nature of instruction in the academy, Medvedev's foes next directed their attention to keeping the very proponent of the academy out of the institution. Late in 1685, the Likhudy challenged Medvedev to a series of debates on religious doctrine. Medvedev accepted the challenge. Controversial statements from his writings and other evidence against him were gathered. The exhausting discussion which followed lasted five years and involved many delicate questions of faith and reason in religion. Joachim feared that the dispute might enlarge into a mass movement comparable to that of the schismatics, as the tenor of the discussions grew more impassioned and vituperative and as the alternate successes and failures of the protagonists were widely discussed not only by churchmen but by laymen—men, women, and children.[46]

---

[46] Nechaev, op. cit., p. 90.

Medvedev supported the Polotskii view, prevalent throughout the Ukraine, that the transubstantiation of the sacrament took place at the moment when the priest repeated the words of Jesus: "Take, eat; this is my body." The Likhudy and the Graecophiles maintained that transubstantiation took place only after the prayer of the priest to the Lord had been uttered to send down the Holy Ghost because of Christ's merits and sufferings.[50] As the debate mounted, Medvedev wrote additional treatises—*Manna, Akos,* and others—to state his views more forcibly. The temperate quality of his earlier works now changed to one of vehemence and indignation as the thrusts of his opponents grew sharper and more telling. Sufficient evidence was finally gathered against him to cause his dismissal as corrector at the Printing Office (1686). The orthodox clergy in the Ukraine were simultaneously compelled, under threat of excommunication, to repudiate his teachings. A rumor spread that Medvedev was plotting to remove the patriarch and take over the office himself. In 1687, Medvedev was forced to retire as a teacher from the Zaikonospasskii School.

The Likhudy brothers meanwhile opened a Graecophile school of their own in Bogoiavlenskii Monastery in Kitai Gorod, Moscow (1685–1686). It enjoyed the full support of the patriarch and rapidly attracted students from the schools of Timothy and Zaikonospasskii Monastery. In October, 1687, it moved into the stone quarters originally intended for Medvedev's school and henceforth became known as "the academy." Although its curriculum was less ambitious than that envisaged by Medvedev, it was nonetheless the most comprehensive in Moscow. For the remaining years of Sophia's regime, its position among Russian schools was preëminent.

It now appeared that everything had again fallen into the hands of the Greeks. They had appropriated Medvedev's plan, recast it to their own liking, and finally excluded him from the academy. But their victory was short lived. Within five years, the Likhudy too fell into disfavor with the Graecophiles. Like other Greeks before them in Moscow, they made no effort to dispel the prejudice against them as foreigners. The character of their instruction, as it developed, differed only slightly from that of the Westerners, for they had studied at Venice and were doctors of Padua University. They had no special knowledge of the sciences, nor were they particularly able instructors. These failures were carefully pointed out by their opponents. Besides, the personal conduct of the Likhudy gave offense. They and their sons rather in-

---

[50] Miliukov, *op. cit.,* pp. 137–138.

advertently became implicated in several unpopular court intrigues. For this even their benefactor, Patriarch Dosifei of Jerusalem, censured them. In 1694, after an inglorious attempt to flee Moscow, they were brought back to the capital and relieved of their offices. The academy thereafter fell into the hands of men of Latin learning—"the foster-children of the Kievan academy."[51]

Thus it was that the government of Sophia felt the impact of the various cultural forces transforming Russia in the late seventeenth century. The reform movement which had germinated during the reigns of Tsars Alexis and Feodor, emerged into clear view during her regency, to attain mushroom growth under Peter.[52] Of Sophia's regime, Miliukov has written: "... the elements of reform in a moderately national spirit were all on hand."[53] This was true. A new stimulus was given to education and a further blow was struck at narrow national prejudice and outlook. The Russians, to a greater extent than ever before, awakened to the need for criticism of the old order with its acceptance of everything on faith.[54] To be sure, Sophia's government, like its predecessor, had taken an uncompromising attitude toward the Old Believers. The decree of 1684 threatened every impenitent follower of the old faith with death at the stake.[55] But nonorthodox minorities in Siberia and outlying areas of European Russia were assured full protection by the regent. The church at Kiev was allowed to continue its teaching of Latin, as it had done under Polish rule, and to publish Latin texts. Also, in 1689, following the Revocation of the Edict of Nantes in France, Sophia offered French Huguenots a sanctuary in Russia with a guarantee that they would be permitted full freedom of faith.[56] These contradictions make it appear that the regent's action against the Old Believers was dictated more by the need to preserve social and political order than to compel religious uniformity.

The regency of Sophia witnessed a growing interest in many Western innovations. Russia became more aware of the attractions of the fine arts, drama, and literature, and of the dress and customs of Western Europe. Western literature in translation appeared in greater abundance—romantic tales, comic stories, collections of anecdotes. Most of the translations were from the Polish, but others came from German,

[51] Platonov, *op. cit.*, pp. 145–146.
[52] Brückner, *op. cit.*, p. 281.
[53] Miliukov, *op. cit.*, Part III, 162.
[54] Belov, *op. cit.*, Part I, p. 101.
[55] *P.S.Z.*, II, 647–650.
[56] *P.S.Z.*, II, 702–703; III, 8–9.

Latin, Czech, and Serbian sources.[57] The taste for foreign articles of clothing and toiletries increased. Polish gloves, fur caps, and soap were in demand. Polish songs became popular. Much attention was given to genealogical investigations, coats of arms, and ancestor portraits in the manner of Western Europe.[58] The generally auspicious atmosphere in which the new regime took over its responsibilities has perhaps nowhere been more enthusiastically described than in the words of a contemporary of Tsar Peter, Prince Boris I. Kurakin:

> The reign of Tsarevna Sophia began with all diligence and equitability so that there never was such a wise government in the Russian state. And the whole state entered through the seven years of her reign into the fullness of great wealth. Commerce was augmented and all kinds of trade; the sciences began and the restoration of the Latin and Greek tongues; and politesse in the Polish manner was practiced among the great nobility and other officers of the court—both in equipages, in the building of houses, and in attire and dining.[59]

This was the keynote upon which Sophia's regime began its activities. Unfortunately its efforts in such directions were repeatedly diverted by issues requiring the government's fuller energies.

---
[57] Gudzy, *op. cit.*, pp. 397, 413, 428.
[58] Platonov, *op. cit.*, p. 146.
[59] *Arkhiv Kurakina*, I, 50.

CHAPTER IV

CHANGES IN NATIONAL ECONOMY

THE WIDENING horizon of Russian culture, so abundantly apparent during the eighties, derived to a marked extent from the closer economic integration of Eastern and Western Europe. Adherents of the economic theory of history, in fact, might find substantial evidence to support the view that the cultural challenge felt by Russia from the West came primarily through trade competition and from association with foreign merchants. The latter had exerted a decisive influence on national economy long before they began to affect the arts and learning. The commercial revolution, the growth of mercantilism, and the Thirty Years' War had sent a wave of traders, adventurers, and political-religious refugees to Eastern Europe. Many had come to Russia. Moscow welcomed them because of their professional skills, adopted many of their techniques, and hoped to learn from them how to meet more effectively the trade competition of their homelands.[1]

---

[1] The collections of official documents have a wide variety of materials on seventeenth century economic history. *P.S.Z.*, II, has a large number of decrees and instructions on customs administration, trade regulations, and peasant labor. *D.A.I.*, X, has materials relating to the iron and textile industries which illustrate the interest of Sophia's government in industrial enterprise. *A.I.*, V, contains many instructions pertaining to the elimination of administrative corruption in the collection of taxes. Among the secondary materials the following have been useful. I. M. Kulischer's *Istoriia russkogo narodnogo khoziaistva* [History of Russian national economy], 1925, and *Istoriia russkoi torgovli do XIX-go veka vkliuchitel'no* [History of Russian trade up to the nineteenth century inclusive], 1923, provide a general survey of Russian domestic economy and foreign trade. P. Miliukov's *Gosudarstvennoe khoziaistva rossii v pervoi chetverti XVIII stoletiia* has an excellent introductory chapter on the basic characteristics of Russian national economy of the seventeenth century. N. Rozhkov's *Russkaia istoriia*, V [Russian History], 1921, provides further critical observations on Russian trade and economy and furnishes some interesting statistical information on Russian trade which is difficult to find elsewhere. G. Kotoshikhin's *O Rossii v tsarstvovanie Alekseia Mikhailovicha* [About Russia in the reign of Alexis Mikhailovich], 3d ed., 1884, gives a colorful contemporary picture of trade in Moscow during the later reign of Tsar Alexis. M. N. Pokrovskii's *Russkaia istoriia s drevneishnikh vremen*, II [Russian history from ancient times], has a good chapter (XII) on Petrine reforms and trade. I. Lubimenko's *Les Relations commerciales et politiques de l'Angleterre avec la Russie avant Pierre le Grand* is useful for its citations of the prices of Russian goods in the European market.

Among the more recent works on economic history P. I. Lyashchenko's *History of the National Economy of Russia*, 1949, provides the best over-all analysis of Russian historical economic phenomena. His work deals not only with the Great Russian area but with the Ukraine, Georgia, Bashkiria, and other outlying regions. The bibliographical notes at the end of each chapter and the bibliographic index at the end of the work give many useful citations to recent works on economic history published in the Soviet Union. Although Lyashchenko is an avowed Marxist his work is distinguished for its scope, documentation, and attention to detail. P. T. Liubomirov's *Ocherki po istorii russkoi promyshlennosti* [Outlines on the history of Russian industry], 1947, briefly analyzes the metallurgical industry and the role of state and

In the generation before Peter, Russia was already undergoing a revolutionary change from natural domestic economy to trade capitalism.[2] Before the seventeenth century, Russia, in the phrase of one historian, was in a stage of "precapitalist" development.[3] A mixed barter-money economy prevailed. Craft industry was poorly organized and trade heavily encumbered by a welter of medieval regulations and practices. Agriculture was still the primary economic activity for the majority of the population, but trade, trade revenues, and royal commercial monopoly provided the state with the largest income. The transition to trade capitalism made great strides during the reigns of Tsars Alexis and Feodor. By 1682 it was well along toward full development. Russia, like most European powers of the seventeenth century, had become increasingly conscious of the importance of precious metals and domestic industry to the welfare and security of the state and was prepared to adopt stronger means to promote them. By the second half of the century, two important trends had appeared: (1) the extraordinary advantages which the foreign merchant had long held in Russian trade were disappearing; (2) substantial gains were registered in the government's effort to bring order into national economy and to free trade from the oppressive restrictions imposed by the medieval spirit of localism.[4]

Russia in the late seventeenth century was a predominantly agricultural country. The great mass of the people and, to a remarkable extent, the nobility and clergy were intimately concerned with agriculture, its needs and requirements.[5] Wealth was still measured in terms of land. The desire to acquire more land was universal. Even the government was "land-minded," not only because of the produce obtained from crown lands, but because it found land a convenient method of disposing of part of its financial obligations. Vast new territories in the

---

private capital in the development of "great" industries in Russia in the seventeenth century. It suffers, however, from a heavy Marxist bias. A. I. Zaozerskii's *Tsar Aleksei Mikhailovich v svoem khoziaistve* [Tsar Alexis Mikhailovich and his economy], 1917, and E. I. Zaozerskaiia's *Manufaktura pri Petre I* [Manufacturing in the time of Peter I], 1947, have additional material on the central government's growing interest in industrial enterprise.

[2] By trade capitalism is meant that stage of early capitalism in Russia when the interests of trade exercised a dominant influence in the formation of national economic policy. The scale of trade became greater. Larger private capital accumulated. Markets and transactions in certain trades became national in scope. The concern for foreign trade increased.

[3] I. M. Kulisher, *Russische Wirtschaftsgeschichte*, I, 444.

[4] K. Lodyzhenskii, *Istoriia russkago tamozhennago tarifa*, pp. 25-29.

[5] C. B. O'Brien, "Agriculture in Russian War Economy in the Later Seventeenth Century", *The American Slavic and East European Review*, VIII (Oct., 1949), 167-174.

Ukraine, Siberia, and the Far East had been incorporated earlier in the century. Many of them were occupied by subject peoples and could not be readily exploited by the state, but in other cases parts of them became crown lands or were granted out to individuals as estates—pomesties or votchinas.

Since money was scarce in Russia during this period the government depended on land to aid it in financing its military projects and to reward its extensive civil service for duties performed for the state. When the government paid an individual for public service or bestowed a special favor upon him or upon a monastery, it was frequently in the form of land. Additional rewards might be given in money, furs, or some other object of esteem, but these were supplementary to land, which represented the substance of the award.[6]

Land also furnished the crown with necessary supplies and additional revenues. The tsar like the clergy, engaged in commercial as well as subsistence farming in the seventeenth century.[7] Specialized crops were cultivated for marketing and for furnishing the court commissary with basic food commodities. During the reign of Tsar Alexis, one of the responsibilities of the Office of Secret Affairs (*Prikaz Tainykh Del*) had been the administration of the imperial farms where cereal crops were grown, large herds of domestic animals maintained, and various agricultural experiments conducted.[8] The estates of Tsar Alexis, it was estimated, brought him an annual income of 200,000 rubles.[9]

The need of the government for greater revenue was chronic. State income was derived from two main sources—direct and indirect taxation. Direct taxes yielded less revenue than indirect taxes, though during the course of the seventeenth century the income from direct taxes tended to increase.[10] Direct and indirect taxes represented an accumulation of unsystematic revenue procedures formulated over many generations under highly divergent conditions. Government trade and taxes on trade furnished the state a substantial income, but it was insufficient in time of war. And since war and preparation for it engaged the

---

[6] See, for example, the citations of awards given to various diplomatic representatives of the seventeenth century in "Inquiries conducted in the Appointment Office in 1686", *Vremenik imperatorskago moskovskago obshchestva istorii drevnostei rossiiskikh*, V (1850), 1–10.

[7] A. M. Bol'shakov and N. A. Rozhkov, eds., *Istoriia khoziaistva rossii v materialakh i dokumentakh*, I, 194–201.

[8] *Ibid.*

[9] P. I. Lyashchenko, *History of the National Economy of Russia*, p. 213.

[10] P. Miliukov, *Gosudarstvennoe khoziaistvo rossii v pervoi chetverti XVIII stoletiia*, p. 78.

energies of the state for a substantial part of the century, the treasury had continually to deal with the problem of deficits.[11]

National income figures for the late seventeeth century are difficult to establish, since only fragmentary information about the budget existed before 1680. Besides, historians who have examined the documentary materials do not agree on the statistics. The Russian historian Miliukov, for example, conducted painstaking research on the problem. After deducting the current state funds in circulation, beginning with the budget of 1680, he estimated that the actual income and expenditures of that year were as follows:[12]

income .... 1,897,026 r.
expenditure .... 1,489,951 r.

N. Rozhkov, on the other hand, estimated national revenue in 1680 as 1,220,000 rubles and expenditures as 1,125,000 rubles. Some 44 per cent of the national income, according to Rozhkov, was derived from direct taxation and 56 per cent from indirect taxes.[13] These figures make an interesting comparison with those of Gregory Kotoshikhin, the seventeenth-century official, who estimated the annual monetary income of the royal treasury during the early sixties to be 1,311,000 rubles, exclusive of the income from Siberia.[14]

Two factors contributed directly to national financial instability: the absence of a budget before 1680, and inadequate tax machinery. Not until 1680 did a genuine national budget exist. Informal estimates of national income and expenditures were computed earlier, but no official statement of anticipated income and expense was made before that year. In this Russia was not far behind such countries as France and certain Germanic states. But the fact that no census system had been instituted before 1678–1679 upon which to base budgetary estimates made financial calculations awkward and faulty.

The machinery for state tax collection was also in need of overhauling. The taxation system of Sophia's time emanated largely from

---

[11] N. Rozhkov, *Russkaia istoriia v sravnitel'no-istoricheskom osveshchenii*, V, 63–65; P. Miliukov, *Ocherki po istorii russkoi kul'tury*, Part I, 149, 152, 199.
[12] Miliukov, *Gosudarstvennoe khoziaistvo rossii* ... , p. 77. At the same time Miliukov furnishes other estimates of income and expenditure for 1680, based on the inclusion and exclusion of particular items. In his *Ocherki po istorii russkoi kul'tury*, Part I, 157, he cites the total expenditure for that year as roughly 1,500,000 rubles.
[13] Rozhkov, *op. cit.*, p. 67.
[14] G. Kotoshikhin, *O Rossii v tsarstvovanie Alekseia Mikhailovicha*, p. 138: "All told the annual monetary income into the royal treasure that is collected at all *prikazes* from the entire estate except that paid in towns is approximately 1,311,000 rubles (not counting the Siberian income)."

methods developed during the reigns of Tsar Alexis and Tsar Feodor. The treasury's ordinary revenues consisted of assessed income (*okladnye dokhod*) and nonassessed income (*neokladnye dokhod*).[15] Okladnye income, which was fixed in advance, was definite enough in yield for the government to rely upon in making its budgetary estimates.[16] The sources of assessed revenue included customs and excise dues, direct imposts and special taxes to meet particular needs. Neokladnye income yielded less calculable amounts of revenue and consisted of levies upon private transactions (state seal and licensing fees), upon petitions to official administrative offices, and upon documents granted in the form of legal decisions (judicial fees).[17] In general the government regarded the income of the current year as the guide for its allotment for the subsequent year. If, however, revenues remained smaller over a period of years, adjustments were made, but the largest amount of taxes collected in any one year over a period in which fluctuations occurred was regarded as the norm to be followed. Under such procedures deficits were frequent and the government appeared to be as powerless in its struggle with them as in its attempts to stabilize allotments.[18]

During Tsar Feodor's reign an initial tax reform was attempted (1681) when four of the principal state taxes—quitrent (*obrochnyia podati*), the Strel'tsy tax (*streletskiia den'gi*), the transport-service tax (*iamskiia den'gi*), and ransom money (*polonianichnyia den'gi*)—were reduced to three. These had been levied separately in different parts of the state without much uniformity. In certain districts all four were imposed on the population; in others only two or three were collected. The decree of 1681 combined the transport-service and ransom money taxes into one tax. It provided that each taxpayer pay two but no more than two of these taxes. Quitrent (*obrok*) was to be gathered from all lands of the state and also from all trade and craft-industrial enterprises. In other words, the whole population upon whom direct assessment rested—namely the peasantry and the artisan-trading classes—paid quitrent. The Strel'tsy tax was to be paid by all towns and by the northern districts of the state. The transport-ransom tax was to be paid by all districts other than those of the north and not by the towns. Thus, all towns and northern districts paid quitrent and Strel'tsy dues, whereas remaining districts paid quitrent and the transport-ransom

---

[15] Miliukov, *Gosudarstvennoe khoziaistvo rossii* ..., pp. 3–4.
[16] V. O. Kliuchevsky, *A History of Russia*, III, 225; G. V. Lantzeff, *Siberia in the Seventeenth Century*, p. 127.
[17] Kliuchevsky, *op. cit.*, p. 229, Rozhkov, *op. cit.*, p. 64.
[18] Miliukov, *Gosudarstvennoe khoziaistvo rossii* ..., pp. 9–10.

tax.[19] Although this represented only one step toward better unification and order in taxation, the trend toward reform is important to note.

The interests of commerce down to the middle of the seventeenth century received scant consideration from the state. Trade was largely conducted on a regional basis.[20] In domestic trade, the medieval concept of private right and prerogative prevailed. Highways and navigable rivers were articulated into sections which stood under private control, their overseers stubbornly refusing to yield privileges which successive tsars had confirmed. Merchants paid license fees, numerous excise taxes, market tolls, and charges for warehouse and drayage services. The corruption of some local officials in exacting trade revenues was a subject of frequent complaint by native and foreign merchants alike. The government acted slowly in remedying these evils. The principle of special privilege remained strong.[21]

In foreign trade native merchants also suffered disadvantages. Government controls and the privileges still held by foreign residents in Moscow greatly hampered trade.[22] During the reign of Tsar Alexis Mikhailovich a series of statutes, largely resulting from the fervent petitions of Russian merchants, attempted to remove some of the abuses created by the inequitable customs apparatus as well as some of the extraordinary privileges enjoyed by foreigners in trade. The most important decrees were those of 1649, 1654, and 1667. Special privileges long enjoyed by Englishmen in trade with Russia were revoked by the decree of 1649.[23] The trade statute (*Torgovy Ustav*) of 1654 provided for the payment of customs dues in rubles rather than in various petty forms, including some payable in kind. At the same time the collection of taxes by tax farmers was abolished.[24] In 1667, the New Trade Statute (*Novo-Torgovy Ustav*) brought foreign as well as domestic trade under closer government supervision. Export duties were separated from import duties and foreigners were prohibited from engaging in direct retail trade with the population.[25] But the large profits and generally favorable opportunities open to the foreign trader in Russia continued at the expense of the Russian producer and consumer.[26]

---

[19] Rozhkov, *op. cit.*, p. 65.
[20] Lyashchenko, *op. cit.*, p. 219.
[21] P. Shchebal'skii, *Pravlenie Tsarevny Sofii*, p. 82.
[22] Lodyzhenskii, *op. cit.*, p. 18–20.
[23] *Ibid.*, p. 26.
[24] *Ibid.*, p. 27.
[25] *Novo-Torgovy Ustav*, *P.S.Z.*, I (Apr. 22, 1667) 677–690; Lyashchenko, *op. cit.*, p. 227.
[26] Lyashchenko, *op. cit.*, p. 227; V. Barbour, *Capitalism in Amsterdam in the 17th Century*, pp. 39, 115–116, 119.

The Russian merchant also found himself circumscribed by royal trade monopoly and by the encroachment of the state in many channels of trade. The sale of alcoholic beverages, the production of salt, the manufacture of tar, hemp, and certain types of leather goods were government monopolies in the seventeenth century. The export fur trade with Asia virtually amounted to a monopoly, since the government controlled the choicest pelts and accumulated from tribute (*iasak*) such vast stores of furs as to discourage most traders from anything more than a local trade.[27]

But the encumbrances to trading did not discourage a large percentage of the population from entering small trade. Foreign residents in Russia almost uniformly took note that "everyone engaged in trade." In the smaller towns artisans, small merchants, peasants, and local residents conducted a sizable trade in handicrafts. The boyars openly bought and sold goods. In many towns, booths were reserved for the agents of the clergy—abbots, bishops, and sextons. The Strel'tsy took advantage of the bartering privileges allowed them to round out their meager salaries from the crown. Even the tsar traded through guest merchants in the larger towns and cities, and was referred to by some as "the first merchant of the state."[28] It was a highly localized trade for most, often a secondary occupation only, but every class from the highest nobility to the lowliest peasant engaged in it.[29]

The conception of profit in trade and the determination of price in Russia differed in certain respects from that of Western Europe. In contrast to the merchant of the West in the seventeenth century, the Russian adhered to the medieval concept of a just price for his labor and trouble in bringing his merchandise to market. The notion of profit as a primary goal often appeared to the West European to be strangely lacking in the Russian trading mind. This came from no unselfishness on the part of the Russian trader, but as a result of different values in determining the market price of goods. Foreigners noticed with astonishment the low prices of particular Russian articles such as silver buttons and leather goods, and alternately labeled the Rusian "dull," "stubborn," "crafty," and "capable of all kinds of swindles."[30] Few foreigners understood that the price of edibles was low in Russia and that the native

---

[27] R. H. Fisher, *The Russian Fur Trade 1550–1700*, p. 210; Kulisher, I, *op. cit.*, pp. 417–418; P. Mel'gunov, *Ocherki po istorii russkoi torgovli IX–XVIII v.v.*, p. 179.
[28] Kulisher, *op. cit.*, pp. 342–343, 345; Lyashchenko, *op. cit.*, pp. 219, 222–225.
[29] J. Mavor, *An Economic History of Russia*, I, 119.
[30] M. N. Pokrovskii, *Russkaia istoriia s drevneishnikh vremen*, II, 253; Lyashchenko, *op. cit.*, p. 227.

craftsman expected his labor to feed him and little else. He thought more in terms of how much food his labor would buy rather than in terms of the amount or quality of the work involved. Thus in transactions he was often prepared to accept only a fraction of profit rather than to exploit the demand for particular articles in the Western market.[31]

The price of Russian goods at home and abroad also varied. As an illustration, hemp sold in Russia for 33 kopecks a *pud*.[32] In Holland the same measure sold for the equivalent of 50 kopecks and in Spain for one ruble. Flax was valued at 82½ kopecks a pud in Russia, at one ruble in Holland, and at two rubles in Spain. Wax sold for two rubles 31 kopecks the pud in Russia, for three rubles in Holland, and six rubles in Spain. Rosin, cable rope, and other Russian products sold at proportionally higher prices abroad than in Moscow.[33]

The government in seventeenth-century Russia had not yet found the means to provide a stable monetary system to meet the demands of trade. The principal monetary units were the ruble, half ruble, and fractional units such as the *grivennik, altyn*, kopeck, and *den'ga*. There were few gold coins, and the silver ones were of foreign origin. Foreign countries, in fact, supplied Russia with a large part of its currency. Spanish doubloons, Italian ducats, German thalers, Dutch, English, and other foreign money circulated freely. The German silver thaler (*Joachimsthaler*) or *efimok*, which had originated in Bohemia in the sixteenth century was the most common larger coin in Russia.[34]

Gold coin was in great demand by the state. It was curious that in an age when the quest for gold was still alive, and in a country as rich in gold as Russia later proved to be, greater attention was not given to gold mining. Instead, all kinds of devices such as the reminting of coin and the reduction the metal content of money were resorted to in an effort to obtain more of the circulating medium. The imported thaler, during the reign of Tsar Alexis, was sometimes taken over by the tsar's treasury and counterstamped with an image of Saint George the Victorious, the letter "M" for Moscow, and an oblong stamp bearing the

---

[31] Pokrovskii, *op. cit.*, p. 255.

[32] A pud roughly equaled 36 pounds avoirdupois; 100 kopecks one ruble; see Alexandrov, A. *Polnyi russko-angliiskii slovar*, p. 754.

[33] "... the ruble of the second half of the seventeenth century equaled seventeen rubles of 1882." Kliuchevsky, "Russkii Rubl' XVI-XVII vv.", *Opty i issledovaniia*, p. 171; I. Lubimenko, *Les relations commerciales et politiques de l'Angleterre avec la Russie avant Pierre le Grand*, pp. 269–270.

[34] Mel'gunov, *op. cit.*, p. 191; Fisher, *op. cit.*, p. 131n.; The den'ga and altyn ceased to circulate after the seventeenth century. One ruble equaled 200 den'gas; one altyn equaled six den'gas.

date in Arabic numerals. It was then circulated as Russian coin. The government made about 6 per cent profit in the operation.[35]

The demand for currency produced other extraordinary developments. Counterfeiting flourished. In the late fifties the government attempted for several years to establish the use of copper coin at a forced ratio with silver. The new coin at first enjoyed public confidence but then gave rise to counterfeiting and to financial manipulating on the part of a number of government officials. The market became flooded with copper coin, trade and industry were critically affected, and a virtual financial panic ensued. As the scandalous activities of certain tsarist officials and prominent government leaders came to light the fury of the people was vented in the so-called "copper riots" of 1662. The government vigorously suppressed the uprising, but in the following year suspended the issue of the copper coin and ordered a return to the silver monetary standard.[36]

Money in Russia was not infrequently borrowed from the Church. The monasteries were rich in capital from donations of the faithful and from profits in business enterprise. The tsars gave them monetary gifts for special favors and as acts of piety. The boyars gave them money as a form of insurance against a day when they might fall into royal disfavor. The clergy were among the few social groups in the state wealthy enough to arrange loans and to extend credit. During the seventeenth century, the Church engaged in the loan business on a wide scale, often lending money at interest rates varying from 20 to 150 per cent.[37]

Like most social classes in Russia, the trading population was rather highly subdivided. Each had its special privileges and obligations. The Guests (*Gosti*) were the privileged merchants, who controlled the greatest capital. They conducted trade for the tsar as well as for themselves and administered the key offices in the supervision of government business enterprises. According to Kotoshikhin, there were about thirty Guests in 1650, and no evidence has appeared that their number was greatly augmented a generation later. A merchant became a Guest when he was called upon by the government to perform some special state service, such as serving as officer in charge of the Sable Treasury or as a sworn man at the customs' house in Moscow or at Arkhangel. While holding such office, he was free to conduct his own business.

---

[35] Mel'gunov, *op. cit.*, p. 192; Rozhkov, *op. cit.*, p. 62.
[36] A. Brückner, "Das Kupfergeld in Russland 1656–1663", in *Finanzgeschichtliche Studien*, pp. 61–65.
[37] Kulisher, *op. cit.*, pp. 381–382.

According to Kotoshikhin, each Guest conducted "...about 20,000, 30,000 or 100,000 rubles worth of business of his own annually."[38]

Below the Guests were the guild merchants of the Guest and Cloth Hundreds (*gostinnaia sotnia, sukonnaia sotna*) and traders of the suburbs or ordinary townsmen (*posadskie liudi*).[39] The merchants of the Guest and Cloth Hundreds supervised the collection of royal taxes in the cities and towns as associates or sworn men. There were about two hundred of them in Moscow.[40] The traders of the suburbs conducted their business in particular faubourgs assigned them in larger towns and cities. A group of them was called upon each year for imperial service as lesser customs officials and sworn men. They also served in taverns and in designated places of trade as collectors of internal revenue. The collection of taxes before 1654 was often farmed out to them. Those who succeeded in collecting a larger sum for the imperial coffers than that agreed upon received high praise from the government, whereas those who failed for some obvious reason—inertia or drunkenness—were severely punished, and the difference between the amount of taxes guaranteed by them and what they collected was taken out of their salaries.

The traders of the suburbs corresponded in most respects to the burghers of Western Europe. Groups of them were to be found in almost every town and city of Russia. They bartered in the commercial rows according to the type of merchandise sold, and on certain days of the week sold foodstuffs in the open markets, in public squares, on bridges, and in the plazas before churches. The public inconvenience thus created occasionally caused the government to impose restrictions on vendors. During Sophia's regime the government decreed (1683) that fish, meat, and caviar could not be sold beyond the Stone Bridge in Moscow but only "in the regular shops where such sale is permitted."[41] In 1685, the sale of all foodstuffs was prohibited in the public tower beyond the Stone Bridge and only permitted "in places provided for their sale."[42]

The lives of merchants in the trade quarters were circumscribed. Once having entered a *sloboda*, a trader could leave it only with difficulty. Each had a responsibility for his share of the state tax (*tiaglo*) and could evade payment only by entering a monastery or becoming a slave. Marriage between the members of one suburb and another was discouraged.[43]

---

[38] Kotoshikhin, *op. cit.*, p. 157; Lyashchenko, *op. cit.*, p. 224.
[39] G. V. Lantzeff, "Moscovite Russia" in *Handbook of Slavic Studies* (L. I. Strakhovsky ed.), p. 208; Lyashchenko, *op. cit.*, p. 224.
[40] Kotoshikin, *op. cit.*, p. 157.
[41] *P.S.Z.*, II, 559.
[42] *Ibid.*, p. 689.
[43] Mel'gunov, *op. cit.*, pp. 185–186.

On the other hand, the government placed no restrictions on the type of business in which a trader chose to engage. Wholesale and retail exchange might be conducted simultaneously in different goods and in different parts of the quarter." The men of the trade quarters were able businessmen, and in spite of the social restrictions placed upon them their number slowly increased in the seventeenth century.

The centers of Russian trade were widely dispersed. Because of its unique political and geographic position, Moscow was a focal point for larger commerce and had the most diversified markets and wealthiest merchants. Geographically, Moscow "was the crossroads of two great waterways and trunk lines of trade, the Caspian-Baltic axis of rivers and portages, and the west-east route from the Western Dvina to the Volga."⁴⁵ Two smaller streams, the Neglinnaia and the Yauza, supplemented traffic moving along the Moscow River to the capital. The presence of the tsarist court in Moscow alone stimulated a wide business activity. Besides the various business enterprises profiting from government patronage, the city was a natural center for foreigners seeking trade concessions from the tsars and for those called upon to perform economic service for the state. The richest merchants dwelt in Moscow. The agents of foreign traders permanently resided in the city.

Trade in Moscow was centered in the Trade Rows facing Red Square and in the district of the city known as *Kitai Gorod*. It also flourished on a smaller scale in two other parts of the city—*Belyi Gorod* and *Zemlianoi Gorod*.⁴⁶ Kitai Gorod (literally Chinatown), enclosed by a low brick wall, was larger in size than the Kremlin and contained many of the offices (*dvory*) that performed special services for the tsar. A Court of Foods (*Kormovoi dvor*) served as the court commissary. The Grain Court (*Khlebennyi dvor*) prepared bakery goods for the imperial household. The Treasury (*Kazennyi dvor*) cared for the bullion of the state, for the costly raiment of the royal family, and for the gifts received by the tsars from individuals and foreign powers.⁴⁷

Foreign merchants in Moscow generally traded along Varvarka Street in the Guest Court (*Gostinyi Dvor*) north of the trading rows. Late in the seventeenth century, Korb mentioned the Persian bazaar, where Armenians, Tatars, and Persians offered their goods for sale.⁴⁸ Kotoshikhin wrote that between fifty and one hundred Greeks came there

---
[44] Kulisher, *op. cit.*, I, 341.
[45] R. J. Kerner, *The Urge to the Sea*, p. 36.
[46] V. N. Bochkarev, *Tri Veka*, p. 250.
[47] Kotoshikhin, *op. cit.*, pp. 80–81.
[48] J. G. Korb, "Dnevnik Ioanna Georga Korba", *Chteniia*, no. 3 (1867), p. 264.

annually and brought "all kinds of goods—tableware, gold vessels, and silverware . . . brocades and horse harnesses." First offered to the tsar's treasury "as gifts," those not accepted for the tsar were sold to "people of any rank."[49]

Although Moscow was undoubtedly the most impressive city from the standpoint of the character and scale of its trade, there were other centers equally vital to the economic life of the state. Arkhangel was a great entrepôt for the import-export trade with Western Europe. In the second half of the seventeenth century it reputedly furnished the treasury with as high as 70,000 rubles in customs' revenue annually.[50] A Moscow Guest merchant and two associates from the guest hundred supervised the Arkhangel markets, which was indicative in itself of the town's economic importance. Pskov and Novgorod were prominent staple centers for goods directed to the Baltic ports of Riga and Reval. Smolensk and Viazma served as outposts for commerce with Lithuania, Poland, and the German states, though they had suffered greatly from the struggle with Poland over the Ukraine.[51] Nizhni-Novgorod conducted a lively exchange in grain, salt, and fish of the Volga region and with Kazan acted as a transit point for commerce with Siberia and Central Asia. Merchants from the West brought their merchandise to Nizhni-Novgorod and exchanged it for the products of Khiva, Bokhara, and occasionally India, though Astrakhan occupied first place as an oriental mart in Russia. Astrakhan was a spacious, well-populated city in the late seventeenth century, with a substantial foreign population. In Siberia, the towns of Tobolsk and Eniseisk were outstanding trade centers in the late seventeenth century, particularly for furs. Tobolsk conducted an important general trade with China and the Kalmyks. In Tobolsk Russian merchants exchanged their goods for Chinese silk, tea, spices, and porcelains. Eniseisk with the adjacent ostrog of Makovsk was the center of an active fur trade with trappers from the Stony Tunguska and Angara rivers and Lake Baikal.[52] In the Far East, Nerchinsk was the fur capital and also a center of unauthorized trade with the subject peoples of China. But in the eighties, economic activity at Nerchinsk had all but ceased because of strained diplomatic relations between Russia and China.[53]

Besides the urban centers cited above, two annual fairs in Russia acquired economic prominence in the late seventeenth century. The fair

---

[49] Kotoshikhin, *op. cit.*, p. 165.
[50] Bochkarev, *op. cit.*, p. 245. See also Miliukov, *Ocherki po istorii* . . . , I, p. 114.
[51] Mel'gunov, *op. cit.*, p. 195.
[52] Fisher, *op. cit.*, pp. 170–171.
[53] Bochkarev, *op. cit.*, p. 242.

at Tikhvin was visited by Swedish, English, and German merchants. The Makar'ev fair near Nizhni-Novgorod saw a sizable exchange of goods between European Russia and Siberia and served as a model for the Nizhni-Novgorod fairs of the nineteenth century.[54]

The peasant population in villages and towns often engaged in a communal production of goods. On monastery lands and on private estates, the abbot or landlord would organize the local peasantry on a semifactory basis for the production of specialized products.[55] Such enterprises might be dictated by an abundance of certain raw materials in the vicinity, by the unusual skill of the local peasantry in a particular craft, or by the local demand for a certain type of goods. Some of the workers were paid in money or in kind or both; others contributed their labor as part of the dues owed the landlord for their use of a household and tillage land. The boyar, B. I. Morozov, one of the great entrepreneurs of the seventeenth century, paid his skilled laborers in wages, as did the abbots of Belo-Belozersk and Bodin monasteries. At the town of Velikii Ustiug along the Moscow-Arkhangel trade route, and at Nizhni-Novgorod, wage earners found lucrative employment in the shipbuilding industries and salt-mining enterprises of the Stroganovs. Many landlords found such enterprises more rewarding than keeping their peasants fully employed in agriculture. Certain towns and villages whose peasant labor was organized in part under this arrangement, attained wide economic importance for the quality of their merchandise and the quantity of their output. Shuia and Iaroslav, for example, gained a reputation for their textiles, Kaluga for its felt, Tula for its metalwares. These products developed a market at home and abroad.

In domestic trade the government of Tsarevna Sophia pursued a policy closely akin to that of its predecessors. Attention was given to protecting traders from the oppressions of local officials, to the removal of customs barriers, and to the development of infant industries. Certain factories were subsidized by the government in an effort to free Russia from dependence on the foreigner. Restrictions on trade were removed wherever possible, without sacrificing the benefits of trade controls to the crown. In all directions great progress was registered, and changes introduced which pointed toward those of the succeeding regime.

A genuine effort was made during Sophia's regency to stamp out the corruption of royal officials in the collection of customs duties. The appointment of lesser officials to the customs office was more carefully

---

[54] *P.S.Z.*, II, 735–737; Kulisher, *op. cit.*, p. 320.
[55] Lyashchenko, *op. cit.*, pp. 218–219, 224–225.

checked. In one case the voevoda of Viatka was forbidden to appoint more customs officials, "... because many officials had acquired their offices by application or bribery, and many of them take extra bribes which causes the population extreme hardship."[56] The voevoda of Chernigov, suspected of responsibility for similar practices, was told that if he took bribes he would be fined and disgraced, and the warning was simultaneously issued that "... any voevoda who takes bribes will be fined and disgraced."[57] Customs officials were asked to check their expenditures closely, particularly for such items as "repairs for buildings," and were instructed to send their accounts to Moscow for auditing.[58] The voevoda of Povenetsk was ordered to select revenue collectors only from among "... good, righteous, and well-to-do men." If a collector were charged with bribery and the charge proved, the accuser gained the former's property.[59] Customs officials were enjoined on all sides not to oppress the trading population. Government agents were to be sent to the provinces to report on such matters.

An important encouragement to internal trade during Sophia's regency came through the abolition of the customs barrier between Great Russia and the Ukraine. A large part of the Ukraine had been returned to Moscow in 1667, but the customs barrier that had long existed between the two regions remained. This had discouraged a normal flow of goods between the two. It had also encouraged a spirit of separatism in Little Russia. Shortly before Golitsyn's first Crimean Campaign (1687) the customs barrier was finally removed. The beneficial effects of this decision were felt at once. An active trade sprang up between Great and Little Russia. The craft industries of both found new markets and new incentives were created for production. More important for Moscow was the genuine political gravitation of the Ukraine toward Russia, which bore fruit during the Great Northern War of the next century.[60]

Russia's taste for the commodities of Western Europe grew steadily in the late seventeenth century. Western textiles, armaments, and mechanical instruments had been in demand since the sixteenth century. By the mid-seventeenth century the variety of imports greatly expanded.[61] During the eighties, however, the threat of war in the West and the abrogation of special privileges to the foreign trader in Russia,

---

[56] *A.I.*, V (June 20, 1682), 140–141.
[57] *D.A.I.*, X (Oct. 15, 1682), 139.
[58] *P.S.Z.*, II, 654, 671.
[59] *A.I.*, V, 215.
[60] Shchebal'skii, *op. cit.*, p. 82.
[61] Barbour, *op. cit.*, pp. 39, 115–116.

combined to keep the supply and demand of imports apart. Although the amount of imports continued to increase, the demand generally exceeded the supply.

Sophia's regency grasped the problem and renewed the efforts to free Russia further from economic-military dependence on the West. The metallurgical industry—an object of particular government interest because of its relation to armaments—was given special attention. An iron foundry had operated at Tula near Moscow since 1632. In the sixties, other iron plants had been established at Kostroma, east of Iaroslav, and along the Sheksna River. Iron masters, peasants, and prisoners of war were engaged in these enterprises.[62] Golitsyn's building program for Moscow and his later military commitments pointed to the need for increased iron output. Iron production was consequently augmented by the award of government contracts to the Marcelis plants at Tula and Koshir. Between 1684 and 1685, Christian Marcelis, a Dutchman in Russian service, furnished the government with over 2,700 sheets of cast iron for repairs in the Kremlin, and with 1,000 corrugated metal sheets and 200 puds of iron bar for the new roofing of Granovitaia Palace. In July 1685, 5,000 cannon shells for a military campaign against the Crimea were ordered.[63]

Somewhat earlier (1682) Sophia's government took steps to promote the textile industry. In November, 1682, Abraham Paulus (Arnaut Paulssen), a "master of velvet manufacture" from Hamburg, was subsidized by the government to produce "velvet, satin and other silken cloths."[64] Paulus had come to Moscow late in Tsar Feodor's reign to investigate the opportunities for such an enterprise and had returned west (probably to Germany) in 1681 to recruit skilled labor for the undertaking. In December, 1681, he returned to Moscow with eighteen craftsmen, their wives, and children. His factory opened the following year. After many trials and disputes between Paulus and the government and between Paulus and his workers, modest amounts of velvet, damask moiré, and other luxury fabrics in demand by the court and nobility were produced. In 1684, a Dutchman, Matthew Tarbet, received a similar government contract to found a textile plant in Moscow. Tarbet was to produce velvet primarily and was to employ Russian apprentices so that they might learn the trade.[65] He brought machinery, tools, and colors with him from Holland and engaged artisans from Brandenburg-Prussia and

---

[62] *D.A.I.*, XII, 283; Kulisher, *op. cit.*, I, 391.
[63] *D.A.I.*, XII, 15–16, 283.
[64] *Ibid.*, X, 173–179.
[65] *Ibid.*, XI, 109–113.

Austria. His output of cloth soon exceeded that of Paulus. He remained in Russia until 1688 when most of his craftsmen and former apprentices left him to found establishments of their own. One of his apprentices, Ivan Parfienov, was given raw silk, dyes, and other materials by the government in April, 1689, and ordered to produce silk for the court.[66]

By the time of Sophia's regency foreign trade had undergone marked progress from that of the earlier century. The time had passed when only small quantities of goods were exchanged. Imports and exports acquired a mass character suggestive of trade in the eighteenth century. Large quantities of paper, metalware, and indigo were regularly imported in contrast to the small amounts of specialized goods—glassware, musical instruments, and medical supplies—of the earlier century. The export of furs, leather goods, tar, hemp, salmon, wood, and cereals simultaneously increased.[67]

In its foreign-trade policy Sophia's government followed two main objects: the extension of trade relations with nations abroad, and better trading conditions for foreign merchants in Russia. As the handicraft production of the early seventeenth century was paralleled by a semifactory production of goods in the larger towns, on the manors of wealthy noblemen, and on monastery lands, the government felt a greater responsibility to seek outlets for Russian crafts abroad. A few manufactures—leather goods, mittens, silver buttons—had acquired a modest foreign market in the Baltic and Middle East. The government sought to increase their sale and to awaken interest in other commodities.[68]

Between 1684 and 1688 Golitsyn arranged favorable commercial relations with Sweden, Poland, England, Brandenburg-Prussia, Saxony, and the Netherlands. Russian embassies were sent to eleven European capitals.[69] Golitsyn regarded the strengthening of Russo-Polish and Russo-Swedish trade as fundamental *a sine qua non* to Russia's economic progress, and a particular effort in his diplomacy was directed toward the end of better commercial relations with those two states. Trade relations with Warsaw and Stockholm had existed on relatively favorable terms since the sixties, but their political relations remained strained because of Russia's growing interest in the Baltic trade, and because of Moscow's advance in the Ukraine. By a treaty with Poland in 1686, the

---

[66] *Ibid.*, X, 193–195.
[67] Pokrovskii, *op. cit.*, II, 274; Barbour, *op. cit.*, pp. 115–116, 119.
[68] Pokrovskii, *op. cit.*, II, 253–255.
[69] G. K. Babushkina, "Mezhdunarodnoe znachenie krymskikh pokhodov 1687 i 1689 gg.", *Istoricheskie zapiski*, no. 33 (1950), p. 170.

favorable trade agreements between Moscow and Warsaw were reaffirmed. From 1688 on, permanent residencies were established in Poland and in Russia.[70] The merchants of both states were permitted to bring their goods freely to the designated trading centers of the other country. They were to pay customs duties and to observe carefully the trade regulations of the nation in which they conducted their business, but their trade was in no way to be discouraged or delayed.[71] Polish merchants henceforth traveled to Moscow and Russian merchants to Warsaw, Vilno, and Cracow for purposes of business. In 1684 trade relations between Moscow and Stockholm were reaffirmed on a "free and unhampered" basis. Swedish merchants were permitted to exchange their goods freely in all Russian cities open to foreign trade and Russian Guest merchants could trade likewise at Stockholm, Reval, Riga, and Narva and even build their own trade courts if they so desired.[72]

Golitsyn also sought to arrange a commercial treaty with the Chinese emperor. Russo-Chinese relations had posed a tantalizing problem for Moscow throughout the seventeenth century. Repeated efforts on Russia's part to establish diplomatic relations with Peking had failed. Since Russia and China were neighbors and had a long boundary in common, it was essential that some kind of agreement be arranged. When Sophia's regime began, such a goal seemed even more remote as the final struggle for control of the Amur River valley developed into open warfare. Golitsyn, nevertheless, gradually overcame these obstacles and arranged a commercial agreement with China by the Treaty of Nerchinsk (1689). Trade on a formal treaty basis between Russia and China was thus authorized for the first time.[73]

To improve the conditions of foreign trade at Arkhangel the regency gave attention to the correction of a number of local abuses. After the curtailment of trade privileges for Dutch and English merchants in Russia in the reign of Tsar Alexis, the foreigners suffered further discouragement from trading in Russia because of abuses at the hands of the voevodas of Arkhangel and the Dvina River. Since Arkhangel was the main port of entry for traders from those countries, the problem, from their standpoint, took on large proportions. The voevodas, it appeared, not infrequently assigned unskilled workers to service the

---

[70] *Ibid.*
[71] *P.S.Z.*, II, 781; Bochkarev, *op. cit.*, p. 241.
[72] Bochkarev, *op. cit.*, p. 241.
[73] Hsuan-Ming Liu, "Russo-Chinese Relations up to the Treaty of Nerchinsk...", *Chinese Social and Political Science Review*, XXIII, 423–437; *Sbornik dogovorov rossii s Kitaem, 1689–1881* gg., art. v, p. 5. The details of this treaty will be examined in a later chapter.

foreign vessels. The port and pilot fees they exacted were sometimes exorbitant. Early in 1682 King Charles II of England formally protested the many "vexations" and "delays" suffered by his merchants in their trade in Russia. Some pilots, he asserted, were drunkards or so unskilled that they frequently ran English vessels aground. The Dutch complained of similar annoyances, particularly of the restrictions placed upon them in the selection of pilots and of the excessive service fees charged them by the voevodas.[74]

Sophia's government acted promptly. In a decree of June, 1682, foreign merchants were allowed a choice of pilots and their activities were placed under the jurisdiction of the Guest merchants of the Customs Office rather than under the voevodas.[75] Assurances were expressly given both governments that their merchants would henceforth be favored with every consideration.

Besides these efforts to promote trade, both internal and external, Sophia's government gave attention to three internal problems immediately affecting national economy. These had to do with fugitive peasants, irregularities in land titles, and the completion of a census. Although there is no evidence to show that Sophia was more successful than her predecessors in dealing with them, there can be no denying the fact that she met them squarely.

The oppressions suffered by the mass of Russian peasantry in the seventeenth century have already been outlined in chapter i. The plight of the peasant had shown itself among other ways in mass escape to frontier lands. During the reign of Tsar Alexis, thousands of serfs fled the estates of their landlords to seek new freedom and opportunity in Siberia, the Zaporozh'e, or some other outlying area beyond the reach of the law. Some settled in frontier towns and became petty traders, craftsmen, or hunters; others joined the Cossacks or hired themselves out to new landlords. These migrations had serious effects on many of the districts evacuated, since they meant great losses of labor to landowners and in turn reduced the tax revenues of the state. The Law Code of 1649 and the decrees of 1662 and 1667 had imposed increasingly severe penalties for such flights, but the problem had continued. Landowners in the Ukraine successfully harbored fugitive serfs without incurring the penalty of the law. The voevoda of the Verkhotursk and Tobolsk districts reported in 1683 that in spite of his best efforts "many

---

[74] *D.A.I.*, XI, 177–182.
[75] *Ibid.*, p. 183; *P.S.Z.*, II, 675–677; ". . . the *Voevoda* of the Dvina is to have no jurisdiction over foreigners in any merchant affairs or in the hire of workers or pilots."

fugitive peasants with their wives and children" passed through his districts during 1680–1682, and that the migration had not ceased.[76]

To check this migration of peasant labor more effectively, Sophia's government inaugurated a new campaign December, 1682, to seek out fugitive peasants and return them to their home villages. Toward that end all vagrants were ordered to be carefully observed and travel barriers erected at certain key towns along the Siberian route—Perm, Solikamsk, and "other places where needed, so that no one on horseback or on foot be permitted from Russia into Siberia without our sovereign's traveling charters."[77] Police agents were placed on special duty in those towns to effect the return of fugitive peasants, and to see that the voevodas properly administered the punishments prescribed for those found guilty of illegal travel.

Sophia's government in the same year attempted to correct many of the irregularities that existed in land titles. Landed property in Russia did not enjoy the benefits of primogeniture. When a landed estate changed hands, its boundaries were altered, more often than not, by a division of the land among the heirs. In the case of pomestie estates,[78] the confusion was particularly great. At the death of an individual estate holder (*pomeshchik*) the land comprising the pomestie estate passed in part to his children and in part to the treasury for transference to other service men. When a new owner achieved an advance in rank for whatever reason, his allotment or estate in tenure was increased. Whenever a landowner transferred from the Novgorodian nobility to that of Moscow, a new grant of land followed and a new shift took place in his landed holdings.[79] To complicate matters, many property deeds and land markings had been lost or destroyed. In the Strel'tsy disorders of 1682 important government survey files had disappeared. Landmarks used in denoting boundaries had also been altered or destroyed through natural causes. Streams changed their courses, forests disappeared before the ax or fire, tillage lands were converted into pasture. The Land Juridical and Estate Offices were burdened with complaints and lawsuits, many of which were "beyond settlement."

Landed property reached a point so chaotic in 1682 that Sophia's government felt ready to act. A far-reaching investigation of land ownership was ordered in August, 1682. The further distribution of land was

---

[76] *P.S.Z.*, II, 483, 491, 551–552.
[77] *Ibid.*, pp. 481–483, 502, 551–552.
[78] Lands originally belonging to the treasury, given to individuals for life tenure with the obligation to perform state service.
[79] Shchebal'skii, *op. cit.*, p. 78.

temporarily halted. Lands acquired from the Tatars was not to be parceled out to Russians as estates. The sale of votchinas was to be more carefully recorded and informers were encouraged to report all irregularities in land ownership.[80]

A more comprehensive decree followed in 1683. Surveyors were dispatched to all parts of the empire with instructions to resurvey all lands, to reëxamine land grants and certificates of ownership, and to collect petitions of complaint and evidence about irregularities in land titles. Boundaries were to be recorded in detail, and new boundary posts erected wherever required. Anyone found demolishing the new landmarks was to be fined, flogged, and jailed. The government used Strel'tsy regiments to protect the surveyors while carrying out the assignment, and instructed all provincial governors to lend aid in executing the measure.[81]

Sophia's government also gave support to the completion of a national census, which supplemented the investigation being conducted on the movements of the peasantry. Between 1678 and 1681 census books had been compiled for the nobility and clergy, with records of the number of peasants held by each group. The census records of the peasantry, however, were incomplete because of insufficient information furnished by the nobility. In December, 1682, the regent decreed that new affidavits be gathered from the Church, the nobility, and various government agencies showing more carefully the number of peasants each held under its jurisdiction. The peasants listed in the previous records were first to be accounted for, with information furnished as to where they had come from, and in what villages they were finally registered.[82] Then all other peasants were to be accounted for with similar information furnished about their place of origin and whereabouts.

The economic policies of Sophia's regime thus carried on those of her two predecessors, Tsar Alexis and Tsar Feodor, and foreshadowed many of the reforms generally credited in origin to the succeeding generation. Under Sophia, trade relations with Russia's principal neighbors in Europe and Asia were strengthened. Residencies were set up in Moscow and abroad on a permanent or semipermanent basis. A modest but genuine effort was made to free foreign and domestic trade from administrative corruption and from certain encumbrances resulting from

---
[80] *P.S.Z.*, II, 471–472, 501.
[81] *Ibid.*, pp. 524–525.
[82] *P.S.Z.*, II, 483; "Concerning the taking of affidavits from clerks and military officials with regard to the number of souls held according to the census books of 1678 and concerning the new additions thereafter."

antiquated taxation practices. The customs barrier between Great Russia and the Ukraine was abolished. During Sophia's regency, as well, Russia appropriated more of the technical skill of Western Europe and inclined further toward its economic philosophy. Western technicians were encouraged to enter Russian service and to aid in the development of national industry.

In all these changes the point to be emphasized is the long-range nature of the economic revolution in progress during Sophia's regime. As Miliukov has suggested, the Muscovite state of the seventeenth century was suffering economic growing pains. Its production of wealth had not kept pace with its political growth. Its economic illness did not reach a decisive phase until the reign of Peter the Great, but "the crisis of the Petrine period was in preparation during the entire seventeenth century."[63] The contributions of Sophia's regency to these changes were both direct and substantial. To summarize—the localized handicraft character of Russian economy in the late seventeenth century was rapidly being paralleled by larger-scale trade and industrial enterprise. A national market existed in certain trades, large private fortunes were in process of formation, state factories were developed which acquired some of the characteristics of industries. The towns were becoming increasingly important as commercial-industrial centers. The population of entire villages and of entire sections of certain towns was engaged in the production of specialized goods—textiles, ceramics, and metalware. Russian crafts appeared in larger quantity in foreign markets and greater attention was given such trade by the state. In general, there was an over-all trend to promote better order and uniformity in trade, to simplify the taxation system, to establish an annual budget, and to harness the manpower resources of the state toward greater economic stability and national security.

[63] Miliukov, *Gosudastvennoe khoziaistvo rossii* ..., p. 2.

Part III
FOREIGN AFFAIRS

CHAPTER V

THE "ETERNAL PEACE" WITH POLAND

FOREIGN RELATIONS in many ways provided the stimulus for all the innovations leading to the reform epoch of Peter the Great. The late seventeenth century began a climactic period in Russian foreign policy, when events might be seized upon for the advancement of long-standing national designs or neglected on the basis of the country's unpreparedness for foreign ventures. Russia was at peace in 1682. A truce with an age-old foe, Poland, had been signed in 1667, bringing the Russians further gains in the struggle for the Ukraine. In 1681, a war with the Crimean Tatars had also terminated on the basis of a truce, which promised better relations with the Tatars and Turks and temporary stabilization of the southwestern frontier.[1]

As a periphery power in European politics, Russia's relations with

---

[1] N. Rozhkov, *Russkaia istoriia*, V, 57. A great amount of documentary material relating to the Peace with Poland (1686) is located in *P.S.Z.*, II, and in *D.A.I.*, XI. The full text of the Treaty of Moscow, for example, is contained in *P.S.Z.*, together with many references to the negotiations preceding the treaty and the steps taken by Moscow to implement the stipulations of the agreement. *D.A.I.*, XI, has much information on Moscow's relations with the Cossacks and on Polish intrigues in the Ukraine. *R.I.B.*, XXI, furnishes materials on Russian relations with the Crimean Tatars, and *Sbornik imperatorskago Russkago istoricheskago obshchestva*, XXXIV, has some information on the French reaction to the proposed Holy Alliance against Turkey.

Several of the secondary sources are of particular interest. N. N. Bantysh-Kamenskii, *Obzor vneshnikh snoshenii Rossii*, II, III, IV (Survey of the foreign relations of Russia) gives a well-defined picture of the larger developments and shifts in the diplomacy of the larger powers in Eastern Europe (1683–1686). M. Immich's *Geschichte des Europäischen Staatensystems von 1660 bis 1789*, 1905, is still a convenient single-volume reference on European diplomacy of the period. Patrick Gordon's diary for 1685–1686 has some key references to conversations between Gordon and Prince V. V. Golitsyn about the military aspects of the Crimean campaign. For Russian relations with Turkey and Moscow's interest in the Balkans see S. Zhigarev, *Russkaia politika v vostochnom voprose eia istoriia v XVI–XIX vekakh*, I (1896), and J. W. Zinkeisen, *Geschichte des Osmanischen Reiches in Europa*, V, (1850).

Among the more recent books *Istoriia SSSR*, I (History of the USSR), 1948, edited by B. D. Grekov, has a useful survey chapter (XIII) on peoples of the Volga area, Asia, and the Crimea in the seventeenth century. Section 4 of his chapter deals specifically with the Ukraine. M. M. Bogoslovskii's *Petr. I: Materialy dliia biografii* (Peter I: Materials for a biography), 1940, has a general account of the political background of Golitsyn's Crimean campaign but adds little that is new in the way of interpretation or analysis. Both Grekov and Bogoslovskii provide helpful bibliographies with each of their volumes showing the status of more recent research on the subject in the Soviet Union. N. A. Smirnov, "Rossiia i Turtsiia v XVI–XVII vv" in *Uchenye zapiski Moskovskogo universiteta*, 1940, reappraises Russo-Turkish relations during the period. G. K. Babushkina, "Mezhdunarodnoe zhachenie krymskikh pokhodov 1687 i 1689" (International significance of the Crimean Campaigns of 1687 and 1689), in *Istoricheskie zapiski, Akademiia Nauk SSSR, Institut istorii*, no. 33 (1950), is an even later and, on the whole, excellent analysis of the political aspects of the campaigns of 1687 and 1689.

Western nations had for centuries been limited and tenuous. The custom of maintaining permanent envoys abroad had not yet been adopted. The volume of foreign relations was still so small that no permanent embassies were required. Instead, the Russians contented themselves with sending special missions to foreign countries as they were needed. Lack of ties with the outside world kept Moscow poorly informed of external events just as the foreigner was ignorant of Muscovite affairs. The Russians relied heavily on foreign journals and pamphlets as well as upon intelligence gathered by agents (often Greek Orthodox churchmen) in Poland, Turkey, and the Balkans, for essential knowledge of Western Europe.[2] Such unsatisfactory methods of gaining information, along with the general indifference of the West toward Moscow and the restrictive political and economic policies of Poland and Sweden, perpetuated the unhappy concept of a Muscovite hermit nation.

In the year 1682, the principal political questions in Europe revolved around the ambitious territorial designs of Louis XIV in the Rhineland and in Spain, and the incursion of the Ottoman Turk into the Habsburg Empire—questions calling for concerted action on the part of the other European states. Russia's relations to these events at first appeared remote. The possibility of enlisting Moscow's support directly or indirectly against France appeared dubious and of questionable advantage. Winning its support against the Turk, on the other hand, seemed more possible on the basis of expediency. The Russian peace with the Crimean khan of January, 1681, had provided for a twenty-year truce. This had been reconfirmed in August, 1682, at Bakhchisarai.[3] It committed the Russians to continue paying tribute to the khan in return for guarantees from him, as well as from the Turk, to maintain peace.

---

[2] V. P. Potemkin, *Istoriia diplomatii*, I, 249; N. F. Kapterev, *Kharakter otnoshenii Rossii k pravoslavnomu vostoku* . . . , p. 345.

[3] *P.S.Z.*, II, 460–462: "The Oath Charter of the Crimean Khan given to the Russian Envoys concerning the inviolability of the 20-year peace according to former conditions. . . . A loving greeting from the Khan to the tsars. In the year 1091 (1681) January 3 . . . Our Great Sovereign brother Feodor sent Vasilii Tiapkin and Nikita Zotov to our Great Khan for a treaty and for the renewal of the former peace and friendship. . . . And we concluded a treaty with them and renewed our friendship . . . and now, owing to the death of Feodor, we once more conclude a treaty concerning the same thing as had been written in the charter of oath. . . . Beginning with our prophet for 20 years henceforth, we are to be at peace. There are to be no evils nor wars nor losses, and as it has been written in the charter of oath given to Tiapkin, we shall remain as we are. We shall build no towns nor fortifications . . . and from the year 1091 (1681) forward, tribute is to be sent us with no decrease compared to past years . . . and the sultan on his part also will not be in any war with you and will order all his subjects to cause no damage to you, . . . and you on your part are not to call your men from the Ukrainian cities, and are not to detain our men and are to remain firm by your oath . . . Written in the Great Capital of ours, Bakhchisarai, this 10th day of August, 1682."

But guarantees from the Tatars, as past experience had shown, could not be relied upon. Even when his subjects were in a peaceful mood, the khan was unable to dissuade them from capricious attacks on Cossack settlements along the frontier. Also, the Turks, with their newly acquired stronghold in Podolia, might turn their effort to recapture the Polish Ukraine, once their enemies in Hungary and the West had been defeated.[4] The Turkish Grand Vizir, Kara Mustafa, had sponsored a separatist movement in Hungary under Imre Thököly in 1681 and had renewed the war against Austria and Poland in 1682. Where this might lead next could not be foretold.[5]

The principal designs of Russia's European policy since the days of Ivan Groznyi had been access to the Baltic and the stabilization of the Ukrainian frontier. The attainment of the former meant a struggle with Sweden, which jealously guarded its southern Baltic position, whereas the accomplishment of the latter involved war with Poland over the Ukraine and the pacification of the Tatars, whose repeated inroads into Cossack territories kept the region between the lower Don and Dnieper in continual unrest.

The decision as to which of these goals to pursue first had come to a head during the reign of Alexis Mikhailovich. Under the guidance of Ordin-Nashchokin, Russia's primary effort was directed against Sweden. Nashchokin's policy appeared to have been dictated in part by personal sentiments, since as a native of Pskov he had long cherished dreams of incorporating the coastal area along the Gulf of Riga into the Russian empire. But he was also convinced that friendship with Poland was essential to Moscow's well-being and that the Ukraine was not worth the sacrifice a war of conquest would entail at the time.[6] Thus the war with Sweden over long-standing Baltic issues was renewed in 1656.

Sweden, like Poland, had utilized Russia's political weakness in the first decade of the seventeenth century to wrest Karelia and Ingria from Muscovite control. In 1656, Russia, taking advantage of a coalition against Sweden, embarked on steps to recapture these territories. During the campaign which followed, several fortresses along the western Dvina temporarily fell to the Rusians. A siege of Riga was begun, but the war went badly for the Russians and ultimately ended in a stalemate. By the Treaty of Kardis (1661), peace was reëstablished on the basis of the status quo ante bellum. Moscow's designs on Sweden's mari-

---
[4] G. K. Babushkina, "Mezhdunarodnoe znachenie krymskikh pokhodov 1687 i 1689," *Istoricheskie zapiski*, no. 33, pp. 159, 161, 171.
[5] *Ibid.*
[6] S. F. Platonov, *Moskva i zapad*, p. 120.

time provinces thus remained unfulfilled, and the strained relations between the two countries continued undiminished. The Russians asserted that Sweden had ignored its treaty obligations and had disregarded the tsar's titles to areas which had been outside the dispute between the two countries.[7] All in all, the failures attending the Baltic campaign, as well as the influence of new counsellors on Tsar Alexis, turned the attention of Moscow once more to the Southwest.[8]

The foremost event in Russia's southwestern position in the seventeenth century had been the incorporation of large areas of the Ukraine into the empire. To accomplish this goal had required protracted wars and negotiations with Poland, ending in the Truce of Andrusovo (1667) for thirteen and one-half years. The truce had been periodically renewed after 1669 but on a similar short-term basis. The Russians thus held the eastern bank of the Dnieper as well as Smolensk, Novgorod-Seversk, Chernigov, and Kiev. Poland, nonetheless, refused to regard these cessions as final and repeatedly countered all Russian efforts to establish them as permanent. Poland also engaged in continual intrigues with the Cossacks to recapture their loyalty and lands.

Moscow's acquisition of further Ukrainian territory had interesting political repercussions. It not only underscored Poland's declining power and Russia's mounting strength in Eastern Europe but posed the question of new political alignments based on the tsar's expanding position.[9] Sweden almost immediately sought to draw the Lithuanian nobility closer to Stockholm; Turkey began to reconsider its position north of the Danube[10] and the political future of its vassals, the Crimean Tatars.[11] Two European coalitions, anti-Turkish and anti-Swedish, began looking to Russia as a desirable ally. The countries involved—Poland, Saxony, the Papal States, Brandenburg-Prussia, the Holy Roman Empire (Austria)—sought to win Russia to their side.[12]

---

[7] N. N. Bantysh-Kamenskii, *Obzor vneshnikh snoshenii Rossii*, IV, 198–200.

[8] Platonov, *op. cit.*, p. 122.

[9] Max Immich, *Geschichte des europäischen Staatensystems von 1660 bis 1789*, p. 43: "The other European states also had begun to reckon with Russia as a factor in European politics, and they commenced to enter relations with Russia according to their friendly or unfriendly attitude toward Poland or Sweden"; Babushkina, *op. cit.*, p. 162.

[10] Johann W. Zinkeisen, *Geschichte des Osmanischen Reiches in Europa*, V, 139: "For in Constantinople they [the Turks] had recognized the dangers which the growing power of the tsar, who was irresistibly driven to the South, could bring to the [Ottoman] Empire."

[11] *R.I.B.*, XXI, 602: "A Report of Prince K. Cherkaskii how he was ordered to march with his troops to the place where the Crimeans wished to construct a fort, and how he was to engage them in an encounter, and to prevent them from building that fort"; "Dela Tainago Prikaza (1683)."

[12] Babushkina, *op. cit.*, p. 162.

The position of Sophia's government in May, 1682, clearly called for the establishment of peaceful relations with foreign powers on all sides. Golitsyn realized the strength to be gained from recognition abroad of his government's status as the legally constituted regime and dispatched charters of amity to Poland, Sweden, the Empire, Brandenburg, and other states in line with traditional Muscovite practice. In May, 1682, the diak N. Seniukov departed for Warsaw with formal greetings from the young tsars to the Polish king, Jan Sobieski.[13] The Polish king received him courteously, asserting that he had recently made statements regarding Poland's friendly disposition toward Russia at the Grodno Diet. In the same month, D. Simonovskii arrived in Berlin with a declaration of Russian friendship for Brandenburg and then proceeded to the Netherlands and England.[14] Nikita Alekseev, in like manner, was dispatched to Sweden and Denmark;[15] Seniukov, completing his assignment at Warsaw, set out for Vienna. In such manner, the new regime opened its relations with the West.

Within a year the political scene in Eastern Europe suffered radical changes. A series of events presaged far closer ties with the West than any Russia had heretofore established. War between Austria and Turkey broke out in 1682. While Imre Thököly, the Hungarian nationalist now in the pay of Constantinople, led a force into Austrian Silesia and the Pasha of Buda seized Tokay in northern Hungary, the Ottoman mobilized his full forces along the Sava and Danube rivers for a thrust toward Vienna. In the summer of 1683, the famous siege of the Austrian capital began. Poland entered the struggle in March, 1683, agreeing to raise an army of 40,000 men in return for military and financial aid from the Empire and diplomatic support in collecting long-standing loans from the Spanish Habsburgs.[16]

The imminent fall of Vienna before the armies of the Turkish Grand Vizir, Kara Mustafa, gave all Europe pause. Hasty efforts began to mend broken political fences between neighbors and to erect political bulwarks against Islam. Even before the siege of the great city began, a Polish mission led by Jan Zembotski came to Moscow with the proposal that a Russian embassy in Warsaw at that time be empowered to treat of affairs "not included in former treaties" and to settle certain difficulties "which had been set aside for special commissions to decide."[17]

---

[13] Bantysh-Kamenskii, *op. cit.*, III, 153.
[14] *Ibid.*, IV, 18.
[15] *Ibid.*, p. 198.
[16] J. Szujski, *Dzieje polski podug ostatnich badań*, IV, 85; *Archiv für österreichische Geschichte*, CIII, 278.
[17] N. Ustrialov, *Istoriia tsarstvovaniia Petra Velikago*, I, 126.

The Elector of Bavaria, who usually aligned himself on the side of Louis XIV against the emperor, decided the time had come to establish closer relations with the German emperor and took a first step in that direction by arranging a betrothal between himself and an Austrian archduchess. Louis XIV, who had earlier contemplated sending an embassy to Moscow to dissuade the Russians from collaborating with his enemies, now decided to abandon the plan.[18]

The failure of the Turks to capture Vienna seemed like an act of Providence to Western Christendom and gave new strength to the united resistance against them. Something like a crusading fever swept Austria, Poland, and other countries and aroused a determination to force the Turks below the Danube and out of Europe. To effect such a plan attention was directed to finding aid from all possible quarters, and in the over-all search for allies the gaze of Warsaw and Vienna inevitably came to rest on Orthodox Christian Moscow. The support of the Muscovites might be hopefully solicited, since their interests in the Crimea and in the area between the Dnieper and Danube continually clashed with those of the Turk and his vassals, the Crimean Tatars. In September, 1683, a Roman Catholic archbishop, Sebastian Knabe, who had been preaching the Roman faith in Armenia, arrived in Moscow with the outline of such a proposal.[19] Two months later an Austrian courier, Johann Gevel, announced the forthcoming entry of an imperial German embassy into Russia to discuss the necessity of a military alliance between the emperor and the tsars. This was followed by the arrival of a Polish envoy, Jan Okrassa, who came ostensibly to announce the great "imperial" victory at Vienna, but also to suggest the desirability of an offensive alliance against the Turkish sultan. The time had come, he argued, for all Christian sovereigns to unite in forcing the Turk out of Europe, and if the opportunity were not seized, they would "be responsible for it to God."[20]

The proposals might earlier have puzzled the Russians and been ignored as impractical, but with the victory at Vienna, and the serious

---

[18] *Sbornik imperatorskago Russkago istoricheskago obshchestva*, XXXIV, 401–408; *Monumenta Historica Poloniae*, III, 691, Letter of Louis XIV to Pope Innocent XI, Aug. 26, 1683.

[19] Szujski, *op. cit.*, IV, 98.

[20] C. Chowaniec, "Z dziejow polityki Jana III na Bliskim Wschodzie, 1683–1686," *Kwartalnik historyczny*, 1926, p. 152: "Now is the time which the centuries have awaited, and if we do not take this opportunity we shall be responsible for it to God. . . . "; see also Shchebal'skii, *op. cit.*, p. 89, for the statement of the Polish King: ". . . this infidel people [the Turks] at some time or other with the blessing of the Most High God, will be humbled and crushed by a Christian hand, provided that all Christian sovereigns desire that. . . . The time is come for the expulsion from Europe of the enemies of the Holy Faith."

losses sustained by the Turks, the suggestion began to pose certain advantages. Golitsyn, as principal minister and head of the Great Foreign Affairs Office, could not deny the many strong arguments for preserving peace. That Russia was unprepared militarily and financially for military ventures, and that anything like a failure in war would react drastically against the new regime were obvious factors. Conversely, a successful war would result in gains so brilliant as to offset exposing the state to renewed political instability. Golitsyn weighed the opposing arguments carefully. Early in 1684, he asked Patrick Gordon, commander in chief of the Russian army at Kiev, to prepare a memoir on the subject—the advantages and disadvantages of a war against the Crimea.[21] As a Westerner and promoter of closer ties with Europe, Golitsyn could not escape a friendly disposition toward the venture. The possibility of arriving at a final settlement with Poland about Kiev and other cities, the termination of frontier strife with the Crimean Tatars and of the payment to them of an annual tribute—to say nothing of the closer ties established with the West through the Balkans and the Mediterranean—all represented compelling arguments to Golitsyn. He could see nothing to be lost by a discussion of the matter and soon agreed that his government would participate in the proposed conference.[22]

An initial meeting between the Russians and Poles took place January 7, 1684, at Andrusovo. Prince Odoevskii, Buturlin, M. Romodanovskii, and Chaadaev represented the Russians, and the envoys Grzymultowski, Oginski, and Chometowski, the Poles. Golitsyn gave his men explicit instructions. He showed particular interest in reaching a final settlement—"an eternal peace" with Poland—and instructed his representatives to insist upon this as a precondition to an alliance. Under no conditions were Kiev or the Zaporozh'e to be returned to Poland, and in future, Orthodox Christians in Polish territories were to be protected from persecutions. The Russian commitment in the alliance should not go beyond a campaign against the Tatars; no outright aid should be pledged against the Turks.[23]

The Polish envoys, as it developed, had equally strong demands to

[21] Platonov, *op. cit.*, p. 135; Alexander Brückner, *Beiträge zur Kulturgeschichte Russlands*, p. 313.
[22] S. Zhigarev, *Russkaia politika v vostochnom voprose*, I, 96: "Unquestionably it would have been more advantageous for Russia to concentrate all its attention on affairs of internal policy, but she had no opportunity to undertake these affairs while her borders were removed from the sea and were open to the attack from the Crimean Tatars who despite even the peaceful mood of its government were unable to maintain their treaty obligations strictly."
[23] Bantysh-Kamenskii, *op. cit.*, III, 154.

make before coming to a final settlement with Moscow. A military alliance against Turkey, they insisted, must precede any final disposition of the boundary question. The Ukraine was to be set up as an independent state. The two positions immediately proved irreconcilable. Some thirty-eight sessions were held, marred by much bickering and vituperation. On February 12 the conference ended in deadlock. The Poles accused the Russians of transplanting Poles to Russian soil, of harboring the Ukrainian nationalist leader Peter Doroshenko, whom they regarded as a Polish fugitive, and of refusing the Cossacks permission to enlist as mercenaries in the Polish army fighting against the Turk.[24] Their position, they concluded, was "... not yet so desperate as to be able to yield to all the demands of the other side."[25] The Russians, on their side, charged the Poles with disregard for the tsar's titles—an oversight of great consequence to the Russians owing to the many areas over which the tsars' titles to sovereignty were challenged. The Cossacks added fuel to the fire by accusing the Poles of raiding Zaporog lands and of violating certain articles of the Truce of Andrusovo.[26] Because of the deadlock, the Truce of 1667 nominally continued in effect, and further discussion about outstanding differences between the two countries was postponed until June, 1691.[27]

The German emperor's commission arrived in the Russian capital May 24, 1684. Baron Sebastian von Blumberg, Ignatius von Gwarient, Johann Zierowski, and Georg von Koch were the principal envoys. The Austrians had journeyed through Poland early in 1684. Upon nearing the Russian border, they encountered such heavy snows that their entry into Russia was postponed until spring. On May 27, the young tsars received them in audience—a formal meeting in which von Blumberg confined himself to a brief congratulatory statement on the occasion of Tsar Ivan's marriage to Praskovia Saltykova. Not until two days later was the subject of the alliance broached. Von Blumberg, in the presence of both tsars, began his proposal by depicting the political and military position of Turkey as that of "an incurably sick man"—the metaphor generally associated with nineteenth-century Russian diplomacy.[28] Expanding upon the theme at great length, he concluded by inviting the

[24] *D.A.I.*, XI, 42–47.
[25] *Ibid.*, p. 49: "... The Turk has not yet grasped the Poles by the neck, and they [the Poles] are not yet so desperate as to be able to yield to all the demands of the other side for the sake of an 'Eternal Peace!'..."
[26] *Ibid.*, pp. 74–77.
[27] *P.S.Z.*, II, 578–579.
[28] K. A. Viskovatov, "Prizyv Rosii na bor'bu s Turtsiei, 1684 g." *Russkaia Starina*, II (1878), p. 446.

Russians to join Poland and Austria in a military alliance against the Porte. The court gave no immediate reply to the proposal but referred the matter to the Duma, with Prince Vasily V. Golitsyn as chairman.

Early in June the Austrians were informed of the breakdown in the negotiations with Poland—a development of which they had no doubt already had knowledge—and of the decision that no pact could be entered into without a previous arrangement with Poland regarding the western boundaries. Discussion over this matter lasted several days, with the Austrians waging a losing fight to persuade the Russians to accept something less than "a permanent boundary settlement" with Poland as a precondition to an alliance. They finally abandoned the effort and by June 7 agreed to use their influence in persuading Poland to yield this point, saying that they believed their efforts would be successful and that if necessary they would seek the help of Pope Innocent XI in the endeavor.[29]

Golitsyn had meanwhile begun to wrestle more seriously with the many complexities involved in such an alliance and spent long hours deliberating the difficult question of peace or war. He held conversations with Gordon and others on the advantages and disadvantages of a Crimean campaign.[30] Gordon, whose military judgment Golitsyn respected, appeared to encourage such an undertaking. He felt that the obstacles could be overcome and that, with a proper force, the Crimea might be delivered into Russian hands "in a year, or two years at the most."[31] The words of Krizhanich regarding the true direction of Russia's foreign policy may also have entered Golitsyn's mind.[32] In the end he yielded to the arguments for an alliance. By mid-June he agreed that if if a peace with Poland could be arranged, Russia was prepared to enter the war. The Russians would conduct a campaign against the Crimea to prevent the Tatars from rendering aid to Turkey when it was at-

---

[29] Viskovatov, *op. cit.*, II (1878), 445.

[30] Brückner, *op. cit.*, p. 313; P. Gordon, *Tagebuch des Generals Patrick Gordon...*, II, 4.

[31] Gordon, *op. cit.*, p. 11: "... With a force of 40,000 infantry and 20,000 cavalrymen one can easily lay waste the Crimea in a year, or two years at the most"; Brückner, *op. cit.*, pp. 314–315.

[32] Iurii Krizhanich, *Russkoe gosudarstvo v polovine XVII veka*, Part V, pp. 117–118: "It would be advantageous to this land to expand its boundaries to the South, not to the North nor to the East, nor to the West.... The Northern countries are cold, marshy, unfertile, and are deprived of many things which are needful. Thus there is little profit in conquering them.... The Crimea, however, and the Nogai lands, are full of God's gifts of all varieties.... Wars with Poland and Lithuania have been unprofitable. In our efforts against the Tatars the Lord has given us success in Kazan, Astrakhan, and in Siberia. Therefore... it is advisable for this land to keep peace with all the Northern, Eastern, and Western peoples, and to fight against the Tatars only."

tacked by Poland and Austria. This satisfied von Blumberg. His mission prepared to depart. In thanking Golitsyn for his decision and taking leave of his hosts, Blumberg once more elaborated upon the decline of the Ottoman empire and of the glories to be won in expelling the Turk from Europe. His words strike a familiar note to students of the Near Eastern Question and furnish a remarkable forecast of Turkey's future and of Russia's later role in the dismemberment of the Turkish empire. Turkey, according to von Blumberg, was doomed and in a short time would be "converted into a corpse." The time had come for Russia to help strike it down and to prepare the way for the possession of great lands. The Black Sea beckoned Russia and "the Red Sea with impatience awaits to embrace you. ... All Greece and Asia await you."[33]

Golitsyn's decision to reopen negotiations with the Poles and to enter a limited military alliance against Turkey was not as ill advised and shortsighted as has been suggested when one recalls the immediate political events in the Ukraine and abroad. Poland and Austria were at war with the Turks and had resolved to press the struggle against them at all costs until they retreated below the Danube and possibly out of Europe. Whether Moscow joined the coalition or not, the war would be prosecuted. Under such circumstances Golitsyn felt it necessary to insure the loyalty of the Cossacks and to reach a new settlement with Poland, in the event of a serious Turkish defeat. Moscow could ill afford a loss of prestige among the Cossacks by failure to support a venture which preëminently promised to further their security and interests in the Zaporozh'e and Don areas. The loyalty of the Cossacks to Moscow in 1684 was still unpredictable, and their nationalist spirit strong. Doroshenko's efforts to unite the Left Bank and Right Bank Dnieper Cossack territories into an independent state had been a recent reminder to Moscow of the spirit of separatism yet alive in the Ukraine.

The actions of Poland in connection with the Cossacks had meanwhile

[33] Viskovatov, *op. cit.*, II, 447: "Turkey has been crushed by its own weight and striving to free itself, not without shock to its internal organs, of all that burdens its stomach, overflowing with the number of its dominions, drunk with the mass of riches of its country. Now is a convenient time to continue the route to the waters of the Euxine Sea. The obstacles on the route are not great; few heavy locks hang on the gates. Even fewer obstacles are present on the road to the Meotuskii marshes and the Black Sea, and the Red Sea with impatience awaits to embrace you with outstretched arms. All Greece and Asia await you. The hour has struck to go into the Crimea, where up to this time the road has presented only difficulty for you. ... Take, lest you be taken from! The Turk clutches first with one hand toward the East, then with another toward the West, not knowing where to affix the splendor of his far-flung might. ... The sultan's sword has grown dull. I assure you that the present sultan is an old woman, not knowing how to weave, but only how to cry. Break Turkey, then, with your mighty arms! Your sword will open the way to the possession of great lands."

given Moscow further reason for alarm. With the breakdown of Russo-Polish conversations in February, 1684, reports came to Golitsyn of new Polish intrigues among them. His friend, Alexis Shein, touring the Ukraine in July, 1684, reported that the Zaporog and Don Cossacks, as well as the Kalmyks of the Lower Volga area, intended to aid Poland in the war against the Tatars, whether Moscow participated in it or not.[34] Colonel G. Donets, a Cossack officer, reported that the King of Poland had written the Don Cossacks, urging them to join in the march against the Tatars. Sobieski's letter had been read at a Cossack council circle and then had been forwarded to the Kalmyk peoples. Gunpowder, cloth, lead, and grain had been sent to the Cossacks by the Polish king.[35] The fact that the Cossacks always bore the immediate brunt of attacks from the Crimea gave unusual interest to such a proposal, especially when it was accompanied with gifts.

From the standpoint of political events abroad the projected alliance also appeared expedient. During the summer of 1684, Golitsyn had sent Savva Sandyrev into Lithuania and Poland to obtain intelligence on Polish affairs. All information about the progress of the war against Turkey was to be gathered. Sandyrev was to learn how much aid the Polish king had given the emperor, whether the French king was planning to aid Vienna, and what his price would be for such aid; whether Polish and Lithuanian troops had committed any unfriendly acts against their German confederates; whether Sobieski was still leading his troops in person; and whether the morale of the Polish army was high.[36] His reports came to Golitsyn in cipher. The Polish king, according to Sandyrev, was not lending the emperor aid at the moment. The Turks had sought to make peace with the Poles, but Sobieski, upon the advice of the emperor and the Roman pontiff, had refused. The Poles counted heavily on the support of the Zaporog Cossacks in the struggle and would welcome an alliance with Russia more than ever. As for the French king—it was reported from the *szlachta* that Poland and France had "fallen out" because of French intrigues in Turkey against the emperor, and because of Louis XIV's design to use the Turkish war as a means of furthering his ambitions to attain the imperial crown.[37]

Along with Sandyrev's report came dispatches of grave military and political reversals for Turkey.[38] It appeared that other European powers

[34] *D.A.I.*, XI, 175.
[35] *Ibid.*, pp. 254–255.
[36] *Ibid.*, pp. 141–146.
[37] *Ibid.*, pp. 148–149.
[38] Zhigarev, *op. cit.*, I, 95.

were showing interest in the struggle. Emperor Leopold had concluded a twenty-year military alliance with Venice. Pope Innocent XI had sent the Poles 2,000,000 thalers for mercenary troops and had urged the Spanish king, Charles II, to send the emperor aid in ships and money. In August, 1684, Rome sent a personal appeal to Moscow, urging adherence to the alliance.[39]

By the end of summer, the reports of Polish intrigues among the Cossacks had been well authenticated. Sandyrev reported in September that 12,000 Cossacks had come from the Zaporog and trans-Dnieper regions to lend support to the Polish king. One of their colonels had told Sobieski that 40,000 more awaited to join.[40] Golitsyn immediately sent a formal protest to Warsaw, saying that the Truce of Andrusovo had been violated. The Poles at first ignored the claim, then denied it, and finally dismissed it by saying that the Cossacks in the Polish forces had volunteered for service on their own initiative through "Christian love and zeal for the sake of Christian peoples ... and these [acts] are worthy not of reproach, but of praise."[41]

During the following year, tension between the two courts increased. The Polish envoy, Jan Zembotski, came to Moscow in June, 1685, with a complaint against the inhabitants of Seversk for their raids on certain Polish towns.[42] Moscow appointed a commission to settle the dispute[43] but charged the Poles with new intrigues to lure the Kalmyks to their side as they had the Cossacks.[44] Poland replied in December that a new embassy would come to Moscow to settle all disputes between the two countries and discuss once again the matter of "an eternal peace."

The new embassy—comprised of the Polish envoys Grzymultowski, Oginski, Przymski, and Potocki with their staffs—arrived in Moscow in February, 1686.[45] Golitsyn arranged to receive them with courtesy and with a certain show of force by way of a military review. Feodor Shak-

---

[39] Bantysh-Kamenskii, *op. cit.*, II, 238.
[40] *D.A.I.*, XI, 149–152.
[41] *Ibid.*, pp. 153–155.
[42] Bantysh-Kamenskii, *op. cit.*, III, 156.
[43] *P.S.Z.*, II, 677–678.
[44] *D.A.I.*, X, 453–454: Oct. 30, 1685: "An accusation against the Polish king for breaking the peace treaty by his efforts to lure to his own side the Kalmyks, who are Russian subjects, and also by calling the Don Cossacks to enter his service.... It is known to you, our brother, that both in the Andrusovo and Moscow Truce agreements, recently concluded and ratified at a commission in 1684, it has been stipulated that we are to be with you in brotherly friendship and love.... On your side, our brother, an obvious breach of the agreement has occurred. In 1684, you sent your envoys from Cracow with letters to our subjects—the Kalmyk Taishas. You also sent letters to the Don Cossacks and invited them to join your service.... For what reason do you break the articles of the treaty? May you hereby know that such action is improper...."
[45] S. M. Solov'ev, *Istoriia Rossii s drevneishikh vremen*, XIV, 985.

lovityi, chief of the Strel'tsy Prikaz, led a parade of select Strel'tsy regiments before them. A reception was given in their honor in Granovitaia Palace. In the formal negotiations that followed, Golitsyn himself led the discussions, assisted by B. F. Sheremetev, P. Voznitsyn, I. Volkhov, and other nobles. The possession of Kiev loomed as the initial stumbling block in negotiations at this second meeting. Golitsyn insisted that its cession to Moscow must be recognized by Poland on a permanent basis and not on a temporary one of two-year renewal periods. The Poles would only agree to this for the price of 200,000 rubles. The Russians expressed astonishment at their demand, since they had understood the free and permanent cession of Kiev was to be part of the price for their campaign against the Tatars. But having long been inured to the payment of tribute in connection with diplomatic bargaining they offered 100,000 rubles and then 140,000 as a final offer for the ancient Russian city. Seven weeks passed in deliberating matters and in resolving minor disagreements in the interpretation of past treaty arrangements and the recognition of the tsars' titles.[46] No progress appeared. Two viewpoints, wrote Prince Boris Kurakin, the youthful friend of Tsar Peter, now appeared at court; one, led by Tsarevna Sophia and Prince Golitsyn, urged that the negotiations with Poland be continued; a second, led by the boyars P. Prozorovskii and F. P. Saltykov, held that the discussions should be terminated and a war started against Poland and not the Tatars.[47]

The negotiations continued under great tension. Unable to reach an agreement about Kiev, the Poles called for their passports, March 27. These were granted and a farewell audience arranged with the tsars. With their baggage packed and their carriage awaiting them, Grzymultowski suddenly postponed the departure. He notified Golitsyn that the price for the cession of Kiev would be reduced to 150,000 rubles and a new treaty settlement presented. Tsarevna Sophia, upon the advice of Golitsyn, agreed to renew negotiations, but only by letter. Two days later, the Poles sent Golitsyn a new proposal. Kiev would be ceded for a reduced price of 150,000 rubles, but the lower Dnieper towns of Cherkassy, Kanev, Chigirin, and others must be returned to Poland. Golitsyn was unprepared for such a compromise. Within the week he requested that the envoys leave the capital. Preparations for their departure again took place, but once more they lingered. On April 7, after further awkward delays, negotiations were resumed. This time the

---

[46] Ustrialov, *op. cit.*, I, 161.
[47] F. A. Kurakin, *Arkhiv kniazia ... Kurakina*, I, 52: "This difference of opinion lasted six months"; see also Szujski, *op. cit.*, IV, 100.

Russians came forward with a proposal drawn up by P. Voznitsyn, I. Volkhov, S. Lavretskii, and K. Nefimov. Discussion of its terms filled two more weeks with angry disputes over titles, extravagant accusations, and recriminations.[48] It now appeared that both sides were prepared to make concessions. On April 21, a compromise settlement was announced,[49] and five days later, April 26, 1686, the "Treaty of Eternal Peace" between the two countries was signed and ratified.

Diplomatically speaking, the treaty was the most important achievement of Tsarevna Sophia's government. It stabilized the Russo-Polish frontier as never before and established the terms of the Truce of Andrusovo as permanent. The treaty comprised thirty-three articles[50] and abrogated all former treaty arrangements between the two countries with regard to the regions concerned. Peace was to be established "forever"—strong testimony to the credulity of the age and to the mutual desire for peace between Russia and Poland. The principal provisions were as follows:

1. Kiev, Smolensk, Dorogobuzh, Roslavl, the Zaporozh'e, and other designated places, with their suburban areas, were ceded to Russia outright.

2. Russia gave Poland 146,000 rubles solely "out of friendship and love," and not as payment for Kiev and other concessions.

3. All disputes over land ownership in the frontier area between Chernigov and Starodub were to be settled by a joint commission of Russian and Polish judges.

4. Trade was to flourish freely between the two countries at Warsaw, Cracow, Vilno, Moscow, and Smolensk. No delays were to be suffered by merchants on account of customs and local restrictions.

5. The towns of Kanev, Cherkassy, and Chigirin were not to be rebuilt or refortified.

6. Roman Catholics in Russia and Russian Orthodox Christians in Poland were not to be persecuted or molested in any way.

7. Russia was to join Poland in an offensive-defensive alliance against Turkey and the Crimean Tatars. Russian forces were to be used to besiege the Crimea, blocking a union of Turkish and Tatar forces.

8. Russia was to sever all diplomatic relations with Turkey and the Crimea immediately.

---

[48] Szujski, *op. cit.*, IV, 100: "Nothing was more shameful than these negotiations. Nothing was more exasperating than this criminal folly of Grzymultowski's, and the brutality and effrontery of the Russians...."

[49] Ustrialov, *op. cit.*, I, 167.

[50] *P.S.Z.*, II, 767–768 contains the full text of the treaty.

9. Neither country was to conclude a separate peace with the enemy without the knowledge and consent of its ally.

10. Both countries agreed to seek the support of "other Christian monarchs" against the Turk and to notify adjacent states immediately of the existence of the alliance.

11. The Polish king agreed not to enlist the services of any of the inhabitants across the Russian border and to refrain from designating himself as ruler of any of the towns ceded to Russia.

12. The titles of the sovereigns of both countries were determined to the general satisfaction of both nations.

These represented substantial gains for Moscow at the price of a campaign which, it was believed, involved few hazards. Much attention was given in the treaty to the manner in which its stipulations were to be fulfilled. At the conclusion of the agreement, Grzymultowski and his assistants were given 10,000 gold pieces to take home to their sovereign. On their arrival in Smolensk in June, they received 100,000 rubles as part of the payment "of friendship and love for Poland." The remaining sum was to be paid at Grodno in February, 1688.

The conclusion of the treaty was received enthusiastically in Russia and somberly in Poland.[51] In Moscow, Sophia proclaimed that her father and brother had held Smolensk, Chernigov, and the Ukraine only temporarily "... and thrice they swore to return Kiev to Poland." Her government had obtained it "forever," without ceding Poland a single town or place.[52] "And according to this treaty, their Russian majesties received many additional titles famous among all Christian sovereigns...."[53] The Russian plenipotentiaries, Golitsyn, Sheremetev, and others were highly praised for their diplomatic efforts and lavishly rewarded in money, landed estates, serfs, and costly gifts. In celebrating their triumph, the tsars even "deigned to touch the goblets given their representatives."[54] In contrast to the warm reception given the treaty in Moscow, the Polish Diet learned of its terms with "profound disappointment." King Sobieski supposedly wept when he heard the price Poland had finally paid for the alliance.[55]

---

[51] Ustrialov, *op. cit.*, I, 169.
[52] De la Neuville, "Zapiski de la Nevillia," *Russkaia Starina*, LXXI, Part I, 443.
[53] *P.S.Z.*, II, 786–789.
[54] *P.S.Z.*, II, 799–803.
[55] Szujski, *op. cit.*, IV, 100: "The King (Sobieski) swearing to this treaty ... the Pact of Eternal Peace with Moscow, which took away from the Polish Republic the most important places on the border, nullified numerous victories bought with the nation's blood, established Moscow's superiority over Poland,—all for miserable money and uncertain aid—wept bitterly, and the Polish Diet of 1688 received it with profound disappointment."

Poland's principal gain in the treaty had been the commitment of Moscow to lead a campaign against the Crimean Tatars. The Russians were to break off diplomatic relations with the Tatars promptly and to place the Crimea under siege. Within three months of the signature of the treaty, Moscow notified the Tatar khan, Selim Girei, of the tsars' new alignment. "It is your will," the khan replied. "You are the ones who have broken the peace, and for that you are responsible to God. As for us, we are ready for either friendship or enmity."[56]

During the summer of 1686, Tatar raids into the Ukraine were renewed. Sobieski, who had undertaken a campaign into Moldavia,[57] suffered defeat near the Pruth River and called upon the Russians to launch their campaign in the east. The call to Moscow came earlier than expected. During the treaty negotiations Russia had taken care to indicate 1687 as the year when operations against the Crimea would begin. Nevertheless, a token Russian force under Colonel Kosagov was dispatched to the Lower Dnieper for preliminary operations. In September, 1686, the diak V. Klobukov went to Warsaw with the Russian plan of campaign. Sobieski approved the plan. In the same month, Tsarevna Sophia issued a decree calling for large-scale preparations against the Crimean khan.[58] The Russians justified the campaign on the basis of unprovoked Tatar raids on Cossack settlements during 1684 and 1685, in which it was declared many inhabitants had been tortured and killed and others dishonored.[59] The khan had refused to amend these evils and had detained the Russian envoys sent to gain redress for the incidents. The latter had also been imprisoned and molested in various ways.[60]

Article 14 of the Treaty of Moscow had provided that both powers seek to gain the support of "other Christian monarchs" in the struggle against the Porte. The Russians, who took this provision in earnest, prepared to send embassies abroad to France, Spain, Denmark, Sweden, and Brandenburg in search of such aid. These missions suffered grave disappointments in every case but are of interest in the light of Western diplomatic strategy and their relation to the later travels of Tsar Peter.

If the French king, Louis XIV, had been deceived into believing that he might somehow engage Moscow in an anti-Austrian bloc in 1683,

---

[56] As quoted by Ustrialov, *op. cit.*, I, 190.
[57] Solov'ev, *op. cit.*, XIV, 986.
[58] *P.S.Z.*, II, 812.
[59] *Ibid.*, pp. 835–838.
[60] *P.S.Z.*, II, 837: "... The tsars seeing such shame on God's name, such destruction and slavery of Christians, and asking God for favor and aid, have decreed that, for the many violations of the truce by the khan, their boyars and *voevodas* with their armies are to be sent from Moscow against the Crimea...."

Golitsyn in 1686 was equally mistaken in seeking to draw France into an anti-Turkish coalition.[61] The Russian envoys, Prince Ia. F. Dolgorukii, I. E. Myshetskii, and K. Alekseev, with approximately one hundred and fifty attendants arrived in France in July, 1687. They were met by M. Storf, the French king's aide.[62] Their sudden arrival without formal announcement had come at an awkward time, politically speaking. Louis XIV was in the midst of enforcing the Revocation of the Edict of Nantes and of insuring himself against the repercussions of his unpopular religious policy abroad. The French could find little to be gained even in granting the Russians a hearing. From the day of their arrival, the Russian envoys met only rebuffs. Upon their entry into France at Dunkerque, their baggage had been seized and sealed by the customs officials. It was to be kept under seal until their arrival in Paris. En route to Paris the Russians broke the seals and began bartering various items with the local inhabitants. When French customs officers sought to stop them, they resisted, and one of the ambassadors threatened a French customs officer with a knife. Upon their arrival in Paris, M. Storf drew attention to this unseemly conduct and impressed upon the envoys the necessity of observing French diplomatic etiquette.[63] There were other unpleasantries. Louis XIV refused the Russians an audience but sent them gifts and a letter informing them it would be useless to open negotiations. This decision the envoys refused to accept and insisted on being received by the king. The French tried starving them, removing their baggage, and isolating them, but they refused to depart the kingdom. Louis finally yielded ground and granted them an interview with his foreign minister, Colbert de Croissy, to be followed by admission to the royal presence.

The discussions between the envoys and the French foreign minister began September 1, 1687, at St. Denis. They proved barren. The Russian proposal that France enter the war against the Porte[64] was parried by a declaration of de Croissy that the French king never declared war without good reason. France, he stated, had only recently renewed her former capitulations with the Ottoman empire, and French trade in

---

[61] A. F. Malinovskii, "Bytnost vo Frantsii u Korolia Ludovika XIV polnomochnym poslom kniazia Iakova Fedorovicha Dolgorukogo," *Trudy i letopisi*, VII, 90: "At the time of the siege of Vienna the French army marched up to the borders of the empire and, if the Sultan had succeeded in capturing this capital, Louis would have marched on the German empire, would have enslaved the electors and all the imperial officials."

[62] Bantysh-Kamenskii, *op. cit.*, IV, 83–84.

[63] *Recueil des instructions données aux ambassadeurs et ministres de France depuis les traités de Westphalie jusq'à la révolution française*, VIII, 83.

[64] *Sbornik* . . . , XXXIV, 12.

the Levant would suffer ruin by such an enterprise.[65] Besides, de Croissy added, since France was in serious danger of attack from her neighbors, she had need of all her troops and could send only a token force against the Turks at that time. He reminded the Russians that in 1664 King Louis had sent a force of French troops to aid the emperor in his war against the Porte, and these had been given miserable treatment—poor camp sites, inadequate provisions, and highly vulnerable positions during times of attack.[66]

Dolgorukii, finding no encouragement for direct military support, sought to obtain the neutrality of France during the campaigns to follow. Would the French, he asked, agree to refrain from attacking any of the confederates in the coalition? De Croissy gave an evasive reply. If the allies would give his government "no legitimate cause for war," France would be pleased if they continued to use their arms in defeating the infidel.[67] He then veered the conversation to the matter of permitting French Jesuits to travel in Russia. Would the tsars agree to admit them to Russia? Dolgorukii stated that he had no instructions on the matter.[68] The discussions ended.

During the next several days further misunderstandings occurred in connection with diplomatic immunity, diplomatic ceremony, and the tsars' titles. The envoys asked for their passports. These were promptly given, and they departed for Spain, September 5, 1687. The unpleasantries connected with the Dolgorukii mission created a lasting bitterness on both sides and for twelve years all diplomatic connections between Moscow and Versailles ceased.[69]

Arriving in Spain, the Dolgorukii mission received more courteous treatment but obtained no more tangible satisfaction from the Escorial than from Versailles. Charles II praised the Russians for their efforts on behalf of Christendom but politely declined to join their coalition or

---

[65] Malinovskii, *op. cit.*, p. 102: "... Prince Dolgorukii learned from the Greek Metropolitan, who had come to Paris with the Turkish ambassador, that the king had received the Mohammedans with great affection, and had ordered them housed at the same place as the Russians...."

[66] *Sbornik* ..., XXXIV, 13.

[67] *Ibid.*, p. 14.

[68] Malinovskii, *op. cit.*, p. 106.

[69] Malinovskii, *op. cit.*, p. 112: "When the Grand and Plenipotentiary Russian envoys returned from Spain and presented their daily record of everything that had passed in France, the Tsars Ivan and Peter Alekseevich, in conjunction with the Tsarevna Sophia, hearing their report, decreed, and the boyars ratified, that imperial charters should be sent to the Roman emperor, to the Spanish and English kings, to the Venetian Republic, to the Estates General of the Netherlands, and to Louis XIV, himself, concerning the inimical actions of the French king ... and of his obvious preference for the friendship of the Turkish sultan."

to lend them two or three million thalers for the prosecution of the war on the ground that he was already aiding his cousin, Emperor Leopold, by sending a fleet into the Mediterranean. Unable to sway the Spaniards any more than they had the French, the envoys once again had to admit defeat and departed for Moscow.

In other quarters as well, Russian efforts to enlarge the alliance proved unavailing. Later attempts to win allies took place by diplomatic correspondence. The English king, Charles II, offered Moscow "his best prayers,"[70] but no more. The Danish king, Christian V, agreed to aid the cause with his fleet "in case of extreme necessity."[71] The Swedish king, Charles XI, congratulated the tsars on their alliance but excused himself from lending active aid "because of the great distance of Sweden from the Turkish Empire."[72] Duke Cosimo III of Florence would give no financial support to the enterprise "because he was planning to aid the Venetians."[73] Even Russia's efforts to form closer ties with the belligerents, Austria and Venice, suffered defeat.

A Russian embassy composed of B. P. Sheremetev, I. Chaadaev, P. I. Nikiforov, and I. Volkov arrived in Vienna in March, 1687, to arrange a formal alliance with the emperor, as suggested by von Blumberg. Leopold I congratulated them on the conclusion of the Polish alliance, assured them of his close military coöperation in future engagements, and promised to make no separate peace with the Turks without the consent of his allies, Poland and Venice. But the matter of a formal alliance with Moscow soon bogged down. The ostensible reason appeared to be disagreement over the tsar's flamboyant titles. The Austrian ministers refused to concede the title of "majesty" to the tsars without the consent of the great princes of the German Empire. Four months passed in laboring this and other matters, until the Russian embassy departed for Moscow, July, 1687.[74] Frequent exchanges of dispatches between the two courts took place in connection with the war, but after four months of effort, the Russians had obtained nothing more than the good will of Vienna.[75]

---

[70] Bantysh-Kamenskii, *op. cit.*, I, 122–123.
[71] *Ibid.*, p. 235.
[72] *Ibid.*, IV, 202.
[73] *Ibid.*, II, 247.
[74] Max Immich, *Papst Innocenz XI, 1676–1689*, p. 21.
[75] Zhigarev, *op. cit.*, I, 98–99: "The allied actions of Russia with the Western powers against the porte (1686) were significant only in the respect that from that time on, the Vienna court for a long time becomes our constant ally in the wars against Turkey, and the Graeco-Slavic peoples of the Balkan peninsula, rising against the Turkish government at the sight of the successes of Austria, Poland, and Venice, took courage and entered relations with Russia, persuading her to come to their help in the struggle for freedom."

At the conclusion of the Vienna mission Prince Sheremetev sent the diak I. Volkov to Venice to converse with the Doge Marcantonio Giustiniano about the war. Volkov was instructed to learn the degree of effort the Venetians planned to expend in the struggle, to gauge what their reaction would be toward a separate peace with the Turks, and to gather other vital information.[76] The Venetians welcomed Volkov but adroitly evaded answering his principal questions. Friendship between the two states augured well, however, and in the following year Golitsyn appointed a Greek, I. Likhudius, to serve as permanent Russian representative to the Republic. Likhudius performed his task with enterprise. As a promoter of Russian interests in the Balkans and Near East he ranks with Iurii Krizhanich, Patriarch Dionysius of Constantinople, and the Wallachian Hospodar Constantine in imagination.[77]

Although the diplomatic missions described were unrewarding from an immediate point of view, they had great significance for later Russian history. The West was apprised as never before of Moscow's changing position in European affairs. Russia's expanding political interest, its preparedness to enter alliances as a European power, and its desire to establish closer relations with the West had been clearly demonstrated. Occasions would arise in the following century when Russia, because of internal disorders, would remain on the sidelines of larger European politics. But the West could not again, as in the past, ignore Moscow as an influence in Europe. The term "hermit nation" no longer applied. The Treaty of Moscow signalized the change; the diplomatic missions confirmed it.

The Permanent Peace was the most positive single achievement of Tsarevna Sophia's regency. It marked the rise of Moscow as the primary Slavic power in Europe in place of Poland. It stabilized the Russo-Polish frontier and made permanent many earlier territorial gains. Moscow's decision to pursue its interests southward toward the Black Sea was in line with policies outlined by earlier Romanovs and followed by Sophia's successors.

---

[76] *Pamiatniki diplomaticheskikh snoshenii*, X, 1285 ff.

[77] *Ibid.*, pp. 1331–1337: "Translation of a letter from Likhudius, the Greek, to Vasilii V. Golitsyn.... November 27, 1688: Many of the high officials of this Republic have asked me whether the Great and most Sovereign Moscow tsars wished to be crowned on the throne of Constantinople. I ... answered then in the following words, 'Truly they wish this.' And they told me that no more appropriate time than the present could ever be found ... and that it is fitting that you (the Russian sovereigns) should desire this.... And if the Great Moscow tsars will be rulers of Constantinople possessing, by God's aid, great strength the like of which no other monarchs of the world possess, the Turk will never be able to approach the boundaries...."; N. S. Derzhavin, "Russkii absoliutizm i iuzhnoe slavianstvo" in *Izvestiia Leningradskogo gosudarstvennogo universiteta*, no. 1, 63–64.

CHAPTER VI
THE TREATY OF NERCHINSK

THE PREOCCUPATION of Sophia's government with the war against the Crimea coincided with critical developments in another hemisphere—Northeast Asia. Negotiations with Poland and Austria had hardly begun when a controversy with China over the Amur River area reached a stage where Moscow's whole position in the Far East was threatened. This crisis forced the government to decide in which direction Russian foreign policy could best be served and also brought up the possibility of a two-front war.

Russian expansion into Asia in the seventeenth century followed the same general pattern laid down in the sixteenth century. Small detachments of men—Cossacks, peasants, and *promyshlenniki* (private traders and hunters, similar to the Canadian *coureurs de bois*)—under the jurisdiction of a few government service men, set out largely on their own to reduce the heterogeneous Paleo-Asiatic tribes dwelling in the vast land mass between the Yenesei River and Penzhinskaya Bay to the position of tribute-paying subjects of the tsar. The incentive, as in the sixteenth century, was fur—the most important single item of trade in Russia.[1] The hunter and fur trader usually preceded the government official to the far corners of the East. During the reign of Tsar Alexis settlement had begun along the Pacific and along the tributaries and upper reaches of the Amur River in the area east of Lake Baikal. Between 1648 and 1666, Irkutsk, Selenginsk, and Barguzin were founded in the lands of the Buriat and Evenki (Tungus). These peoples at first stubbornly resisted the Russian advance, but ultimately admitted Muscovite control in preference to Mongol domination. Late in the seventeenth century an important Russian penetration took place along the Shilka and Amur rivers. The expedition of Vasilii Poiarkov (1643–1646) and of Erofei Khabarov (1649–1651) had quickened Russian interest in those areas, and within thirty years (1654–1683) Nerchinsk, Albazin, and Aigun were established.[2]

---

[1] R. H. Fisher, *The Russian Fur Trade*, p. 230.

[2] Two documentary collections have supplied the bulk of materials for this chapter. *D.A.I.*, X, has numerous reports of the voevodas to their superiors, instructions from them to subordinate officials, as well as instructions from the Moscow government to the voevodas about Russian relations with China, Mongolia, and the native tribes of the Amur area. Many of these show the mounting tension in Sino-Russian relations, the difficulties of the eastern ostrogs, and the necessity for an agreement with China. Volume XI of *D.A.I.* has some material on the Chinese attacks on Albazin. The Russian text of the Treaty of Nerchinsk may be found in *P.S.Z.*, III, and in *Sbornik*

In the movement along the Amur the Russians encountered larger tribes, the Daurians and Duchers, who were subjects of the Chinese emperor. More civilized than the natives to the north and to the west, they boasted fertile grain fields, many village settlements with populations up to a thousand people, and a rich trade with China. The subjugation of the Daurians and Duchers to a tribute-paying status by the Russians, with a demand for their grain, aroused the serious enmity of China. The emperor resolved to oust the Russians entirely from the Amur. In 1653, as a preliminary, Emperor Shun Chih ordered the Daurians and Duchers to destroy their dwellings and to emigrate to Manchuria where he might protect them more readily.[3] The order for evacuation presented a serious problem to the Russian settlers in those areas, who had come to depend upon the native tribute in grain for sustenance. The larger issue of a struggle with China over control of the Amur was also raised. In 1670 the Manchu dynasty further advised the Russians of its intentions by militarizing the Amur and parts of Northern Manchuria. Military fortifications were erected at Kirin, Aigun, and other places; dockyards, wharves, and granaries were built at vantage points along the Amur. Reconnaissance expeditions appeared near the Russian settlements, investigating land and water routes to the upper reaches of the Amur.[4] In September, 1682, the emperor sent a military force under Deputy-Lieutenant General Lang-tan and Duke Peng-chun to Ta-huerh and So-lun under the pretext of a deer-hunting expedition. They were to notify the Russians at Nerchinsk of their

---

Dogovorov Rossii s Kitaem (Collection of Treaties of Russia with China). The Latin and Manchu texts of the treaty may also be found in *Sbornik*.

Among the secondary works N. N. Bantysh-Kamenskii's *Diplomaticheskoe sobranie del mezhdu rossiiskim i kitaiskhim gosudarstvami s 1619 po 1792-i god* (Diplomatic collection of affairs between the Russian and Chinese states from 1619 to 1792), 1882, though somewhat antiquated has a wide assortment of information on Russo-Chinese friction along the Amur, the Chinese attack on Albazin, and the Golovin mission to Nerchinsk. Hsuän-Ming Liu's article on "Russo-Chinese Relations up to the Treaty of Nerchinsk" in the *Chinese Social and Political Science Review*, Jan.-Mar., 1940, and V. S. Frank's article on "The Territorial Terms of the Sino-Russian Treaty of Nerchinsk, 1689" in *The Pacific Coast Historical Review*, Aug., 1947, are recent appraisals of the critical Russian-Chinese agreement of 1689. D. M. Lebedev's *Geografiia v Rossii XVII veka* (Geography in Russia of the XVII century), 1949, has a substantial chapter on Russian embassies to "eastern lands" which includes a section on the Spafarii mission to Peking (1675–1676), and descriptions of the Amur area in the late seventeenth century. M. N. Pavlovsky, *Chinese-Russian Relations*, 1949, has three essays on the role of Mongolia in Sino-Russian relations, Jesuit influence in Chinese diplomacy, and Russian émigrés in China, all of which are primarily concerned with the seventeenth century. For a short, clear account of commercial relations between Russia and China during this period see chap. xi of R. H. Fisher's *The Russian Fur Trade, 1550–1700*.

[3] V. I. Ogorodnikov, *Tuzemnoe i russkoe zemledelie na Amure, v XVII v.*, p. 72.
[4] N. N. Bantysh-Kamenskii, *Diplomaticheskoe sobranie del* ..., p. 23.

presence and to make a thorough survey of approaches to the Russian settlements by land and water.⁵

In 1682, the voevoda at Albazin, I. Semenov, reported that Chinese agents had begun to trample grain fields in his area and to make careful observations of the Russian fortifications. He anticipated an attack on Albazin within a year.⁶

A settlement of these differences by negotiation appeared unlikely in 1682. Russia's diplomatic relations with China had been troubled and irregular and had not attained a point of development where matters of mutual concern could be readily discussed by diplomatic representatives. No permanent embassy was maintained by Moscow in Peking, and special missions from the tsar to China had been uniformly unsuccessful.

Moscow's primary interest in China was trade. Travelers, traders, and government agents coming to Moscow from China had sharpened the Russian desire for Eastern luxury goods. In 1618, Ivan Petlin and Andrei Mundov were sent to Peking to arrange trade relations on a formal basis. Without gifts for the emperor, they failed to obtain an audience and were sent home. Nearly forty years later, Feodor I. Baikov (1654–1658) and Ivan Perfil'ev (1658–1662) were sent to China with gifts on a similar mission. They also failed to observe diplomatic custom and returned to Moscow empty handed. Baikov was asked to leave when he refused to present the tsar's gifts to the emperor before being received by him or to kowtow in his presence. The Perfil'ev mission failed because a letter from the tsar to the emperor "showed a lack of humility and courtesy."⁷

In 1667, Russo-Chinese relations became further strained. Gantimur, a Tungus tribal chief, had been an ally of the Chinese in opposing the Russian advance along the Nercha River. In 1667, he forsook his allies and joined the Russians. Gantimur's strong influence among his own people impelled the Chinese to ask for his extradition. The Russians refused. The voevoda of Nerchinsk, Daniel Archinskii, reportedly aggravated the issue in 1670 by suggesting that the Chinese emperor accept Russian suzerainty. Only a rebellion in the southern provinces of China (1673–1680) prevented the Chinese from taking military action at that time.⁸

⁵ *Edicts and Proclamations of the Manchu Emperor, Kang-hsi, A. D. 1662–1721*, XVI, 2, v. and 3, v. Translated from the Chinese by Wei Lin.
⁶ *D.A.I.*, X, 229.
⁷ Hsuän-Ming Liu, "Russo-Chinese Relations up to the Treaty of Nerchinsk...," *Chinese Social and Political Science Review*, XXIII (Jan.–Mar., 1940), 403–406; see also D. M. Lebedev, *Geografiia v Rossii XVII veka*, p. 126.
⁸ *Ibid.*, pp. 397–398; M. N. Pavlovsky, *Chinese-Russian Relations*, pp. 127–131.

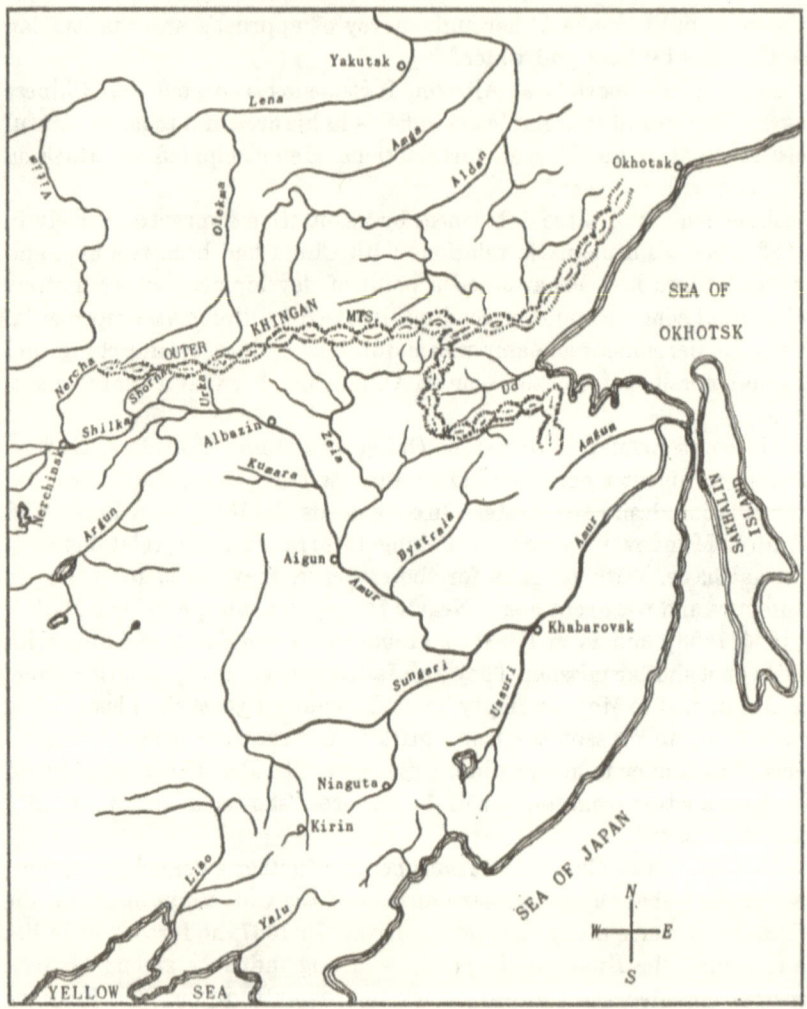

Map 1. Russian settlements in the Amur River Area in the Late Seventeenth Century

In 1675, Tsar Alexis, apprehensive over these developments, appointed a Greek, Nikolai G. Spafarii, as envoy to China. The latter was instructed to establish diplomatic and commercial relations with China on terms carefully outlined by Moscow, and to arrange other matters affecting the two countries.[9] Spafarii arrived in Peking in May, 1676. A dispute again arose over diplomatic ceremonial. Several months passed

[9] Hsuän-Ming Liu, *op. cit.*, pp. 407–408.

in an effort to resolve the difficulty, during which time both sides agreed to minor concessions. But Spafarii finally returned to Moscow without a treaty.

By 1680, tension along the Amur had reached a breaking point. No military support had come from Moscow, and the voevoda of Albazin, I. Semenov, had been compelled to seek help from the voevoda of Nerchinsk. In January, 1683, Feodor Voeikov, the voevoda at Nerchinsk, wrote Alexander Saltykov, the voevoda of Eniseisk, of the grave position of Albazin and the other Daurian settlements.[10] There were, he wrote, only 202 military men in the combined ostrogs of Nerchinsk, Telembinsk, and Eravinsk. Nerchinsk had few firearms, and those left by the former voevoda, Pashkov, had been allowed to deteriorate.[11] Semenov at Albazin asked for Cossacks and firearms from Nerchinsk to defend his ostrog from the approaching Chinese attack, but the voevoda of Nerchinsk replied, "I have no firearms to send and can spare no men."[12]

The difficulties of the voevodas were further increased by dissension among themselves and a decline of morale within their ostrogs. Their Cossacks on occasion would attack Chinese settlements in violation of orders and would threaten to abandon the Russian peasants in the ostrog whenever disagreements occurred. Voiekov complained that Semenov ignored instructions and failed to prevent Cossacks and promyshlenniki from traveling along the Amur, or to respect the memoranda he had sent him in connection with administrative affairs.[13]

In December, 1683, the Russians at Nerchinsk received an ultimatum from Peking to abandon the Amur River valley entirely. The various complaints of the Chinese against the Russians were carefully enumerated. The Russians had seized sables and provisions from Chinese traders and trappers, had molested Chinese subjects, burned their homes, and committed many escapades along the Amur. These incidents, it was ordered, must cease, or the Chinese army already stationed in the Amur would begin operations against them.[14]

---

[10] *D.A.I.*, X, p. 227.

[11] *Ibid.*, p. 229: "... there is a scarcity of cannon, shells, pistols, rifles, powder, and lead, and whatever small firearms they do have are poor and unreliable. They explode during firing and injure men."

[12] *Ibid.*

[13] *Ibid.*, pp. 229, 231.

[14] *Ibid.*, pp. 238–239. Letter dated October 19, 1683: "... And I (the Chinese emperor) shall not let you make escapades on the Amur.... And I have ordered wherever they may see you they are to shoot and capture you.... O Russians of Albazin and Nerchinsk, renounce all evil... and go back, and we shall drop all these affairs... and live in peace among ourselves. And if you fail to understand this, and will live along my border, neither heaven nor earth will be able to protect you, and I shall

Sophia's government reacted slowly to the information regarding these developments. Although aware of the growing needs of its new empire in Northeast Asia, the Amur controversy at first rated only secondary consideration. Political events in Moscow explained much of the government's early ineptitude and desire to postpone the issue. The change in government and the threat of a large scale Strel'tsy revolt preoccupied the state in 1682, and when that threat had been overcome other factors intervened to discourage a responsible policy in the East. Sophia's regime required greater stability and wider political support at home before it could deal effectively with an issue several thousand miles to the east. Its strength rested mainly upon the lesser nobles and clergy. The boyars and other higher grades of nobility and clergy had acquiesced to the regency but gave it no real support.[15] Golitsyn had plans for the settlement of Siberia,[16] but they would come later with the backing of the governing classes, an element whose support he had not yet won. Opinion about the Amur was also divided.[17] Among the ruling class it was probable that few felt its importance outweighed that of political issues closer at hand. To embark on a war with China without the support of the nobility, the Cossacks, and other elements would have been inadvisable and impractical. Consequently, Golitsyn sought a solution with China short of war. He encouraged the Eastern ostrogs to cope with events as best they could, and promised them little by way of reinforcements in men and supplies. Voiekov's plea for men and ammunition in 1683 remained unanswered until 1684, when a decree finally ordered ammunition and foodstuffs to go to Eniseisk by the winter route, and 500 volunteers to be sent in the spring. At the same time recruits were permitted to go from Tobolsk to Eniseisk for deployment to the ostrogs farther east.[18]

Throughout 1684, the position of the ostrogs between Lake Baikal and the Amur remained critical. Sable hunting all but ceased along the

---

have no qualms about killing you. It is a long way for you to return, so ponder this carefully and come to me, and I shall favor you greatly."

[15] M. Pomialovskii, "Sofiia Alekseevna," *Russkii biograficheskii slovar'*, XIX, 135–136.

[16] A. Brückner, *Beiträge zur Kulturgeschichte Russlands*, p. 300.

[17] Krizhanich, *Russkoe gosudarstvo v polovine XVII veka*, pp. 121–122 (c. 1670): "I have heard much talk about China... and from some people I have heard that the tsar desires to lead an army against China.... The accursed enemy of the Russian people would thus have Russia stupidly go to conquer China while the Germans and Tatars would gain possession of the Russian state.... The Russian possessions have spread far enough.... It would be more advisable, in my opinion, to hold peace in Siberia with the Daurs and other neighbors...to avoid our starting war with two enemies or with many enemies at once in various lands"; Pavlovsky, *op. cit.*, p. 122.

[18] *D.A.I.*, X, 240; S. M. Solov'ev, *Istoriia Rossii*..., XIV, 1027.

Shilka and Nercha rivers, and the population lived "in constant fear of Chinese and Mongol attack."[19] A dispute between the Russians and the Mongol khan, Sain Ochiroi, also threatened to throw the weight of Mongolia to the side of China.[20] For some years the Russians had been gathering tribute from the Buriat tribes of the Oka- and Selenga-river region—peoples whom the Mongols regarded as their subjects. The Mongol khan protested the practice; the Russians successfully delayed the issue by referring the matter to Moscow and by arranging lengthy conferences with the Mongols. But the Mongols finally became unwilling to await Moscow's decision longer.[21]

Simultaneously, a Chinese attack threatened Albazin.[22] In August, 1684, a Chinese fortified town eight days distance from Albazin had arisen. The new voevoda of Albazin, Aleksei Tolbuzin, ordered an earthen embankment and a fifteen-foot moat built around Albazin as a further defense, but his supply of firearms and gunpowder remained small.[23]

In May, 1685, the Chinese attack upon Albazin began. A Chinese force of about ten thousand men under the command of Deputy Lieutenant General Lang Tan left Aigun late in the Spring. The Russian force at the ostrog under the command of Tolbuzin numbered 450 men with three hundred guns and three cannons. Chinese couriers arriving at Albazin in June ordered Tolbuzin to surrender the ostrog, but he refused. Within a few hours the bombardment of the fort began. The siege lasted ten days. During the first three days of the attack Tolbuzin lost a quarter of his men. Outnumbered, exhausted, with his ammunition almost gone and with no relief in sight, he decided on the tenth day to accept the relatively favorable surrender terms offered by the Chinese. Albazin was to be abandoned and the Russians permitted to retire to Nerchinsk unmolested. Arrangements having been agreed upon, Tolbuzin and his men departed for Nerchinsk and the Chinese took over the ostrog. The latter removed all foodstuffs from the fort, razed its buildings by fire, and then returned to Aigun.[24]

---

[19] *D.A.I.*, XI, 189.
[20] *D.A.I.*, X, 243: Report of Ivan Porshenikov to the voevoda of Enisei, 1684: "... We are living in the Selinginsk ostrogs in great fear of the Mongols, because there is an extreme scarcity of men here, and very little gunpowder and lead, and no reserve firearms. There are only one hundred and thirty-three service men in Selinginsk. Of these sixteen were sent to Nerchinsk, and about forty are going by water to Irkutsk for grain supplies. There are about twenty men at the Udinsk ostrog, and thus only about fifty or sixty men remain in the Selinginsk ostrog."
[21] *D.A.I.*, X, 245.
[22] Pavlovsky, *op. cit.*, p. 122.
[23] *D.A.I.*, XI, 174.
[24] *Ibid.*, X, 258–260.

Lang Tan's victory was short lived. Having defeated the Russians and destroyed their principal fort, he assumed that his work was completed and that the Russians would remain west of the Amur. No precautions were taken to insure the area against their return. Soon after his arrival at Nerchinsk, Tolbuzin learned that though his ostrog had been destroyed, the grain fields around the settlement had been left unmolested by the Chinese. His men suggested that he salvage the grain by sending troops back to the area to guard the crops until harvest. After much persuasion, the voevoda of Nerchinsk, I. E. Vlasov, consented, and in August, 1685, a force of men led by a Cossack colonel, Athanasius Beiton, reëntered Albazin. A spontaneous decision to rebuild the ostrog followed, and in September the work of restoration began and continued undisturbed throughout the remainder of the year.[25]

Inevitably the decision to reoccupy Albazin meant new clashes with the Chinese. As early as March, 1686, Colonel Beiton, conducting a reconnoitering party south of the ostrog, met small companies of Chinese patrols. In several encounters that followed, both sides suffered casualties. Chinese policing and reconnaissance activities were renewed, and in June reports came to Albazin of plans for a second large-scale Chinese operation against the stronghold.

In the summer of 1686 the work of rebuilding the ostrog neared completion. Only the watchtowers of the settlement remained to be roofed.[26] The Russian force at Albazin was increased to 670 men with better equipment. But their number was gravely inadequate. Tolbuzin managed to gather only five cannons and forty puds of gunpowder. He was promised eight additional cannons and one hundred puds of lead from Nerchinsk. The Chinese force descending upon him, from the standpoint of manpower, was overwhelming. Lang Tan, who again held the command, had a cavalry of three thousand men and an infantry of from three thousand to six thousand men. They came from Aigun on specially built river barges manned by slaves. They brought thirty cannons with them but few firearms. Most of the infantry fought with bows and arrows and some even used scythes as their principal weapons.

The second attack on Albazin began July 7, 1686, and lasted five months. It was a better integrated, more serious operation than the first but less decisive in result for the Chinese. Lang Tan's forces again surrounded the settlement and bombarded it heavily. The Russians re-

[25] Bantysh-Kamenskii, *op. cit.*, pp. 39–41.
[26] *D.A.I.*, X, 258.

turned their fire cautiously, to conserve ammunition, and the siege soon went badly for them.[27] The aid from Nerchinsk failed to materialize because of a decision taken there to conserve supplies for resistance against a later Chinese attack. Scurvy disabled many of Tolbuzin's men. The military siege continued throughout the summer and by September the garrison had dwindled to 115 men. Cossack scouts from Nerchinsk reported that the ostrog was undergoing continual bombardment, and that all grain in the surrounding countryside had been destroyed. In September Tolbuzin himself fell in action, struck by fragments from a cannon shell.[28] The command passed to Colonel Beiton. The only encouraging development during the summer was word from Moscow that an armed peace commission had departed for China to negotiate a settlement with the enemy.

In October, 1686, two Russian representatives, Nikifor Venykov and Ivan Favorov, arrived in Peking with a letter from the tsars requesting that the two courts enter negotiations to settle all matters of dispute between the two countries. Pending the arrival of the accredited Russian envoy, it was proposed that the siege of Albazin be raised. To this the Chinese agreed. In December, 1686, Lang Tan's forces retired to a position two miles east of Albazin, and early in 1687 to Aigun. The siege of the ostrog ended with a decimated Russian force still in command.

For the task of arranging a settlement with China, Golitsyn selected Feodor A. Golovin, son of the boyar Alexei Golovin, voevoda of Tobolsk. Young Golovin combined personal vigor and boldness of mind with shrewdness and an instinct which told him when concessions were required. He departed from Moscow in January, 1686, with the title of Great and Plenipotentiary Ambassador.[29] The following year he arrived at Selenginsk. He carried specific instructions about terms to seek but his primary assignment—"to end the dispute with China"—gave him great leeway for diplomatic bargaining.[30] "All bloodshed" must be avoided, read his instructions; in the event of a rejection of his pro-

---

[27] *Ibid.*, p. 257, Albazin, July 12, 1686: "... On July 7 (1686) a great Chinese force came to Albazin by boat and by horseback with firearms and with cannon, and from July 7 to 12 the enemy has gone around Albazin ... and has surrounded Albazin, and has turned its cannon on the town, and is attacking it furiously.... I am sitting besieged, and with me are my soldiers and other men, and there are few men and little ammunition in the town. Please send me men and guns and ammunition from Nerchinsk."

[28] *Ibid.*, pp. 263–265.

[29] Bantysh-Kamenskii, *op. cit.*, pp. 49, 53.

[30] N. Ustrialov, *Istoriia tsarstvovaniia Petra Velikago*, I. 244; Kh. Trusevich, *Posol'skiia i torgovyia snosheniia Rossii s Kitaem*, p. 29: "This peace was to have been reached at any cost...."

posals by the Chinese, he was to make arrangements for another embassy to go to Peking. The Amur River was to be obtained in its entirety, if possible, as the boundary between the two countries. Failing this, compromise boundary lines were to be proposed along certain tributaries of the Amur—the Bystraia or the Zeia River. And if the Chinese still would not yield, as a last concession Albazin was to be designated as the border.[31] Golovin was also instructed to arrange for a commercial agreement with China on as favorable terms as possible.

The discussions between the representatives of both countries were delayed until August, 1689. An initial problem had been failure to agree upon a meeting place. The Russians had wanted the negotiations held at Albazin, the Chinese at Nerchinsk. Delays in travel and differences regarding diplomatic ceremony accounted for further postponement. Prince So E Tu, a member of the Chinese secretariat, and Prince T'ung Kuo Kang, an uncle of the emperor, headed the Chinese delegation. Two Jesuits, John Gerbillon and Thomas Pereyra, served as their interpreters. The Russians regarded the presence of the latter with suspicion, since the Jesuit order had suffered many rebuffs in Moscow in recent years and strained relations existed between Rome and Moscow. The Chinese embassy departed from Peking in May, 1688, with a guard of 800 troops. The emperor had determined not to yield any part of the Amur to the Russians, and had refused to discuss peace terms unless Russia agreed in advance to retire from the area entirely. According to the Chinese, the Amur territory occupied by the Russians was not Russia's, nor was it a neutral zone.[32]

[31] Bantysh-Kamenskii, *op. cit.*, pp. 50–51; "While at the conference with the Chinese ambassadors a border line to the river Amur is to be established without fail and they [the Chinese] are to know that besides this river, which from ancient times has divided both states, no other border will be a stable one, also that the subjects of both states should not run from one bank of the Amur River to the other. They must not collect tribute or *iasak* from the *iasak*-paying people and must not cause them any grievance. The border-line disputes should be settled, the little ostrogs which have been ruined, should be rebuilt, and the people settled in them again. And in case the Chinese are unwilling to have the border-line to the Amur then at least they are to establish the border along the Amur as far as the river Bystraia or the river Zeia which flow into the Amur. But in case they prove to be stubborn then as a last resort they are to designate Albazin as the border. And they [the Russians] are to have the right to trade along the rivers Amur, Bystraia and Zeia, and in case that they are unwilling to settle peaceably then the envoys are to act according to the instructions concerning the mission of the plenipotentiaries—that is to obtain all this by means of a military force."

[32] Hsuän-Ming Liu, *op. cit.*, pp. 413–414: "The Amur has a strategic importance which must not be overlooked. If the Russians descend it, they can reach the Sungari.... If they descend the Sungari to the mouth, they can reach the sea.... If we do not recover the entire region our frontier people will never have peace ... all the rivers and rivulets flowing into the Amur being ours, it is our opinion that none should be abandoned to the Russians.... If the Russians will accede to these points,

At first the discussions progressed slowly. At the opening meeting Golovin proposed that the belligerents return to the status quo ante bellum. Since the Chinese had begun the hostilities, why not return to the situation that had prevailed in 1682? So E Tu rejected this suggestion, citing a long list of grievances against the Russians along the Amur. He reminded Golovin that though the siege of Albazin had been lifted at the request of the tsars, the Chinese claim to the region still stood, because all the Daurian lands had immemorially been subject to the will of the Chinese emperor. Golovin denied this, saying the peoples in the Selenga, Shilka, and Upper Amur valleys had long paid tribute to the tsars. Their great distance from Moscow had made it difficult for Russia to afford them proper protection in the past, but with the establishment of Nerchinsk, Albazin, and other ostrogs they could now be brought under effective Russian control. The Chinese rejected these arguments.[33]

On many days it appeared that the negotiations might suddenly terminate. Both sides indulged in the pretense of abandoning discussions.[34] A serious disagreement developed August 16 when the Russians inquired into the minimum Chinese terms. So E Tu presented a map and drew a line running along the Gorbitsa River, north and east through the great chain of the "Outer Khingan Mountains," probably the Yablonovoi and Stanovoi ranges.[35] He proposed that the region west of the river and north of the mountains go to Russia and the area south of the mountains and east of the river belong to China. The lands east and south of the Argun River should remain under Chinese control, and those west and north of the river should go to Russia. The Chinese further insisted that all Russian building constructions south of the Argun River be removed. Golovin regarded these proposals as inacceptable. He would not commit himself about the Mongolian frontier, asserting that he had no instructions on the matter.

As a counter proposal he suggested setting up the boundary from the source of the Gorbitsa to the mouth of the Amur; the land south of that line going to China and the northern part to Russia. The Chinese

---

we shall in return give up their deserters, expatriate the prisoners, draw the boundary and enter into commercial relations; otherwise we shall return and make no peace with them at all."

[33] *Ibid.*, p. 417.
[34] G. Cahen, *Histoire des relations de la Russie avec la Chine sous Pierre le grand,* p. 48.
[35] V. S. Frank, "The Territorial Terms of the Sino-Russian Treaty of Nerchinsk, 1689," *The Pacific Historical Review,* XVI (Aug., 1947), 268.

plenipotentiary replied by calling a council of war, at which it was agreed to end the discussions, renew the attack on Albazin, surround Nerchinsk, and incite the Mongols to revolt against the Russians. When word of these plans reached Golovin, he decided that further compromises were in order. On August 17 he requested that negotiations be reopened. The Russian military capabilities in the Amur did not exceed fifteen hundred men as opposed to a Chinese force of ten thousand men supported by subject tribes. Golovin proposed that Albazin be surrendered on condition that it be destroyed, and the Argun River be accepted as part of the boundary if the Russian inhabitants dwelling east of the river might remain under Russian protection. The Chinese sent the Jesuit Gerbillon to the Russian camp with plenary powers to continue the discussions.

During the next several days the wide differences between the Russian and Chinese points of view were gradually reduced. Golovin made three specific requests: (1) that an article be inserted into the treaty whereby the Chinese recognize the tsar's various titles in full or in summary form, and whereby both countries would abandon any references indicating the superiority of either sovereign; (2) that a statement be included insuring to the envoys of both countries proper respect from the government to which they had been accredited, and allowing them to present, in person, letters from their respective sovereigns to the heads of the state to which they had been sent; (3) that trade be permitted to exist freely between the two countries, on the condition that merchants conducting such trade be provided with passports. So E Tu successfully evaded the first two issues, pleading a lack of instructions on such matters, but readily accepted the proposal for commercial relations.[36]

A point of larger issue arose in connection with the Ud River valley. So E Tu had loosely designated the boundary to run along the "Outer Khingan Mountain" chain until it reached the sea. These mountains did not extend directly to the coast. As they approached the Sea of Okhotsk, they divided into lesser mountain chains; one turned northeast toward the Russian settlement of Okhotsk, called the Nosse range by the Chinese, and another regarded by the Russians as the mountain barrier intended, veered south and then east, roughly paralleling the Amur River. Between these two ranges was a vast expanse of territory through which the river Ud flowed. The high quality of its sables made this area highly important to the Russians, who had established several colonies

---

[36] Hsuän-Ming Liu, *op. cit.*, pp. 419–421.

there to carry on a fur trade with the natives. In the Chinese draft of the treaty, according to Gerbillon, the eastern frontier was to run along the crest of the "Outer Khingan Mountains to the sea"—the region south of the mountains assigned to China and that to the north to the Russians. On August 22 Golovin refused to accept the Chinese interpretation of the Nosse range as the boundary line.

Once again negotiations seemed to be approaching an end. Gerbillon fortunately intervened and persuaded the Chinese that their demands were unreasonable, since the mountains to which they referred were located over a thousand leagues from Peking.[37] A compromise was arranged August 23. It was decided to leave the territory in question undemarcated until the matter might be referred to the governments of both countries.

During the days that followed, terms for a treaty were gradually drawn together in the Russian, Manchu, and Latin languages, with the Latin text as the authoritative one.[38] In the Russian text drafted August 25—apparently the first to be completed—only the territory south of the Ud River was designated as neutral. The Ud itself and the land north of it were demarked as Russian. When a copy of this version was translated into the Manchu tongue, the Chinese immediately raised objections, and insisted that the Russians revise the Latin draft to agree with the original Chinese intent. For some unexplained reason, when the Russian and Manchu copies accompanying the final Latin text appeared, these alterations had not been made. It has been suggested that the two plenipotentiaries, eager to sign the treaty, may have neglected to correct the discrepancy, or may purposely have left it unchanged for future reference.[39] The Russians may deliberately have substituted a different mountain chain for the one intended by the Chinese to narrow the undivided territory to a comparatively small area and to eliminate the threat of a future Chinese claim to a sizable part of Eastern Siberia.[40] Whatever the reasons, the Chinese envoys were negligent in permitting the Russian version to stand and in leaving the terms of their Manchu version so ambiguous, namely: "... all lands ... south of the Ud River and north of the Khingan Mountains shall remain neutral for the time being...."[41] It is true that the Latin text was generally regarded as official; if the Manchu and Russian

[37] Frank, *op. cit.*, p. 267.
[38] *Sbornik Dogovorov Rossii s Kitaem, 1689–1881 gg.*, pp. 1–6; Hsuän-Ming Liu, *op. cit.*, p. 439.
[39] Hsuän-Ming Liu, *op. cit.*, p. 440.
[40] Frank, *op. cit.*, p. 270.
[41] Hsuän-Ming Liu, *op. cit.*, pp. 427–428.

versions were considered essentially different and unauthoritative, the matter should have been clarified in the Latin text, or the fact should have been recorded that the Latin text was the only authoritative one.

The Treaty of Nerchinsk was signed August 27, 1689. The Russians gave the Chinese one copy in Latin and one in Russian; the Chinese reciprocated with drafts in Latin and Manchu. The Latin versions were then signed and sealed by both parties. A note appended to the Russian copy stated that the Jesuits read the original text in Manchu and translated it "word by word" into Latin. The accuracy of their translation could not be ascertained because "not a single interpreter of the Manchu language could be found among the Daurian cities."[42]

Compared with the Polish treaty of 1686, the Treaty of Nerchinsk was a model of brevity. In contrast to the thirty-three lengthy articles of the Polish treaty, that of Nerchinsk contained only six. Its summary character, in fact, gave it an ambiguity which in the end worked against the Chinese and resulted in what appeared for several generations to be serious losses for the Russians. Articles I and II on the national boundaries had created the principal difficulty. They represented the core of the understanding.[43] According to these articles the eastern boundary between the two nations ran along the course of the Argun River to its confluence with the Amur. It then moved west along the Shilka River to the Gorbitsa River (Kerbichi in the Manchu) which joined the Shilka near the Chernaia (Shorna). From the course of the Gorbitsa, the boundary took a northeasterly direction along "the craggy mountains which begin at the source of this river" and "which stretch as far as the sea [Sea of Okhotsk]."[44] All rivers and streams that rose on the southern slopes of this range and fell into the Amur were to belong to China, whereas those which flowed to the other side were to be Russia's.[45] According to the Latin text, all the territory between the said mountains and the river Ud was to remain undivided until further settlement. Although the mountain range to which the text alluded was not clearly designated, the Russians, it appeared, understood that only the land south of the Ud River would remain neutral, the Ud itself

---

[42] *Ibid.*, pp. 436–437.
[43] The Russian text may also be found in *P.S.Z.*, III, 31–32; the Chinese text is reproduced in *Tung Hua Lu*, VII, 26 K'ang Hsi, 28th year, 12th month, 13th day. An English translation of the latter has been prepared by Chih Pei Sha.
[44] *Sbornik Dogovorov Rossii s Kitaem 1689–1881 gg.*, pp. 3–4.
[45] Frank, *op. cit.*, p. 268: "The Gorbitsa has its source in the great Stanovoy Range. This chain starts in Transbaikalia under the name of Yablonnoy Range ... Seventeenth-century Russian maps assumed, however, that another clearly marked range branched off the Stanovoy proper near the headwaters of the Gorbitsa and ran to the Sea of Okhotsk, reaching it south of the Ud' estuary."

being "under the dominion of the Russian government." The Chinese, on the other hand, assumed that all lands north of the Khingan Mountains and south of the Ud were to remain neutral "for the time being."[46] In effect, the whole area south as well as north of the Ud came under Russian domination and remained so until the Treaty of Aigun (1858) confirmed the change.

Article III provided for the destruction of Albazin and the withdrawal of the garrison to lands within the Russian sphere. Article IV dealt with hunters and fugitives. Hunters individually or in groups were not permitted to cross the frontier; should they do so they were to be apprehended and punished according to their crimes. However, "no excess whatever committed by private persons shall kindle a war between the signatories," stated the Latin text. Fugitives and deserters when apprehended were to be returned to the country of their origin. Fugitives from either side might remain unmolested if they had settled in the country not of their origin before the signature of the treaty. Article V specified that commercial relations were to be established. The subjects of either state, if properly furnished with passports by their government, were allowed to move freely across the frontiers and carry on mutual trade. Article VI stated that friendly relations had been restored between the two countries and that no grounds for uneasiness need exist if the terms of the treaty were faithfully observed.

The conclusion of the treaty gave relief to both sides. Golovin's principal task—to reach a settlement with China short of war—had been accomplished at the price of his secondary purpose—to gain as much of the Daurian lands as possible.[47] The Chinese emperor, on the other hand, had reached an understanding with the Russians for the first time on what appeared to be his own terms. For him the treaty was something of a personal triumph.[48]

The Treaty of Nerchinsk has been adversely criticized by Russian

---

[46] Hsuän-Ming Liu, *op. cit.*, pp. 428–429.

[47] *D.A.I.*, X, 265–266. Golovin wrote Zinoviev, the voevoda of Irkutsk, that "after many stubborn conversations with the Chinese, we, with God's help and the good fortune of the Russian sovereigns, established a peace and a boundary line, and exchanged the negotiated documents with our signatures."

[48] *Edicts and Proclamations of the Manchu Emperor K'ang Hsi (1662–1721)*, XVI, 8 v. On February 17, 1690, the emperor wrote his ministers: "I have diligently exerted myself and have been responsible for all merits and faults in regard to national administrative affairs ... the affair of the pacification of the Russians, both the Manchu and Chinese ministers unanimously said ... was hard to succeed in ... because they (the Russians) were in a region too far from China. But I insisted that this affair could not be allowed to remain undecided. Therefore, I immediately sent high officials to proceed according to my instructions. Russia was accordingly and instantly brought into submission."

historians as a disgraceful blunder, a calamitous loss, and an added proof of the incapacity of Sophia's regime. Ustrialov described it as the "irreparable loss of a spacious, fruitful territory, extremely important by virtue of its position, to the safety and well-being of Eastern Siberia."[49] M. Pomialovskii wrote that the "aimless and disadvantageous Crimean campaigns" had prevented Russia from defending her interests "where it was most vital for them to be defended."[50]

Such judgments ignore key factors. It was true in the seventeenth century as in the nineteenth and twentieth centuries, that the Amur was of great economic and strategic importance to Russia. If Albazin had been retained in 1689 and the Amur River fixed as the Russo-Chinese boundary, Russian penetration to the Sea of Okhotsk, to Kamchatka, the Kurile Islands, the Chinese maritime provinces, and even North America might have developed at a far earlier date.[51] As it developed, Moscow took nearly one hundred and seventy years to acquire what might have been won by a successful resistance at Albazin and a show of strength along the Amur. These arguments must not be underrated. But the Moscow government of 1683 could hardly foresee that such advantages to be gained in the Amur outweighed the rewards of a successful policy in the West. For Golitsyn and others, a final agreement with Poland on the Ukrainian frontier, the elimination of attacks by the Tatars, the winning of a Black Sea foothold, and the establishment of closer ties with the West seemed more immediately desirable and logical objectives than the rewards to be gained by conquering the Amur. The hazards attending a Far Eastern expedition must have loomed large in Golitsyn's mind. Krizhanich and Spafari had warned against them.[52] The problems attending the dispatch of an Amur expedition of ten thousand men with sufficient arms, food, and equipment for an arduous journey across Siberia and a campaign to last several years could not be lightly contemplated, as some historians have suggested. It may be argued that even with such obstacles, Russia had everything to gain by such an undertaking. Moscow's control of the Ukraine was already virtually established and what little remained to be settled with Poland could have been achieved later without effort. But the situation

---

[49] Ustrialov, *op. cit.*, I, 254: "Thus Sophia renounced all claims to the banks of the Amur, which had been in Russia's possession for thirty years; thus the Russians lost a navigable river, which by its confluence into the Pacific might have given a different significance to the whole Siberian region. The Treaty of Nerchinsk was Sophia's last affair. At the time Golovin signed it, her regime was drawing to a close."

[50] Pomialovskii, *op. cit.*, XIX, 139.

[51] Sychevskii, "Istoricheskaia zapiska o kitaiiskoi granitse" in *Chteniia*, II (1875), 10.

[52] Pavlovsky, *op. cit.*, p. 111

was not that simple in 1683. Sobieski's recent victory at Vienna had strongly stimulated nationalist sentiment in Poland. Sobieski's enthusiasm for a new drive against the Turk, and the stubborn attitude of Polish diplomats in discussing a Ukrainian settlement with Moscow, belied the growing contention of Poland's decline and discredited the suggestion that because of Warsaw's preoccupation with the Turk, a permanent settlement with Moscow might readily be arranged.

Once Golitsyn determined to concentrate his main diplomatic effort on the pursuit of Russian interests in the West, only minimum consideration could be given the Amur controversy. As during the previous regimes, the Eastern ostrogs must be maintained largely by the forces stationed in them and would have to meet the Chinese threat as best they could. Moscow could furnish them with little more than verbal encouragement and diplomatic support. Even during the years 1683–1686, when the controversy with China reached its peak, and Russia's entire position in the Far East was in danger, Golitsyn still hoped to find a solution to the problem short of war. It was for that purpose that he sent Golovin to Nerchinsk in 1686–1687. Golovin soon recognized the hopeless plight of Albazin and the slender military resources on which the Russian claim to the Amur depended. If Russia's claim to the region were successfully maintained, additional men and supplies would have to be found. Thus, in the fall of 1688, he supported a request to Nerchinsk for additional "settlers, supplies, and troops" for Albazin.[53] The request came too late. The only hope of the Russians by that year was in the diplomatic front Golovin might put forth in dealing with the Chinese plenipotentiaries. His accomplishments in overcoming many obstacles were striking and deserve greater appreciation than they have been accorded.[54]

The Treaty of Nerchinsk actually won gains for Russia. For the first time a peace with China recognized Russia's right to be in the Far East. The settlement disposed of many long-standing differences between the two powers. It established peace on a basis that was as permanent as the Russians chose to make it. Such an arrangement removed the probability of a two-front war at a time when Russian arms in the West had suffered serious reverses. The Russians, it was true, had not gained the Amur boundary or Albazin as they had desired. But the Chinese failure to define the frontier in the Ud River valley more carefully opened the way for a later reassertion of those claims under cir-

[53] *D.A.I.*, V, 296–298.
[54] Pavlovsky, *op. cit.*, p. 123.

cumstances more favorable to Moscow and, at the same time, eliminated the threat of a Chinese claim for a large share of eastern Siberia, "including the whole Pacific Coast."[55]

The Treaty of Nerchinsk also arranged trade relations between Russia and China for the first time.[56] From 1689 on, increasing numbers of caravans traveled the ancient routes to the East conveying goods from Western Europe, Russia, and the Middle East to Peking and other Chinese trade centers to exchange for the commodities of the Far East. Border towns like Irkutsk and Nerchinsk became filled with Chinese products. The local government service men assumed the role of middlemen in the new trade. Thus the Treaty of 1689 marked a commercial as well as political milestone, enabling Russia to tap a great eastern market with impunity, while consolidating her earlier territorial gains made in northeast Asia.[57]

---

[55] Frank, *op. cit.*, p. 271.

[56] V. P. Potemkin, *Istoriia diplomatii*, I, 231: "The Nerchinsk Treaty of 1689 was essentially a very great success of Moscow diplomacy. It insured the establishment of Russia in the upper basin of the Amur, and opened broad possibilities for Russian trade with China. Russo-Chinese relations were grounded on the basis of the Nerchinsk Treaty down to the middle of the nineteenth century."

[57] S. V. Bakhrushin, *Torgi gostia Nikitin v Sibirii i Kitae*, p. 335: "At the end of the seventeenth century Chinese goods begin to displace furs in Siberia. The Treaty of Nerchinsk of 1689 opened new and broad possibilities in the realm of Russo-Chinese trade."

PART IV

THE LAST YEARS

CHAPTER VII

THE FALL OF THE TSAREVNA SOPHIA'S GOVERNMENT

THE POLISH alliance overshadowed all other political events of Sophia's regency. Even though the alliance ended in military failure the direction it gave Russian foreign policy and the opportunities it suggested for later territorial aggrandizement marked it as a development of first magnitude. Russia's gains through the peace treaty were assured in advance.

Sending an army against the Tatars was the principal step to be taken by the Russians to fulfill their commitment to Poland. Golitsyn had no illusions about the hardships of conducting a campaign in the Crimea. Bakhchisarai, the khan's capital, lay nearly one thousand miles from Moscow. The route to the Crimea led across the Nogai Steppe and the Perekop Isthmus, where stubborn resistance might be put forth against an invader and where dry summer heat could be oppressive and destructive to both man and beast. The siege of Chigirin during the Russo-Turkish war of 1677–1681 had already shown the inherent weaknesses of Muscovite military organization and the problems attached to campaigning in lands as wanting in roads and ostrogs as the Zaporozh'e and the Crimea.[1]

---

[1] *P.S.Z.* and *D.R.V.* have a wide variety of documents on this topic. Volume II of *P.S.Z.* has the principal government decrees relating to the Crimean campaigns, official accounts of the campaigns, Golitsyn's intrigues with the Hetman Mazeppa, Tsarevna Sophia's awards to Golitsyn, and orders and instructions on many other subjects. *D.R.V.*, XI, is less satisfactory as a source because of its organization and its selection of materials but furnishes important details on the Crimean campaign (1687), Tsar Peter's marriage (1689), and Tsarevna Sophia's relations with Feodor Shaklovityi.

The writings of contemporary observers, Gordon, de la Neuville, von Kochen and Kurakin, on many of the leading issues and figures of the day comprise a particularly important source for this chapter. Patrick Gordon's comments upon the Crimean campaign, de la Neuville's speculation about the strength of the Russian arms in 1689, von Kochen's report of Golitsyn's arrival in Moscow (1687) after a serious military defeat, and Kurakin's comments upon the political tension in Moscow (1688–1689) vividly portray much of the atmosphere of the time which is an invaluable auxiliary to the description of events in the documentary materials.

The most critical appraisals of the downfall of Tsarevna Sophia's government are E. F. Shmurlo "Padenie Tsarevny Sof'i" (The Fall of Tsarevna Sophia) in *Zh.M.N.P.*, Jan., 1896, and N. Aristov's *Moskovskiia smuty v pravlenie tsarevny Sofii Alekseevny* (Moscow rebellions in the regency of the Tsarevna Sophia Alekseevna), 1871. For comments on both these works see the *Bibliographical Essay* which follows chap. viii. For a more recent account of the ultimate collision between the Regent Sophia and Tsar Peter see M. M. Bogoslovskii's *Petr I* (Peter I), 1940, and chap. xxiv of B. D. Grekov's *Istoriia SSSR: s drevneishikh vremen do kontsa XVIII veka*, I (History of the USSR: from ancient times to the end of the eighteenth century), 1948. Although

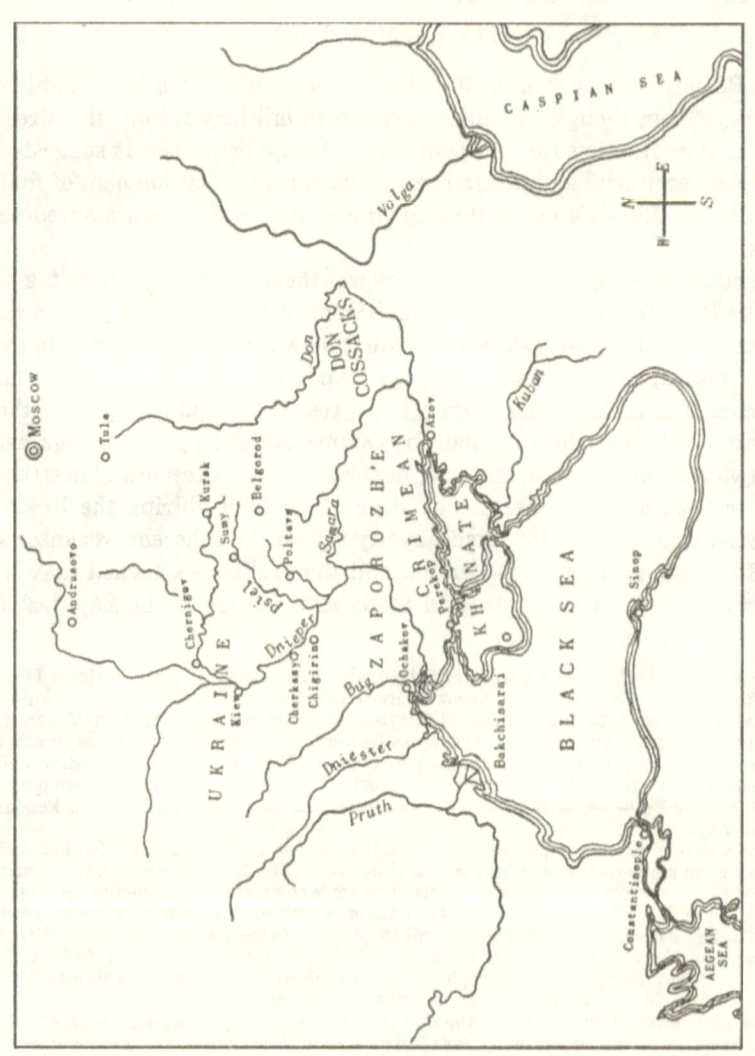

Map 2. The Ukraine and the Crimea in the Late Seventeenth Century

Patrick Gordon, who had participated in the defense of Chigirin, reminded Golitsyn in 1684 of the "discontent, disobedience and obstinacy of the Russian soldiery" and of "the little inclination amongst the greater part of the Russian nation toward war, especially among the Great Ones and Advisors."[2] Golitsyn himself had served in the army in the Ukraine during the sixties and seventies, and had witnessed the dissension which frequently arose over assignments, prerogatives, and military strategy.[3] The abolition of mestnichestvo had aimed in part at eliminating these evils, but they could not be removed entirely so long as large-scale military efforts depended upon the good will of the nobility. All these were calculated risks which Golitsyn had accepted.

Kurakin briefly noted in his memoirs the serious division of opinion toward Poland existing at court in 1686. One party of boyars led by Prince Peter I. Prozorovskii and Feodor P. Saltykov suggested that national arms should be turned against Poland rather than the Tatars.[4] The Dolgorukii and Shcherbatov families strongly opposed the alliance and threatened to undermine it by "draping themselves and their retinue in black" in protest of what appeared to them to be a serious failure in foreign policy.[5] The jealousy and distrust that proverbially existed between the Russians and Poles abated only slightly as a result of the treaty. The fear remained in Moscow that Poland might yet make a separate peace with Turkey to the disadvantage of Russia.

Preparations for the Crimean campaign began methodically. A Boyar Duma assembled in Moscow late in 1686 to consider the number of men required for the campaign, the appointment of officers, and the financing of the enterprise.[6] On September 3, 1686, a decree ordered all courtiers of the table (*stolniks*), courtiers attending to food (*striapchiis*), Moscow nobles, nobles of the Moscow garrison (*zhiltsy*), and warriors of all ranks to prepare for a campaign against the Tatars because "the Khan intended to make war against the Ukrainian and the Little Russian towns."[7] Voevodas throughout European Russia were sent instructions to mobilize the male population in their districts. In November, special taxes were levied upon merchants, peasant households, and church lands.[8]

---

both Bogoslovskii and Grekov tend to minimize the importance of Tsarevna Sophia's regency and to portray it as a relatively inconsequential prelude to that of Tsar Peter, their description of the larger events producing Sophia's downfall is correct.

[2] P. Gordon, *Tagebuch des Generals Patrick Gordon*, II, 5.
[3] Alexander Brückner, *Beiträge zur Kulturgeschichte Russlands* ..., p. 288.
[4] F. A. Kurakin, *Arkhiv kniazia F. A. Kurakina*, I, p. 51.
[5] Brückner, *op. cit.*, p. 319.
[6] *P.S.Z.*, II, 817–820.
[7] *Ibid.*, p. 812. Transliterations of titles slightly modified.
[8] *Ibid.*, pp. 817–820.

An awkward issue arose concerning the selection of a commander in chief. Golitsyn, a statesman and not a military strategist, would have preferred to remain in Moscow. But his opponents could not overlook an opportunity to remove him from the capital and early began an agitation for him to assume leadership of the campaign. Flattering as the suggestion might have appeared, Golitsyn knew it was dictated by a desire to capitalize upon his absence from Moscow. The boyars who so vociferously promoted his candidacy represented to a great extent the same element that had balked at the Polish alliance and earlier at naming Sophia regent.[9] Consequently, Golitsyn found his recommendations for candidates for the supreme army post successfully evaded, and himself thrust into the position of commander in chief to demonstrate his confidence in the campaign and to insure its proper conduct.

The plan of mobilization in 1687 was in accord with the traditional concept of movement along a chain of ostrogs and portages dominating a river system.[10] February 25, 1687, was the date originally set for the completion of military preparations. All troops were to be in the field by March 2, 1687. The main army, under Golitsyn and his associates, Prince V. O. Shcherbatov and V. A. Zmeev, assembled at Akhtyrka on the Vorskla River February 22. But it was late spring before the other forces completed mobilization. A Novgorod army commanded by A. S. Shein and B. Z. Boriatinskii assembled at Sumy on the upper Psël River, a tributary of the Dnieper; a Riazan army under V. D. Dolgorukii and P. D. Skuratov gathered at Khotmyzhsk, on the upper Vorskla; and a Sevsk army led by N. R. Nepluev collected at Krasny Kut on the Omel'nik River.[11] Further delays were created by the late arrival of lower-ranking officers at their commands and by petty arguments over assignments. The behavior of certain high-ranking officers, Princes Boris Dolgorukii and Iurii Shcherbatyi in particular, became so troublesome

---

[9] De la Neuville, "Zapiski de-la Nevillia o Moskovii," *Russkaia starina*, LXXI (Sept., 1891), 444: "V. V. Golitsyn appointed many to this post, but everyone said that since he had concluded peace with Poland he should take command so as to prove the conquest of Perekop as simple as it was supposed to be. Golitsyn did all he could to decline this position because he justifiably thought all blame for the failure might fall on him.... The nobles who confirmed the appointment of Golitsyn were precisely those who disagreed with the idea of a Polish alliance. They understood well that the invasion of the Crimea would be difficult, and tried to get Golitsyn out of Moscow because in his absence they hoped to weaken his power which they deemed had already become too great."

[10] R. J. Kerner, *The Urge to the Sea*, p. 64.

[11] *D.R.V.*, XI, 172–173; N. Ustrialov, *Istoriia tsarstvovaniia Petra Velikago*, vol. I, p. 190; de la Neuville, *op. cit.*, Part I, p. 445.

to Golitsyn that he had to threaten them with confinement to bring them into line.[12] The actual march did not begin until May, 1687.[13]

Moving south from Akhtyrka to the Merl River, a tributary of the Merchik-Vorskla-Dnieper, Golitsyn's army passed through Orel and Poltava to the Samara River. There his forces joined those led by Shein, Dolgorukii, and Nepluev. On May 30, 1687, the Cossack Hetman, Ivan Samoilovich, brought fifty thousand Ukrainian Cossacks to the Samara. The formation used by Golitsyn was as follows: the infantry, forming the base and center of the mass, was flanked on one side by the baggage train and on the other by the artillery, which in turn were covered by the cavalry. The Russian forces descended the Samara into the heart of the Zaporozh'e, crossed the Konskie Vody, a tributary of the Dnieper, and June 13 encamped at Bol'shoi Lug near the Lower Dnieper. From there troop movement became difficult.

In certain areas late rains and floods left the ground a soggy marsh, and in others steppe fires, presumably started by the Tatars, destroyed most of the fodder for the horses and oxen. Unable to bear the heavier loads, many cattle fell by the wayside. At the same time, army rations became depleted; very little foodstuffs could be commandeered en route, particularly after the troops reached the Nogai Steppe. "Up to this time," wrote Ustrialov, "our [the Russian] armies saw only herds of wild boars seeking safety from the steppe fires."[14] The army laboriously advanced across the steppe, coming within sixty miles of Perekop, gateway to the Crimean peninsula. Thus far no contact had been made with the Tatars. The most serious obstacle was the increasing number of steppe fires, which desolated the land and greatly impeded progress. Golitsyn began to doubt the ultimate success of the campaign. A lengthy siege of Perekop and an extended operation in the peninsula suddenly loomed as a larger undertaking than he had bargained for. Each day it became clearer that without reinforcements his forces could not be sustained. Some pretext was required to abandon the campaign.

The loyalty of the Cossacks—of Hetman Samoilovich, in particular—became a topic for much speculation. It was known that the hetman had opposed the Russo-Polish alliance from the beginning, and a rumor circulated that he, and not the Tatar khan had ordered the firing of the

---

[12] Ustrialov, *op. cit.*, I, 194.
[13] Estimates of the numerical strength of the Russian forces vary. Ustrialov, *op. cit.*, I, 192, asserted that the number of men in the "three armies" including Cossacks and the other service men amounted to 100,000; Kurakin, *op. cit.*, I, 64, set the figure at 200,000; whereas de la Neuville, *op. cit.*, Part I, p. 446, placed the figure at 400,000.
[14] Ustrialov, *op. cit.*, I, 198.

steppe. Whatever the cause, Golitsyn resolved to make Samoilovich the scapegoat for what promised to be a most indeterminate military venture. Late in June, Samoilovich was charged with many "contrary acts" against the Russians, among them responsibility for having fired the steppe.[15] Although the rumor was probably false, it was true that the Cossacks had thus far given the Russians only perfunctory military support. Great disaffection also existed among the Cossacks toward their leader. A young Cossack officer, Ivan Mazeppa, had been plotting to overthrow the hetman and to replace him as Cossack leader, and now capitalized on the rumor to gain the support of Golitsyn in fulfilling his plan. Neuville's statement that Golitsyn himself initiated the charge against Samoilovich cannot be proved. In early July Samoilovich and members of his family were captured and July 15 were deprived of their insignia of office. Mazeppa was promptly named his successor. Mazeppa assured Golitsyn, when he took over office, that he would have no communications with the Polish king, the Turkish sultan, or the Crimean khan.[16]

This intrigue against Samoilovich provided Golitsyn with an excuse to turn his back on the steppe. At the end of June he and his forces started for Moscow. On August 16 the Russian armies reached the Merl River, having followed a homeward route similar to the one taken in the advance south. There the troops were liberally paid and then demobilized. Golitsyn quietly reappeared in the capital in early September.[17]

In spite of the obvious failure of the campaign, Sophia insisted upon depicting it as a successful undertaking. On September 5 she conferred upon her favorite and his associates, rewards in lands, money, and gifts. An imperial decree praised them for their services and zeal.[18] According to the decree, Golitsyn and his men had promptly gone to their assigned

---

[15] *P.S.Z.*, II, 890.

[16] *Ibid.*, pp. 878–879: "... I, the slave of God, Ivan (Mazeppa), promise before the Holy Scriptures to the Lord God Almighty ... that I shall be in eternal and constant subjection to the Most Illustrious and Mighty Great Sovereigns and tsars and Grand Princes Ivan Alekseevich and Peter Alekseevich, and to the ... Grand Princess Sophia Alekseevna ..., and I promise not to betray myself and in no affair to communicate with or write to or hold counsel with the Polish king, the Turkish sultan and the Crimean khan. ..."; see *Ibid.*, pp. 863–864, "A Charter of Instructions to the Palace *Voevoda*, V. V. Golitsyn, to deprive Ivan Samoilovich of the rights of Hetman and to expel him from Little Russia ... and to elect a successor ..."

[17] C. von Kochen, "Moskva v 1687–88 gg., Pis'ma Khristofora fon Kokhena," *Russkaia Starina*, iii (1878), 122: Letter from von Kochen to the Livonian Governor-General at Riga (Sept., 1687): "The latest piece of news is that the former generalissimo, Prince V. V. Golitsyn, arrived in town on the 4th of September (1687) late in the evening.... He still remains at the helm of state in his former honor, and besides that, the Tsarevna Sophia Alekseevna, who had completely gained the reins of government, vigorously upholds him. All are of the opinion that in the last campaign from 40,000 to 50,000 men perished."

[18] *P.S.Z.*, II, 885–897.

places, organized their armies, and launched a campaign against the infidel with laudatory zeal. Upon crossing the River Konskaia and advancing to the Akchakrak and Karachakrak streams, the khan and his horde had become filled with terror, and losing their customary daring, had retreated to their strongholds and "burned out the steppe." Golitsyn and his army, continuing the advance, had been unable to engage the Tatars, even though they had approached "to the very closest regions of the Crimean towns." Suffering grievous privations—lack of fodder, dust storms, inadequate food, and failure to meet the enemy—a war council had been held at which it was decided to return to Russia. At a subsequent council meeting, it was agreed to send Leonty R. Nepluev and his forces to seek out an enemy encampment near the Zaporozh'e. The khan had sent his son, Nuradyn Sultan, there with many Turks, Kalmyks, and Crimeans. A battle of several hours duration followed with Nepluev's forces emerging victorious. This was the only encounter with the Tatars, but, concluded the decree, it had prevented the Tatars from attacking Poland and thus had "upheld the peace with Poland."[19] Dutch and German translations of this report were immediately sent abroad for publication.[20] The reasons for this became obvious. The government lacked sufficient strength to support the opprobrium attached to a large-scale military failure, particularly when that failure could be directly assigned to the military incapacity of an unpopular prime minister rather than to the unpredictable elements of war. There was also the necessity of representing the enterprise to Poland as a fulfillment of Russia's military commitment. Much effort and expense had gone into the expedition. If some positive result were to be salvaged, the government felt the necessity of portraying the campaign as a success.

During Golitsyn's four months' absence from the capital, the tsarevna had suffered renewed political threats from her opponents. Her skill in dealing with them and the general fear of further Strel'tsy and schismatic outbreaks had silenced the opposition in 1686. During the greater part of that year, Tsar Peter dwelt peaceably away from the capital with his mother and his principal supporters—the Cherkaskiis, Troekurovs, Lykovs, Urusovs, Boris A. Golitsyn, and an uncle, Lev Naryshkin. According to Kurakin, the Tsaritsa Natalia and her son "did not enter into the government in any way and lived by whatever was given them

---

[19] *Ibid.*, pp. 889–891.
[20] Von Kochen, *op. cit.*, p. 122: "Everyone is worried here [Moscow] by the fact that abroad there is being published in German and Dutch a glorifying description of the campaign in which the causes of the unsuccessful return of the large imperial army will be given in detail."

from the hands of the Tsarevna Sophia."[21] They had not abandoned hope, however, of one day seeing the regent overturned and their own party reinstated to power.

Sophia's actions, particularly after 1686, strengthened this desire. Thus far, the regent's plans to improve her political position had been unsuccessful. Tsar Ivan's marriage to Praskovia Saltykova had not yielded the male heirs Sophia had hoped for. It was now rumored that she planned to obtain the crown for herself and to marry Prince V. V. Golitsyn upon the conclusion of his Crimean campaign. Kurakin mentions this "as the rumor was a public one, but to be sure I doubt if such was her true intention."[22] Her actions, nevertheless, appeared to justify such conclusions. Upon the final arrangement of the Polish alliance in April, 1686, Sophia had taken every opportunity to associate herself with the royal prerogative.[23] Her name, which had previously appeared in public acts along with those of her brothers, was now preceded by the term "autocrat."[24] Special references to her were made in public prayers, her name being heard directly after those of the two tsars. A special crown was made for her to wear during public ceremonies and gold coins and medallions were struck bearing her image. Regal portraits of her appeared, holding the scepter and other insignia of power. Some of these portraits found their way abroad.[25] Her name was also mentioned more frequently in diplomatic discussions, and her appearances at public ceremonies accepted.[26]

The Naryshkins openly resented these changes. Golitsyn's departure for the Crimea signalized their return to political activity. During Golitsyn's absence, Lev Naryshkin and Boris Golitsyn openly ridiculed the tsarevna's pretensions to power, even going so far as to cast doubt upon her legitimacy as the daughter of Tsar Alexis.[27] Ugly stories were spread

---

[21] Kurakin, *op. cit.*, I, 53.

[22] Kurakin, *op. cit.*, p. 53.

[23] *P.S.Z.*, II (Jan. 8, 1687), 842–843: "A decree provides that grant charters be written in the names of Ivan and Peter Alekseevich and the Tsarevna Sophia Alekseevna"; E. A. Belov, "Moskovskiia smuty v kontse XVII veka," *Zh.M.N.P.* (1891), p. 338.

[24] *P.S.Z.*, II, 662, 691; Aristov, *op. cit.*, p. 122.

[25] Kurakin, *op. cit.*, I, 54: E. F. Shmurlo, "Padenie Tsarevny Sof'i," in *Zh.M.N.P.*, CCCIII: I, pp. 54–55.

[26] Von Kochen, *op. cit.*, p. 122: "Day before yesterday (Sept. 23, 1687) Tsar Ivan and the Tsarevna-regent according to the annual custom, went off on a pilgrimage to Troitsa monastery about twelve miles distance from here ... Tsar Peter remained at home"; *D.R.V.*, XI, 164–165.

[27] Shmurlo, *op. cit.*, p. 57: "In proclaiming herself an autocrat, and in carrying out acts not proper to a regent but to a sovereign, Sophia was reaching for that which did not belong to her and Natalia could no longer be silent. Silence would have meant sanctioning these acts, so she began to complain...."

about her relations with Golitsyn and Feodor Shaklovityi, chief of the Strel'tsy office. An anonymous letter, supposedly found in a Moscow suburb, charged her with all manner of vice and corruption. It was further asserted that the Tsaritsa Natalia had been excluded from the palace and was being held in confinement. Neither the attacks of Peter's adherents nor the subtler opposition of the Tsaritsa Natalia deterred the tsarevna.

Impelled by a growing will to maintain her political position, Sophia awaited some act or event that would decide the issue. A suggestion came from Shaklovityi, the man to whom Sophia had turned in Golitsyn's absence. Shaklovityi, whom the tsarevna had raised from the rank of clerk to that of the second highest nobility, had become her boldest adherent, and possibly her lover pro tempore, as Kurakin has suggested.[28] As leader of the Strel'tsy, Shaklovityi adopted ruthless methods against the opponents of the government within his jurisdiction. The solution he proposed in August, 1687, would have repelled Golitsyn. He solicited from several Strel'tsy commanders their reaction to the idea of having Sophia crowned tsaritsa. His plan for achieving this coup involved the seizure of Lev Naryshkin, Boris Golitsyn, and Prince M. A. Cherkasskii should they oppose the move. The Strel'tsy hesitated. They feared the boyars more than ever, and a friendly sentiment among them for Peter and for the patriarch was now beginning to develop. Shaklovityi argued that the boyars had no vitality and that the patriarch could be replaced by a more amenable churchman, but the proposal created no enthusiasm. Reports of Shaklovityi's plot soon reached the Naryshkins and convinced them further of Sophia's surreptitious plans and of the direct intent of her acts. It was clear that the next strong move belonged to them.

With Golitsyn's return to the capital, Tsar Peter ordered that direct information be given him about state affairs.[29] The younger tsar had now reached his sixteenth year, and in stature easily passed for an adult. His interest in the army and the government was becoming more manifest each year. His play regiments at Preobrazhenskoe continued to draw recruits. Although small in number and adolescent in years, their devotion to Peter might make them formidable in a palace revolution. Peter's interest in administrative affairs also increased. In 1688 he began to attend sessions of the Boyar Duma and to address questions to the vari-

---

[28] Kurakin, *op. cit.*, p. 54: "It is necessary to recall that at the departure of Prince Vasilii Golitsyn with his regiments for the Crimea, Feodor Shaklovityi profited greatly from his amorous attachment to the tsarevna, and in those evening entertainments enjoyed her greater confidence than Prince Golitsyn although not so openly."

[29] Shmurlo, *op. cit.*, p. 63.

ous government prikazes. In May, his uncle, Lev Naryshkin, and his friend, T. N. Streshnev, were made boyars upon his recommendation. The impending marriage of the young tsar to Evdokia Lopukhina was openly discussed. The end of Peter's political minority was clearly approaching and with it a new turn in government affairs was indicated.[30]

The political discomfort of the tsarevna's government grew daily after Golitsyn's return. Sophia's efforts to conceal the barrenness of the Crimean venture and to suggest that it had fulfilled Russia's military obligation to Poland were failing as miserably abroad as at home. Even before his return, Golitsyn foresaw the probability of a second campaign against the Tatars. In July, 1687, he ordered Nepluev to build the town of Novo Bogoroditsk at the confluence of the Samara and Dnieper rivers to serve as a supply base for a renewed effort.[31] The town with fortifications designed by a Dutch engineer, Vazal, had been completed by the end of summer.[32]

In March, 1688, the Polish king called upon Russia to renew the struggle against the Tatars. Since great Turkish armies had prepared to move against Poland, he demanded further aid from Russia.[33] Although the request was untimely for Moscow, the prestige of the government demanded that it be fulfilled. In late spring, Golitsyn replied that a second campaign against the Crimea would be undertaken and that preparations for it had already begun. As early as January, 1688, Roman Nepluev and Grigorii Kosagov were named voevodas for the new military venture, and had been ordered to the Ukraine with small forces of troops.[34] By summer, Tatar raids were renewed against Volhynia and the Ukraine. Captives were seized and Kiev threatened. The Poles took no action. The forces of Nepluev and Kosagov avoided combat. Mazeppa's troops remained at Baturin. Shaklovityi had been sent to the Ukraine

[30] Von Kochen, *op. cit.*, May 11, 1688, p. 128: "It seems that the favorites and adherents of Tsar Peter from now on will also take part in the government; a few days ago his mother's brother, Lev K. Naryshkin, was granted the rank of boyar."
[31] Kerner, *op. cit.*, p. 65: "The ostrog Tor on the Velikii Tor built in 1668, and the ostrog Novo-Bogoroditsk on the Byk constructed in 1687 controlled the portage through which the Muravskii Shliakh passed south of the Donets. Here it was possible to check the Tatars in the very beginning of a raid."
[32] Von Kochen, *op. cit.*, Nov. 18, 1687, p. 123: "There is talk about building a fortress on the Samara River in which imperial troops will be stationed under the guise of hindering the Crimean Tatars from raiding the Ukraine. Most are of the opinion that the fortress is being constructed for the purpose of holding the Cossacks in check, and to deprive them of any relations with the Tatars. It is said that the measure was decreed by the new Hetman Mazeppa.... Nothing certain has been heard about the Crimean campaign."
[33] N. N. Bantysh-Kamenskii, *Obzor vneshnikh snoshenii rossii...*, III, 158; Ustrialov, *op. cit.*, I, 213.
[34] *P.S.Z.*, II, 905.

during the summer to investigate the loyalty of the Cossacks. He reported that their support of Moscow could be relied upon, but that the loyalty of the new hetman was less certain.[35] On September 18, 1688, the official proclamation calling for a second Crimean campaign appeared. Able-bodied men of all ranks and categories were urged to support the undertaking which was designed "to prevent the khan from lending aid to the Turkish sultan."[36]

Small incidents in Moscow simultaneously warned of the government's critical position at home. In early September, 1688, an alarm sounded in Moscow in connection with renewed unrest among the Strel'tsy. Although the disturbance was promptly suppressed, it uncovered divided loyalties within the regiments. During the disturbance, Tsar Peter called for support from Patrick Gordon's Butyrki regiment. This Gordon promptly gave. On September 7 Peter asked for five fifers and five drummers from that same regiment. Gordon again complied. Golitsyn showed great displeasure when he learned of Gordon's action, taken without his knowledge.[37] In October, the number of recruits for Peter's regiments took on the character of a wholesale desertion to the Naryshkin party.[38] The tsarevna's supporters and the Naryshkins were now absenting themselves from various ceremonies, including church services, attended by their opponents. In January, 1689, Peter's marriage to Evdokia Lopukhina was celebrated. This event drew attention to the end of the younger tsar's minority and renewed the delicate matter of the succession.[39] These circumstances again suggested the inopportunity of the prime minister's departure from the capital. But the demand for Golitsyn to accept military responsibility for the campaign once more proved overwhelming and in the end he acquiesced.

Disturbing political reports meanwhile came to Moscow from Vienna. The attention of Emperor Leopold I was being seriously diverted from

---

[35] Ustrialov, *op. cit.*, I, 213–215.

[36] *P.S.Z.*, II, 946–949: "...the Holy Roman Emperor, the Polish King, and the Venetian Republic have written the tsars and the Tsarevna Sophia that at this time the Turkish state...is coming to its very last ruination and catastrophe.... They only have small hope in the Crimean khan and his hordes.... The Great Sovereigns... have decreed that their boyars and *voevodas* are to be at their posts for duty, and with...other classes are to undertake this venture and are not to permit the khan to go to the sultan's aid."

[37] Gordon, *op. cit.*, II, 227.

[38] Kurakin, *op. cit.*, I, 57: "Thus gradually by means of these regiments he [Peter] became independent of his sister and gained power. He constantly engaged in military exercises. Among the Strel'tsy he had a special liking for the Sukharev regiment to whom he gave all kinds of rewards. Intrigues on both sides tried to win over the Strel'tsy because they constituted the entire strength...in Moscow, and the whole palace was in their hands."

[39] *D.R.V.*, XI, 194–196; Ustrialov, *op. cit.*, II, 28; *P.S.Z.*, III, 10–11.

the Turkish War by events in Western Europe. In September, 1688, he again found himself at war with France. The French invasion of the Palatinate created a strong desire in Vienna to end the conflict in southeastern Europe as quickly as possible. Secret negotiations had already begun between the Turks and the Austrians, and it appeared that Emperor Leopold might make a separate peace with the Turks in violation of his alliance with Poland. Voznitsyn, the Russian ambassador at Warsaw, had been informed by Zierowski, the Austrian ambassador to Poland, that unless Russian envoys reached Vienna by March, 1689, a peace might be concluded without them.[40] Voznitsyn forwarded the information to Moscow and was instructed to reply that Moscow expressed "astonishment" at such news, and that if a peace were to be arranged with the Porte, Russian interests would have to be preserved.[41] Moscow's interests were outlined as follows: (1) the evacuation of all Turks and Tatars from the Crimea and the cession of that area to Moscow; (2) the cession to Russia of Ochakov, Kazikermen, and other fortresses between the Bug and Dniester; (3) the liberation of all Russian prisoners of war without ransom; and (4) the payment of 2,000,000 gold pieces as an indemnity for recent Tatar raids. In the light of Moscow's contribution to the war such demands, to say the least, were extravagant. Golitsyn had little hope that they would be seriously entertained. But as an indication of Russian aims in the direction of the Black Sea these proposals had great interest, since they directly foreshadowed the acquisition of the Crimea and the territorial gains won by Russia at the Treaty of Jassy a century later. In 1689, Golitsyn no doubt intended only that they discourage a separate peace between Austria and Turkey and delay a settlement until the second Crimean campaign had been launched, when the Russians would be in a better position to push such claims. The immediate effect of Vienna's move on Moscow, however, was to spur military preparations for the next year.

In the plan for the second campaign, all military preparations were to be completed by February, 1689—"before the ice broke." Several armies began assembling in December, 1688. Golitsyn again assumed command of the main army, assisted by Princes Ia. F. Dolgorukii and

---

[40] Bantysh-Kamenskii, *op. cit.*, III, 159.

[41] *Pamiatniki diplomaticheskikh i torgovykh snoshenii moskovskoi Rusi*... VII, 352: "... inasmuch as it is known to us [the Russian tsars], by post and other correspondence, that at the court of your Imperial Majesty there are at present great ambassadors from the Turkish sultan with treaties of peace on honorable and profitable terms for you; therefore we, the great sovereigns... declare to you that in accord with... the obligations of treaties... you should deign to notify us concerning that embassy of the Turkish porte and in accord with our mutual agreement..."; Ustrialov, *op. cit.*, I, 216.

V. A. Zmeev. Supporting him were a Novgorod army of A. S. Shein and F. Boriatinskii, a Riazan army led by V. D. Dolgorukii and A. I. Khitrovo, a Sevsk regiment under L. R. Nepluev, and a Kazan regiment led by B. P. Sheremetev. The Russian forces numbered approximately 112,000 men, excluding Mazeppa's 16,000 Cossacks, who were to join the main armies at the Samara River. Foreign officers like Gordon, Trauernicht, von Graham, Lefort, and von Werden commanded many of the infantry and cavalry regiments.[42] According to Neuville, the Russian artillery possessed seven hundred cannon, but Ustrialov's figure of four hundred and fifty would appear more nearly correct.[43]

The second march for the Crimea began in March, 1689. Golitsyn had hoped for an earlier departure to avoid the danger of steppe fires but the late arrivals of leading commanders once more disappointed him. Golitsyn himself remained longer in the capital than he had expected and did not overtake his troops until they had reached the Psël River at Sumy. Before his departure Gordon counseled him on several matters—the kind of equipment required and the most suitable approach to the Crimea. Gordon suggested the use of battering rams to break down enemy fortifications at Perekop. He advised following the Dnieper route as closely as possible from the confluence of the Samara and the Dnieper River south. But perhaps because of the Scot's growing friendship for Tsar Peter his suggestions went largely unheeded.

Golitsyn's army joined those of Shein and Dolgorukii in April at the Orel River, a tributary of the Dnieper. The months of March and April, 1689, had been unusually cold. The spring thaw had created many floods which made crossing the various rivers and streams hazardous and costly. The value of Novo-Bogoroditsk on the Byk River amply proved itself, because there the Russians were able to rest and procure two months' provisions for the final trek across the Nogai Steppe.

Encounters with the Tatars first occurred in May. On May 13 the movement southeast from the Lower Dnieper began. While crossing the Nogai Steppe on May 15 Sheremetev's Kazan regiment, the smallest in size, was suddenly attacked by a Tatar force of approximately ten thousand men. The regiment was put to flight, opening ground for an attack on the whole Russian baggage train. Golitsyn's forces intervened in time to stop this development, in turn putting the Tatars to flight, but not before they had inflicted considerable damage. This early loss was accounted for as much by disorder among the Russian troops as by the

[42] Ustrialov, *op. cit.*, I, 216–217.
[43] De la Neuville, *op. cit.*, II, 242; Ustrialov, *op. cit.*, I, 217.

surprise tactics of the Tatars. From there on the Russians had free passage to Chernaia Dolina, approximately fifteen miles north of Perekop. On May 16 during a midday rainstorm a large Tatar army from Perekop appeared on the Russian right flank striking Golitsyn's rear formations with great daring and force. Again great confusion was created until Golitsyn's artillery fire stopped the charge. The attack then shifted to the left flank against the Cossack regiments, which sustained heavy damage until the artillery again drove them off. After this second encounter, which lasted eight hours, the Tatars fled, but lingered on the horizon until nightfall. On the following two days, attacks of shorter duration occurred south of Chernaia Dolina. Both sides claimed victories, but the results were indecisive. The advance toward Perekop continued. Serious steppe fires and depleting food and water supplies again harassed the Russians. Much of the heavier equipment and large numbers of horses were abandoned.

On May 20 the Russians came within sight of Perekop. The critical moment in the campaign had arrived. But once more Golitsyn stopped short of his objective. Within a matter of hours after his arrival outside Perekop, the Russians and Tatars entered negotiations. Karaman, an Astrakhan Tatar, served as the intermediary. Whether these discussions were initiated by the khan or Golitsyn cannot be determined, but Golitsyn again appeared to lose faith in the will of his army to execute a successful siege of Perekop. The Tatar khan, on his part, apparently believed he had more to gain by discussion and delay than by a large-scale encounter with the Russians. The Russian terms for a truce were moderate when compared with what had been asked the year before in discussing the peace terms with the Austrians. They included: (1) a guarantee that the Tatars would not molest the Ukraine or Poland; (2) the cessation of Russian tribute payments; and (3) the liberation of all Russian captives. The Tatars delayed replying to these demands and sought to bargain further with their opponents. The khan wanted a tribute for ending the war and evaded the matter of returning prisoners by explaining that many were no longer captives but "had accepted the Mohammedan faith." Golitsyn took counsel with his chiefs of staff on these matters and decided on a retreat without a formal agreement.

The return to Moscow was more precarious than in the first campaign. All along the route north Turkish and Tatar guerilla forces harassed the retreating army. Steppe fires blazed on all sides and no supplies could be found.[44] Had the khan decided to pursue his opponents with

---

[44] Gordon, *op. cit.*, II, 258.

all his forces the Russian withdrawal might have become a rout. Fortunately for the Russians the Tatars had fewer men than Golitsyn estimated. Harried by summer heat, lack of water, and guerilla encounters, the weary Russians covered the ground from Perekop to the Dnieper in four days. The retreat was orderly and well executed though men, horses, and equipment decreased at an alarming rate.[45] At Belozerka, Golitsyn dispatched couriers to Moscow to inform the regent of the army's return. An announcement was simultaneously sent to the Polish king declaring Russia's fulfillment of her treaty obligations. Three thousand men under Volynskii were left along the Samara River to guard against renewed Tatar attacks.[46]

The failure of the second Crimean campaign posed graver difficulties for Sophia. The opponents of the regent had already hinted at what might happen to Golitsyn should his second expedition end like the first. Before his departure in February, 1689, a coffin had reportedly been placed at Golitsyn's doorstep with a sly notation implying that this would be his resting place, should the second campaign fail.[47]

During April and May, 1689, pressure against the government from the opposition became more apparent. The Naryshkins openly accused Shaklovityi of attempts to destroy the leaders of their party—Boris A. Golitsyn, M. A. Cherkasskii, and Lev Naryshkin. The tsaritsa Natalia expressed apprehension about the safety of her son, Peter, the replacement of Patriarch Joachim by Silvester Medvedev, and any change in government leadership. The role of sorrowful widow whose rights had been imposed upon was played more skillfully in 1689 by Natalia than that of potential leader in 1682.[48] Shaklovityi had kept Golitsyn informed of these developments during the Crimean campaign and the latter had asked him to write the truth and to watch Prince Cherkasskii "with an ever vigilant eye," and "if necessary beat him down with the aid of the patriarch and tsarevnas."[49]

Golitsyn gave Sophia an inkling of the misfortunes of the campaign in his early reports to her. In March, 1689, he had commented on the

---

[45] Ustrialov, *op. cit.*, I, 236–237.
[46] De la Neuville, *op. cit.*, p. 247.
[47] N. Aristov, *Moskovskiia smuty v pravlenie tsarevny Sofii Alekseevny*, p. 124; Shmurlo, *op. cit.*, p. 79: "To an impartial observer in April (1689) a general explosion and revolt appeared inevitable in case of the failure of the campaign."
[48] Shmurlo, *op. cit.*, pp. 71–73: Both sides awaited a surprise attack, and each side, apprehensive of taking a decisive step, feared at the same time that any moment might see the final clash.
[49] Aristov, *op. cit.*, pp. 125–126; Ustrialov, *op. cit.*, I, 346–350: "Please answer whether there are any devilish impediments from those (?) ... Supporters of Cherkasskii and Boriatinskii are rebelling everywhere.... Please write me whether there are any libelous anonymous letters. For God's sake write the truth!"

great cold and snow and on the delays in receiving money from Moscow for paying the troops; in April he wrote of the "swollen rivers," broken bridges, and deep mud encountered; and in May he told her of the first engagements with the Tatars. His later reports and particularly those regarding his negotiations with the Tatars, were less than candid, and his failure to attack Perekop was left unexplained. Such information or lack of it in no way marred Sophia's image of her lover. When she received his letter written before Perekop, she rejoiced more at the news of his well-being than of his arrival at his objective, and pleaded for him to hasten back to Moscow rather than to press the campaign. "Don't delay in coming," she wrote, "You have burdened yourself as it is. Had you not labored so, no one would have done it...."[50]

As in 1687, Sophia insisted upon proclaiming the Crimean venture of 1689 a military success before evidence to the contrary could be submitted by her opponents. A month before Golitsyn's return she began to glorify it as a brilliant undertaking. On June 15 it was announced that the Russian armies had won "incredible victories"[51] over the Tatars. On June 18 a laudatory decree heaped praise on Golitsyn and his associates for their military exploits. The decree stated that the khan and all the Crimean, Belgorod, and Turkish armies had sought to prevent the Russians from reaching Kolanchak (north of Perekop), and that on May 17 great battles had been waged "the whole day long." The Russians had battled bravely, killing and capturing many Tatars and forcing them to disperse. Golitsyn and his armies reached Perekop May 20, but before attacking the fortress, scouts had been sent out to locate food, water, and possible places for entrenchment. Everything beyond Kolanchak had been uprooted and destroyed and no water was available "because there were no streams and wells." The Crimean khan not only had failed to give the Russians battle, but had sued for peace "on numerous occasions." On May 21, Golitsyn, upon taking counsel with his associates "as to what to do to preserve our sovereign armies without harm because of the above-mentioned hindrances," decided to retreat

---

[50] Ustrialov, *op. cit.*, I, 236–237: "Letters of the Tsarevna Sophia Alekseevna in cipher to Prince Golitsyn": "My light, my little brother Vasenka, health to you.... Your letters from Koirka near Perekop reached us in safety.... No sooner did I arrive at the monastery of St. Sergei ... when reports arrived concerning the battle. I do not remember how I mounted the steps. I read while walking, and I do not know how to thank ... the Virgin, the Most Holy Mother of God.... Whatever you have written me, *batiushka,* concerning the dispatches to the monastery, I have carried out. ... ; God knows ... how I desire to see you ... don't delay in coming. You have burdened yourself as it is. Had you not labored so, no one would have done it...."

[51] Ustrialov, *op. cit.*, I, 239.

to Kolanchak. Had the Russian armies remained near Perekop even one day longer, they could not have been evacuated without impairment.[52] Golitsyn had been offered peace terms by the khan but had refused them because they would have violated the treaty with Poland. In the return from Kolanchak to Belozerka, though the Tatars did not molest the Russians, "Turkish" forces had attacked them continually and set fire to the steppe. The valiant Russian armies invariably defeated them, killing and capturing many infidels. These activities were corroborated by Golitsyn's associates, and he was therefore to be favored and commended. Not content with this official apologia of her principal minister, Sophia insisted on arranging suitable awards for him and his associates. During late June and throughout July, lengthy discussions took place about such favors.

Golitsyn entered Moscow July 19. The tsarevna paid him tribute by crossing the Moskva River to greet him and his army at the Serpukhovsk gates. Tsar Ivan and the patriarch awaited him at the Kremlin, but Tsar Peter absented himself from the welcoming ceremonies. Relations between the younger tsar and Sophia had grown more strained since July 8, when the two had clashed during a religious procession.[53]

When Golitsyn and his associates came to pay Tsar Peter their respects several days after their return, the young tsar openly reproached them for their military failures. The tsarevna ignored this affront. Special religious celebrations were ordered held throughout Moscow in thanksgiving for the safe return of the Russian armies. Arrangements were also continued for rewarding the "victors."[54] When the rewards were finally agreed upon, Tsar Peter withheld his approval of them for a week, and even when prevailed upon to acquiesce on the matter July 29, he refused to grant Golitsyn and his associates an audience to re-

---

[52] *P.S.Z.*, II (June 19, 1689), 19–21. *A Laudatory Charter given to V. V. Golitsyn for his Crimean Campaign.*

[53] N. I. Kostomarov, *Russkaia istoriia* . . . , II, 505. Tsars Ivan and Peter had been marching bareheaded from Uspenskii Cathedral to the Cathedral of Kazan, accompanied by Sophia, who also appeared bareheaded in the manner of an autocrat. Peter, probably at the suggestion of a member of his suite, suddenly turned to Sophia and demanded that she withdraw from the ceremony. A bitter argument followed, in which the regent held her ground. As the procession passed Arkhangel Cathedral, Peter left the ceremonies and departed for Kolomenskoe.

[54] *P.S.Z.*, II (July 27, 1689), 21–30. "Decree announced . . . to men of various ranks lauding them for their service in the Crimean campaign and granting them estates and monetary increases in salary, and ordering that names of warriors who fell in battle be entered in the church books so that they might be remembered in churches and monasteries and providing that their orphans be rewarded with money and estates"; *Ibid.* (Aug., 1689), 30–31: "A decree providing that additional money and estates be given to soldiers, officers, and others, for wounds suffered in the campaign"; Kostomarov, *op. cit.*, II, 505.

ceive their thanks.⁵⁵ A definite disclosure of intentions between the rival factions was clearly imminent and only some further incident was required to precipitate an open break.

When Tsar Peter came to Moscow July 25 to pay his respects to an elderly aunt, the Tsarevna Anna, on her name day, the regent ordered a special guard of fifty Strel'tsy to stand by to forestall a coup. Preobrazhenskoe by this time had assumed the air of a second capital. A rumor spread that Peter planned to use his private corps of soldiers for an attack on the government.⁵⁶ Extravagant tales, anonymous letters, and partisan street brawls rapidly multiplied. On August 7, Peter suffered a virtual paroxysm of fear when a report came to him after midnight that Strel'tsy regiments, under order of Sophia, were on their way from Moscow to kill him. Literally rising from sleep, without taking time to dress, the young tsar fled in terror to the fortress walls of Troitsa-Sergeiv Monastery.⁵⁷ Sophia vigorously denied any such order, and the Strel'tsy leader, Shaklovityi, also refused to admit any connection with such an attempt on the tsar's life, idly remarking that Peter was "free to run about if he is crazy enough to do so." The affair proved genuinely disturbing to the young tsar and illustrated his credulity of the criminal intentions of his sister.

With the rising political tension in Moscow, the regent took bolder steps to protect her position. The nucleus of Golitsyn's Crimean army remained at hand as a possible source of strength, but its divided loyalties rendered it politically ineffective. Even during the recent military campaign the Cherkasskii and Boriatinskii factions within the army had threatened mutiny on several occasions, and the criticism raised in connection with the awards to Golitsyn from the government had made any aid to the regent from that source most unlikely.⁵⁸ Sophia, consequently, looked elsewhere for support, and her gaze inevitably returned to the Strel'tsy. If the enmity of certain regiments of the Strel'tsy could be aroused once more against the Naryshkins, ways might open for the tsarevna to retain and strengthen her power. Such possibilities were small in 1689 compared to 1682, since Shaklovityi had removed the bolder spirits in the order, and to arouse their interest in what was essentially a family quarrel would be difficult.⁵⁹ But in her extremity Sophia grasped at even that straw. In late July she complained to

---
⁵⁵ Gordon, *op. cit.*, II, 266.
⁵⁶ E. A. Belov, "Moskovskiia smuty v kontse XVII veka," *Zh.M.N.P.*, 2 (1887), p. 329.
⁵⁷ S. F. Platonov, *Moskva i zapad*, p. 149.
⁵⁸ Ustrialov, *op. cit.*, II, 355.
⁵⁹ Belov, *op. cit.*, p. 329.

several Strel'tsy leaders of Tsaritsa Natalia's enmity toward the government and asked for a reaffirmation of their support. They assured her of their favor, and one of them, Stryzhev, even proposed taking action against the Naryshkins.[60] The suggestion never progressed beyond an initial stage, and when report of it came to Peter, Stryzhev's arrest was demanded. This the regent refused. Early in August, hearing of the possibility of a retaliatory measure against her, Sophia barricaded herself in the Kremlin with a guard of seven hundred Strel'tsy.

For the Naryshkins now ensconced at Troitsa-Sergeiev Monastery, the time for settling accounts had arrived. Boris Golitsyn, the spokesman for Tsaritsa Natalia, asked the regent to explain why she had surrounded herself with such large numbers of Strel'tsy guards. Tsar Peter shortly after began summoning various government officials and Strel'tsy officers to Troitsa for conferences. Few of them returned to Moscow. Even Patriarch Joachim, whom the tsarevna had asked to serve as intermediary in the dispute with her brother, left Moscow for Troitsa in August and did not return. Ivan Tsykler, one of the tsarevna's most active adherents in 1682, also joined Peter, furnishing him with information and much misinformation about the government, upon which his supporters capitalized. At first Sophia and Shaklovityi sought to prevent reports of these desertions from spreading in Moscow, but failing this, dismissed them as inconsequential matters. In rapid succession Sophia sent Prince Ivan B. Troekurov, P. I. Prozorovskii, and two other representatives to Troitsa to induce Peter to return to the capital. As a last resort she decided to attempt settling the quarrel herself through a personal meeting with the younger tsar.

Sophia's journey to Troitsa proved futile. The Naryshkins, who knew something of her powers of persuasion over individuals as well as groups were determined to avoid such a meeting. Sophia left Moscow August 30 under Strel'tsy escort. Almost immediately she encountered adherents of Tsar Peter—Buturlin, Troekurov, and others—who sought to turn her back. At Vozdvizhenskoe, Prince I. B. Troekurov informed her that Peter would not see her, and that if she persisted in continuing the journey she would "meet with dishonor." The road from Vozdvizhenskoe to Troitsa lay within range of the cannon bristling from the monastery walls. In vain the tsarevna appealed to the Strel'tsy for a new pledge of support. Her charges against the Naryshkins now appeared even more awkward and unconvincing. Failing to check the tide of opinion against her, she returned sorrowfully to the capital.

[60] M. Pomialovskii, *Russkii biograficheskii slovar'*, XIX, 140.

At the beginning of September the struggle between the regent and the Naryshkins reached its final stage. More of the Strel'tsy regiments were shifting their loyalties to Peter each day. Two such regiments under Colonel Lev Nechaev appeared in Moscow September 1, and demanded in the name of Tsar Peter that Shaklovityi, Medvedev, Petrov, and six other members of Sophia's government be extradited to Troitsa.[61] The regent refused. In a scene eloquent of her personal insecurity, Sophia denounced and threatened them, stating "I will not give over the nine men for whom you have been sent, because if I give nine men, they will falsely incriminate 900 others."[62] The Strel'tsy wavered and in the end took no action. Nechaev returned to Troitsa without his victims. A week later the same regiments returned to the capital to repeat the demand. This time they were successful. The growing number of émigrés from Moscow, the rumors of military preparations at Troitsa, and the steadily declining influence of Sophia now demoralized the Strel'tsy remaining at the Kremlin. The tearful appeals of the regent and her threats of reprisals against further deserters no longer moved them to resistance. The accused were surrendered. Shaklovityi and his cohorts were ingloriously given over to Nechaev. Within the week the family of Tsar Ivan made peace with Peter.[63] A decree was next promulgated excluding the name of the tsarevna from the imperial title. Convinced at last that her political role had ended, the tsarevna announced that all who wished to leave her might go freely to Troitsa. Many availed themselves of the opportunity. Several days later, upon order from Peter, Sophia retired to Novodevichii Convent outside the Kremlin.

Sophia's withdrawal opened the way for a swift prosecution of those individuals most closely associated with her in government. The indictment of Shaklovityi and Medvedev began September 7 on charges that they had rebelled and committed treason against the government. Incriminating evidence was readily produced against Shaklovityi, and September 12 he and several fellow conspirators were executed for having "plotted to beat the tsars, Natalia Kirilovna, and the Patriarch Joachim to death."[64] Medvedev's trial proceeded slowly. His record was

---

[61] Kostomarov, *op. cit.*, II, 507.
[62] Aristov, *op. cit.*, p. 132: ". . . Why should these men be given over? They are good and faithful servants. . . . You all know how I have ruled these past seven years, and how I accepted the government at a most troublesome time. . . . It is not Feodor Shaklovity's head they seek, but mine and that of Tsar Ivan Alekseevich . . ."
[63] Pomialovskii, *op. cit.*, XIX, p. 142.
[64] *P.S.Z.*, III (Sept. 11, 1689), 33–36. "A decree providing that the rebel and traitor, the Strel'tsy leader, Feodor Shaklovityi, and his accomplices be executed; some of his co-conspirators are to be subjected to corporal punishment and exile to

singularly free of political misdeeds. The most damaging evidence against him, aside from his friendship with the tsarevna and Shaklovityi, was the discovery of certain heretical doctrines in his writings,[65] the fact that he had addressed the Tsarevna Sophia as an autocrat, and on one occasion had called Patriarch Joachim ignorant. But what his record failed to produce of a criminal nature, the torture chamber soon supplied, and, in 1691, he too was executed.

Prince V. V. Golitsyn received the most clement treatment. In late August he retired to one of his estates outside Moscow. Criminal charges were leveled against him September 7. He was accused of referring to the tsarevna as "sovereign"[66] [Gosudarynia], of reporting matters directly to her rather than to the tsars, and above all, of being primarily responsible for the failure of the Crimean campaigns. He and his son, Prince A. V. Golitsyn, were deprived of their boyar rank and properties and exiled with their wives and children first to Kargopol (1689) on the Onega River, and then to Pustozersk (1692) on the estuary of the Pechora River. The fact that his cousin Boris Golitsyn was principal spokesman for Tsaritsa Natalia and still entertained sentiments of family loyalty toward him, undoubtedly saved Golitsyn from a harsher fate.

The regency of the Tsarevna Sophia thus terminated. The Crimean campaigns had precipitated its downfall and it is with them that this chapter has been primarily concerned. Although failures from a military standpoint, the campaigns represented an important link in the chain of events which awakened Russian interest in the Black Sea and which later involved Russia in the Turkish Question. Geography, religion, politics, and trade had long beckoned Moscow to throw its weight into southeastern Europe. In 1684 and again in 1687, Austria and Venice reminded the tsars of their singular relationship to the Balkans and Constantinople. The campaigns signalized their awareness of this relationship and of the opportunities it presented.

From a Russian military viewpoint the campaigns were failures. Tsar Peter labeled them as such in 1689 and his judgment has generally been accepted as valid from both a military and a political viewpoint. But Peter learned too of the hazards and disappointments of campaigning

---

Siberia for their villainous attempts on the lives of Peter Alekseevich and his mother Natalia Kirilovna"; *A.I.*, V, 326–327: "... They plotted to beat to death the tsars, Natalia Kirilovna, and the Patriarch Joachim...."

[65] Particularly in Medvedev's theological treatise *Manna* (1687) reproduced in *Chteniia* no. 4 (1896), App. pp. 452–538.

[66] *Ibid.*, p. 388.

against the Turks and Tatars in 1695–1696. Although he captured Azov, in 1696 (after two expeditions), he was compelled to return it to the Porte in 1711. And it was during the course of this campaign that he belatedly credited Sophia's government with having entered the struggle against Turkey in 1687 and 1689.[67]

The Crimean campaigns marked the first coalition war in which Russia was involved. The Russian and Polish armies had agreed to engage in the war jointly. The progress of the Russian army southward from the Samara River was to coincide with operations of the Polish army to the west. For the Poles as well as the Austrians and Venetians, these Russian commitments had an important effect on Turkey. They deflected one of the principal forces upon which the Turks relied for their attack on Poland—the Tatars. Having learned of the Russo-Polish alliance, the Turks abandoned their effort to resume the offensive against Poland and Austria. Turkish forces, instead, were so divided that the emperor and the Venetians were able to win several victories in Hungary, Dalmatia, and the Morea. The Crimean campaigns thus contributed a positive effect in discouraging a further Turkish advance into Europe.[68]

---

[67] G. K. Babushkina, "Mezhdunarodnoe znachenie krymskikh pokhodov 1687 i 1689 gg.", *Istoricheskie zapiski*, 33 (1950), p. 171.

[68] *Ibid.*, pp. 167, 171.

CHAPTER VIII

THE REGENCY OF TSAREVNA SOPHIA ALEKSEEVNA: AN APPRAISAL

IN THE FOREGOING chapters the interest and importance of the years immediately before Peter's reign in Russian history have been demonstrated. Vital changes which affected the cultural outlook, economy, and foreign relations of the country were underway, calling for enlightened and decisive leadership. The period was a critical one, both in the events themselves and their influence on succeeding generations.

Sophia's regency of seven years and four months was a brief span of time compared to the longer reigns of Tsar Alexis and Tsar Peter. Yet it was longer than the reigns of Tsar Feodor and of Tsar Peter's two successors, Catharine I and Tsar Peter II. The regency marked the first rule of a woman member of the Romanov family. It initiated a century of government in Russia dominated by women. Sophia's right to govern and her political methods were questionable. A palace plot similar to that used by many of her eighteenth-century successors brought her to power in 1682. A variety of motives apparently urged her to assume the role of regent—personal ambition, family pride, and disdain for a future behind convent walls or within the terem, living upon the generosity of unfriendly relatives. Yet casting aside the issue of the legitimacy of the rule, it is doubtful whether within the imperial family—during this important period—a more capable regent than Sophia could have been found. That she held a regime together against great odds for seven years demonstrated her capacity.

From a cultural point of view the regency saw noteworthy progress away from the restrictive influences of orthodoxy and Greek scholasticism. Against the stormy background of social and religious conflict, the Byzantine theological tradition in education lost further ground, giving way to secular elements, many of which had come from the West. Moscow's expanding foreign relations, especially with Poland, and the incorporation of the Ukraine exposed the Russians to stronger European influences. Although "Kievan" scholars were not accepted with full confidence in Moscow, their learning and talents were widely utilized, and they provided a healthy intellectual stimulus to Russian education in general. The Zaikonospasskii Monastery School, in particular, illustrated such trends and did much to undermine the unconditional acceptance of Greek instruction and learning. The founding of the Moscow Academy in 1685 represented a culmination of these trends during Sophia's regency. Medvedev, it first appeared, had failed to orient the academy westward, but its curriculum ultimately proved not unlike that which Medvedev had originally planned. Within a decade, in fact, the direction of the academy fell squarely into the hands of men of Latin learning.

In literature, popular tastes, and manners, the regency of Sophia also witnessed significant changes. The cultural outlook largely pointed toward the Latin West as opposed to that of Peter's reign which leaned heavily toward northern Europe and Protestantism. But both regimes showed eclectic tastes in Western innovations and gravitated toward those changes which best adapted themselves to national idiosyncracies and needs. Narrative literature of a secular nature enjoyed a marked popularity throughout the eighties. Collections of apothegms, anecdotes, and novelle were translated into Russian from the Latin and German.[1] Russian dress, home furnishings, and manners showed strong Polish influences. Sophia's assertion of personal freedom and her disregard for court etiquette paralleled Peter's later efforts to free the wives and daughters of the royal family and nobility from outmoded personal restrictions.

Russian economy, too, was changing in the generation before 1689. Like almost every other phase of national life, it suffered growing pains. Under Sophia, national economy was still dominated by the government and the nobility, supported by serf labor. But private enterprise was encouraged in a number of directions. A significant development of craft and industrial enterprises took place. There was an increased interchange of goods among the provinces. Serf economy began to adapt itself to an expanding market.[2] Some types of industry in fact were served almost entirely by serf labor.[3] But the economic development of the state failed to keep pace with its political growth. As in the earlier seventeenth century national income was unequal to the demands made upon it.[4] The crisis reached its peak during Peter's reign, but was building up throughout the seventeenth century.

In all these changes Sophia's government played an active role. The expansion of foreign trade relations, the broadening tastes of the nobility for new commodities, and the growing interest in western technology

---

[1] N. K. Gudzy, *History of Early Russian Literature*, p. 428.
[2] P. I. Lyashchenko, *History of the National Economy of Russia to the 1917 Revolution*, p. 265.
[3] B. D. Grekov, *Istoriia SSSR*, I, 176.
[4] P. Miliukov, *Gosudarstvennoe khoziaistvo Rossii v pervoi chetverti XVIII stoletiia i reforma Petra Velikago*, p. 2.

were all clearly illustrated during her regency. The government made a conscious effort to promote industry, to remove customs barriers, and to protect the trader from the abuses of local administrators. Foreign trade was encouraged by the renewal of trade treaties and the establishment of permanent or semipermanent residents in Moscow and in a number of foreign capitals.[5] Sophia, like her brother Tsar Peter, felt the need of freeing Russia from economic-military dependence on the West. Western technicians were encouraged to enter the country to aid in developing Russian industry. Iron foundries, copper plants, and textile factories were subsidized, and special privileges were granted to those enterprises which would promote greater economic self-sufficiency. In all these activities the regency of Sophia foreshadowed the economic developments of the succeeding reign.

In the realm of foreign affairs, the regency of Tsarevna Sophia occupied an even more important place in Russian history. Expanding foreign relations in many ways provided the stimulus for all the innovations of the reform epoch of Peter. The growing political stature of Moscow in Europe and the firmer position it attained in Asia, set the stage for the role Russia was to play in affairs of the Near and Far East in the eighteenth and nineteenth centuries. The late seventeenth century was truly a climactic period in Russian foreign policy. The need to resolve long-standing disputes with immediate neighbors was imminent. If Moscow's dynamic position in Europe was to be maintained and the opportunities for settling the disputes in Asia to be pressed, bold diplomatic action accompanied by a readiness to apply military force was required.

In the Far East the main problems were an agreement with China over a boundary and the establishment of normal diplomatic-commercial relations. The Russian advance into the Daurian lands had produced conflicts with China, which in the eighties appeared to have gone beyond the stage of peaceful settlement. Russia's failure to abandon the Amur in reply to an ultimatum from Peking had precipitated attacks on the principal Russian outpost in the Amur area—Albazin—in 1685 and 1686. The Russians at Albazin, outnumbered and poorly supported by

---

[5] G. K. Babushkina, "Mezhdunarodnoe znachenie krymskikh pokhodov 1687 i 1689 gg.", *Istoricheskie zapiski*, no. 33 (1950), p. 170: "The first Russian residency in Poland during the seventies was short-lived, but from 1688 on in Poland and in Russia permanent residencies were established 'for mutual military planning against the enemy and for their speedy despatch.'... At the beginning of the eighties a Dutch residency was established in Russia and in 1685 the Swedish ambassador [von] Kochen became officially a resident.... Russian embassies were sent to eleven European capitals."

Moscow, were compelled to enter a two-year period of critical bargaining that resulted in the loss of the Amur. Although momentous and disappointing from the Russian standpoint, this loss nevertheless was offset by gains in other directions. China confirmed for the first time Russia's right to be in the Far East. A boundary between the two states was fixed, with the door left open for later bargaining on the matter of controlling the territory south of the Ud River. Thus, the treaty formalized the division of a huge segment of northeast Asia and its peoples between two giant neighbors. Diplomatic and trade relations were established between Russia and China and the question of the apprehension of fugitives from justice agreed upon. These arrangements brought new stability to Russia's possessions in the Far East and remained in effect for nearly one hundred and seventy years. Moscow apparently recognized these as positive gains at the time. To illustrate, Tsar Peter awarded Golovin, the Russian plenipotentiary at Nerchinsk, highest honors for his services, and later gave him responsible diplomatic missions to perform.[6]

In the light of Moscow's future role in the Near Eastern Question these years were equally important in the West. Geography, religion, politics, and trade had long beckoned the Russians to throw their weight into the struggle against the Turk. In 1684 and again in 1687, Austria and Venice reminded Russia of her singular relationship to the Balkans and Constantinople. But not until the issue with Poland over the Ukraine was resolved could Russia pursue the matter. With the Ukrainian issue settled by the Treaty of Moscow in 1686, attention could be directed to winning a foothold on the Black Sea and to excluding Turkey from Europe. Thus, historically, the question of Russia's relations with Poland over the Ukraine merged with that of Russia's relations with Turkey over the Crimea. In the late seventeenth century, the clash with Turkey came indirectly, with only a half-conscious motion toward the Black Sea. But within a decade—through Peter's capture of Azov—the Russians acquired, temporarily at least, such an outlet. It may, therefore, he claimed, with considerable weight that the Crimean campaigns of 1687 and 1689 signalized Russia's entry into the Near Eastern Question in its modern aspect. Within a century Sophia's successors incorporated the Crimea and won for Russia a substantial littoral on the Black Sea.

Changes affecting many vital aspects of Russian life thus characterized Sophia's regime. In the realm of cultural and diplomatic achieve-

---

[6] *Diplomaticheskii Slovar*, I, 495: M. N. Pavlovsky, *Chinese-Russian Relations*, p. 123.

ments, the tsarevna proved herself a worthy daughter of Tsar Alexis and a distinguished representative of the Romanov dynasty. At home she introduced reforms that were practical in purpose, if moderate in scope. It was unfortunate that the opposition of the powerful nobility prevented her government from proceeding with its larger designs and that the military incapacity of her prime minister Golitsyn overshadowed his genuine talents as a statesman. In both Europe and Asia she and her advisors intelligently pursued Russian national interests. It may therefore be concluded that this important segment of Russian history deserves greater attention from historians than it has heretofore received. It was a government of distinction and promise which held together against great odds. Its policies were both vigorous and enlightened.

BIBLIOGRAPHY

BIBLIOGRAPHICAL ESSAY

SEVENTEENTH-CENTURY Russia with its great unrest and decisive changes has attracted the interest of many prominent historians. A number of distinguished bibliographies exist which, though old and not confined to the seventeenth century, nevertheless still serve as the best guides to the literature of that period. Of these V. I. Mezhov's *Russkaia istoricheskaia bibliografiia za 1865–1876 gg.* (A Russian historical bibliography for 1865–1876) and V. S. Ikonnikov's *Opyt russkoi istoriografii* (An essay in Russian historiography) are of initial interest. Mezhov's bibliography, the older of the two works, provides an impressive list of references to the historical acts, public records, and other primary sources as well as many secondary works. The arrangement of materials is topical. An alphabetical guide to authors and subjects is appended, serving as a helpful cross reference to the citations that appear earlier in full. Ikonnikov's bibliography is a more analytical work. It has excellent chapters describing the materials contained in the former state and private libraries, museums, and many other archival agencies of Russia. A convenient guide to personal and geographical names is also included. Professor R. J. Kerner's *Slavic Europe: A Bibliography* offers the most complete list of titles on Russian history in the Western European languages. Its citations of diaries and travel accounts of the seventeenth century have been particularly useful for the present study. Professor Kerner's more recent work, *Northeastern Asia: A Selected Bibliography*, is an indispensable reference on Russian Far Eastern history and has a large number of titles in the principal European and oriental languages pertaining to European as well as Asiatic Russia.

For Russian foreign relations, certain standard German and French bibliographies have been useful. Dahlmann-Waitz' *Quellenkunde der Deutschen Geschichte* and R. Charmatz' *Wegweiser durch die literatur der osterreichischen geschichte* contain a selective list of titles on Moscow's diplomatic and commercial relations with Austria, Prussia, and the lesser German states. G. Monod's *Bibliographie de l'histoire de France* and E. Bourgeois' *Les Sources de l'histoire de France, XVIIe siècle* have been of particular aid in finding materials on the Dolgorukii mission to France in 1687.

The guides to the more recent literature on seventeenth-century Russia have been less satisfactory, but several useful bibliographical aids must be noted. Volume I of M. N. Tikhomirov's *Istochnikovedenie istorii SSSR s drevneishikh vremen do kontsa XVIII v.* (Guide to the sources of the history of the USSR from ancient times to the end of the XVIII c.) has furnished a number of titles. Tikhomirov has reëxamined many of the materials in the former government prikazes of Russia and has given his own evaluation of them as historical sources. It is interesting to compare his description of the functions of the prikazes with that of the seventeenth-century Russian official, G. Kotoshkikhin. *The Monthly List of Russian Accessions*, the Library of Congress, Washington, gives a record of the publications in Russian, in and outside the Soviet Union, received by that library, as well as by several other libraries since 1948. P. I. Lyashchenko's *Istoriia Narodnogo Khoziaistva SSSR* has recently been translated into English under the title *History of the National Economy of Russia to the 1917 Revolution.* It has a bibliographic index that includes references to recent works on the economic history of the seventeenth century. The citation of materials in Part III of Lyashchenko's work (English translation) on the problems of rural economy, the peasantry, and the city of Moscow is especially noteworthy.

The bibliographies of R. H. Fisher's *The Russian Fur Trade* and G. V. Lantzeff's *Siberia in the Seventeenth Century* are particularly recommended to students of the seventeenth century in the United States. Both contain highly selective lists of publications most of which may be found in American libraries. The book reviews and bibliographical references in such periodicals as *The Slavonic and East European Review, The American Slavic and East European Review, The Russian Review, Voprosy Istorii, The American Historical Review* and other comparable historical journals also serve as practical guides to recent books. For references to the periodical literature of the late nineteenth and early twentieth century, N. A. and V. N. Ul'ianov's *Ukazatel zhurnal'noi, alfavitnyi, predmetnyi, sistematicheskii, 1896–1906 gg.* (Guide to periodical literature, alphabetic, topical, systematic, 1896–1906) is a standard work. The list of articles compiled by Sergius Yakobsen for *The American Historical Review* under the Modern European History Section—Russia and Slavic Europe—furnishes still another clue to recent materials.

The primary sources for late seventeenth-century Russian history consist of the official documentary materials found in government archives and include the large collections of laws, treaties, and decrees issued to the various government offices. Because research in the Russian archives has been impractical for the present study, the standard collections of government documents published by the Archeographic Commission and the Imperial Chancellery have been the principal sources relied upon. Of these the *Akty istoricheskie* (Historical Acts) and its Supplement (*Dopolneniia k aktam istoricheskim*), as well as the *Pol'noe sobranie zakonov* (Complete Collection of Laws), have provided the greatest number of documents dealing with all phases of Sophia's regime. Those in *Akty istoricheskie* discuss commercial, financial, and religious questions of the seventeenth century. Its *Supplement* has an even greater amount of materials on Russian industrial development, relations with minority peoples, and diplomatic relations. Volumes II and III of *Pol'noe sobranie zakonov* contain many documents covering a wide range of subjects and are particularly strong on matters pertaining to minority groups, the Strel'tsy, the Church, the Crimean campaigns, and economic reform. The materials on the Strel'tsy uprising of 1682 may be supplemented by others in Volume IV of the Archeographic expedition's *Akty sobrannye v bibliotekakh i arkhivakh rossiiskoi imperii arkheograficheskoi ekspeditsiei imperatorskoi akademii nauk* (Acts collected in the libraries and archives of the Russian Empire by the Archeographic Expedition of the Imperial Academy of Sciences). For information on the more personal activities of Tsarevna Sophia and the young Tsars Ivan and Peter Alekseevich, the *Dvortsovye razriady* (Court Registers) published by the Imperial Chancellery, though antiquated, still supply considerable detailed information.

For the foreign relations of Russia, a number of official collections have been valuable. The *Pamiatniki diplomaticheskikh snoshenii* (Memorials of diplomatic relations), a publication of the Imperial Chancellery, has two volumes on Russo-Austrian relations, which include materials on the years 1682–1689. The Academy of Science has a four-volume work on Russian relations with Italy, which contains material on the Russo-Polish alliance of 1686. Russian relations with France in 1687 are dealt with in *Sbornik imperatorskago russkago istoricheskago obshchestva* (Collection of the Imperial Russian Historical Society) and F. Martens' *Recueil des instructions donées aux ambassadeurs et ministres de France: Russie*. The Ministry of Foreign Affairs' *Sbornik dogovorov Rossii s Kitaem* (Collection of Treaties of Russia with China) contains the Russian, Latin, and Manchu texts of the Treaty of Nerchinsk.

Besides these larger collections of documents, a substantial amount of seventeenth-century material may be found in the journals of the historical society of Moscow University, *Chteniia* and *Vremennik*, as well as in the historical periodicals *Zh.M.N.P.*, *Russkaia starina*, and *Russkii arkhiv*. Some documentary information on Prince V. V. Golitsyn and the Treaty of Moscow appears in *Vremennik*. De la Neuville's *Relation curieuse de Moscovie*, which is difficult to obtain in most historical libraries in the United States, has been reproduced in *Chteniia*. The principal writings of Silvester Medvedev and the diaries of Patrick Gordon and Johan Korb also appear in *Chteniia*. Other documentary materials dealing with a wide variety of subjects are scattered in the *Russkii arkhiv* and *Zh.M.N.P.*

The official Russian documents of the late seventeenth century have a peculiar stamp. Their style and phraseology give the impression that they all might have been composed by a small group of men. Excessive attention is directed to the titles of the sovereigns. These occupy great space in many documents and are sometimes repeated to the point of monotony, particularly if the matter pertains to foreign affairs. In diplomatic negotiations the dignities of the tsar's office are carefully observed, if not exalted. The arguments for and against a position Moscow may assume on a particular issue also tend to be laboriously explained and justified. In the orders to the voevodas and other officials there is often a great amount of complaining and scolding for administrative failures and unseemly behavior.

Of the secondary materials, many deal with phases of Sophia's regime but few attempt to analyze it as a whole. Among those in the latter category, several deserve particular attention. P. Shchebal'skii's *Pravlenie Tsarevny Sofii* (Regency of the Tsarevna Sophia) which appeared almost a century ago was more of a romantic biography of Sophia than a serious study of her government. Shchebal'skii saw the regent in a less critical light than did earlier historians and recognized her exceptional talents and achievements, but he heavily censured her for her treatment of the Naryshkin family. Small space was given to Russian foreign relations, and social and economic conditions were touched upon only lightly. Volume I of N. Ustrialov's *Istoriia tsarstvovaniia Petra Velikago* (History of the Reign of Peter the Great), 1858, was devoted almost entirely to the years of Sophia's regency. Ustrialov recognized Sophia's abilities but criticized the ineptitude of her regime and especially Golitsyn's conduct of foreign affairs. Ustrialov concentrated on the political history of the period. Volume 14 of S. Solov'ev's *Istoriia Rossii s drevneishikh vremen* (History of Russia from the earliest times), which first appeared in the early sixties, also dealt almost exclusively with the late seventeenth century. Two chapters were devoted to Sophia's government. It was portrayed more favorably than by Ustrialov, but did not depart essentially from the interpretation of the regime as little more than an interlude between the reigns of Tsars Feodor and Peter.

In the late nineteenth century several articles appeared in Russian historical journals, attracting wider interest in Sophia's regime. N. Aristov's lengthy article "Moskovskiia smuty v pravlenie tsarevny Sofii Alekseevny" (Moscow Rebellions in the Regency of Tsarevna Sophia Alekseevna), published in *Varshavskikh Universitetskikh Izvestii* (Warsaw University Bulletin), 1871, went even further in whitewashing particular aspects of the regent's government and attacked many sentimental notions heretofore entertained about Sophia's opponents. Aristov saw the struggle of 1682 as primarily between rival parties rather than between Sophia and Peter. He gave great attention to evaluating the strength of both factions and to the chronology of events in 1682. Six years later, A. E. Belov's article, "Moskovskiia smuty v kontse XVII veka" (Moscow rebellions at the end of the XVII century), appeared in *Zh.M.N.P.* Belov was chiefly interested in the intellectual implications of the Strel'tsy uprising. The events of 1682 had significance for him only in the light of the intellectual ferment in Muscovite society of the late seventeenth century which they illustrated. Belov brought to light much new information on Sophia's relations with her principal officials and showed her to be a more effective political leader than had previously been acknowledged. In the late nineties Sophia's regime was further examined by E. Shmurlo in an article in *Zh.M.N.P.* entitled "Padenie Tsarevny Sof'i" (The Fall of the Tsarevna Sophia). Shmurlo, like Aristov, saw the events of 1682 primarily as a party conflict. Like Belov he advocated greater attention to the cultural implications of the period. The immediate events in Moscow which led to Sophia's downfall were examined. Shmurlo urged that further research be undertaken in the archives at Vienna and Rome for new light on the international influences affecting the events of 1682–1689.

Among the secondary materials providing a helpful general background of the period, two coöperative works published in Moscow before the Revolution must be mentioned: *Moskva v ee proshlom i nastoiashchem* (Moscow in its Past and Present) and *Tri Veka* (Three Centuries). The first, edited by D. N. Anuchin, has several ably written chapters on important aspects of Muscovite social life by P. N. Miliukov, V. V. Nechaev, and S. F. Platonov. Nechaev's chapter in Volume III of the first work on Moscow in the sixteenth and seventeenth centuries has several very illuminating passages. Nechaev also has contributed a useful chapter on Russian culture of the later seventeenth century to *Tri Veka*, edited by V. V. Kallash. V. N. Bochkarev and S. K. Bogoiavlenskii have also written distinguished survey chapters on Russian trade, markets, and military organization for the latter publication.

In the following bibliography the works cited are primarily those used in preparing this book. Only a few titles of topical importance have been included which the author has not had occasion to use. The works comprising the bibliography have been arranged as follows: (1) bibliographical aids, (2) sources, (3) contemporary accounts, (4) secondary works, and (5) articles and essays. For the sake of economy, the two most frequently cited periodicals have been shortened to the form used in the text, namely: *Chteniia v imperatorskom obshchestve istorii i drevnostei rossiiskikh pri moskovskom universitete* (Readings in the imperial society of Russian history and antiquity at the University of Moscow) to *Chteniia*, and *Zhurnal ministerstva narodnago prosveshcheniia* (Journal of the ministry of public education) to *Zh.M.N.P.*

BIBLIOGRAPHY

BIBLIOGRAPHICAL AIDS

Bourgeois, Emile. *Les Sources de l'histoire de France; XVIIe siècle (1610–1715)*. Paris, 1913–1934. 7 vols.

Charmatz, Richard. *Wegweiser durch die Literatur der osterreichischen Geschichte*. Stuttgart, 1912.

Dahlmann, Friedrich C. [Dahlmann-Waitz]. *Quellenkunde der deutschen Geschichte*. Leipzig, 1931–32.

Dorosh, John T. *Guide to Soviet Bibliographies*. Washington, 1950.

Ikonnikov, V. S., *Opyt russkoi istoriografii* [an essay in Russian historiography] Kiev, 1891–1908. 2 vols. in 4.

Kerner, Robert J., *Northeastern Asia: a Selected Bibliography*. Berkeley: University of California Press, 1939. 2 vols.

———. "Russian Expansion to America: Its Bibliographical Foundations," *Papers of the Bibliographical Society of America*, XXV (1931), 111–29.

———. *Slavic Europe: A Selected Bibliography in the Western European Languages, comprising History, Languages and Literatures*, Harvard bibliographies, library series 1. Cambridge, Mass.; Harvard University Press, 1918.

Lambin, P. P., *Russkaia istoricheskaia bibliografiia* [Russian historical bibliography]. St. Petersburg, 1861–1884. 10 vols. in 5.

Mazour, Anatole G., *An Outline of Modern Russian Historiography*. Berkeley: University of California Press, 1939.

Mezhov, V. I., *Russkaia istoricheskaia bibliografiia za 1865–1876 g.g.* [Russian historical bibliography for 1865–1876]. St. Petersburg, 1882–1890. 8 vols. in 4.

———. Supplement: *Bibliographie des livres et articles russes d'histoire et sciences auxiliares de 1800–1854*. St. Petersburg, 1892–1893. 3 vols.

Monod, Gabriel J. J., *Bibliographie de l'histoire de France ... depuis les origines jusqu'en 1789 ...* . Paris, 1888.

Shvedov, O. I., *Istoriki SSSR* [Historians of the SSSR]. Moscow, 1941.

Tikhomirov, M. N., *Istochnikovedenie istorii SSSR s drevneishikh vremen do kontsa XVIII v.* [Guide to the Sources of the history of the USSR], vol. 1. Moscow, 1940.

Ul'ianov, N. A. and V. N., *Ukazatel' zhurnal'noi literatury, alfavitnyi, predmetnyi, sistematicheskii, 1896–1906 g.g.* [Guide to periodical literature, alphabetic, topical, systematic, 1896–1906] 2d ed. Moscow, 1913. 2 vols.

Viktorov, A. G., *Opisanie zapisnykh knig i bumag starinnykh dvortsovykh prikazov, 1584–1725 g.g.* [Description of the record books and papers of the old court prikazes, 1584–1725]. Moscow, 1877–1883. 2 vols.

SOURCES

Akademiia nauk, St. Petersburg, *Akty, sobrannye v bibliotekakh i arkhivakh rossiiskoi imperii, arkheograficheskoiu ekspeditsieiu imperatorskoi akademii nauk* [Acts collected in the libraries and archives of the Russian empire by the archeographic expedition of the Imperial academy of science]. St. Petersburg, 1836. 4 vols. Index, St. Petersburg, 1838.

Akademiia nauk, *Rossiia i Italiia: Sbornik istoricheskikh materialov i izsledovanii, kasaiushikhsia snoshenii Rossii s Italiei* [Russia and Italy: Collection of historical materials and studies touching upon the relations of Russia with Italy]. St. Petersburg, 1907–1911. 4 vols. in 2.

Arkheograficheskaia kommissiia [Archeographic Commission]. *Akty arkheograficheskoi ekspeditsii* [Acts of the archeographic expedition]. St. Petersburg, 1836. 4 vols.

———. *Akty istoricheskie* [Historical acts]. St. Petersburg, 1841–1842. 5 vols. Index, 1843.

———. *Dopolneniia k aktam istoricheskim* [Supplements to the historical acts]. St. Petersburg, 1846–1872. 12 vols. Index, 1875.

———. *Rozysknyia dela o Fedore Shaklovitom i ego soobshchnikakh* [Tribunal affairs regarding Feodor Shaklovityi and his accomplices]. St. Petersburg, 1884–1893. 4 vols.

———. *Russkaia istoricheskaia biblioteka* [Russian historical library]. St. Petersburg, 1875–1927. 39 vols.

Arkhiv inostrannoi kollegii [Archive of the Foreign College, later Ministry of Foreign Affairs]. *Sobranie gosudarstvennykh gramot i dogovorov* [Collection of state charters and treaties]. Edited by N. N. Bantysh-Kamenskii, A. F. Malinovskii, and others. Moscow, 1813–1894. 5 vols.

Chumikov, A. A., "Materialy dlia istorii russkoi torgovli" [Materials for the history of Russian trade], *Chteniia*, no. 4 (Oct.–Dec., 1875), Part 5, 160–164.

Forsten, Georgii V., comp. *Akty i pis'ma k istorii baltiiskago voprosa v XVI i XVII stoletiiakh* [Acts and letters relating to the history of the Baltic question in the XVI and XVII centuries]. St. Petersburg: Zapiski istoriko-filologicheskago fakul'teta imperatorskago S.-Peterburgskago universiteta, XXI, XXXI, 1889, 1893. 2 vols.

France. Commission des archives diplomatiques. *Recueil des instructions données aux ambassadeurs et ministres de France depuis les traités de Westphalie jusqu'à la revolution française: Russie.* Edited by Alfred Rambaud. Paris, 1890. 2 vols.

Martens, Feodor. *Recueil des traités et conventions conclus par la Russie avec les puissances étrangères.* St. Petersburg, 1874–1909. 15 vols.

Novikov, Nikolai, comp. *Drevniaia rossiiskaia vivliofika, soderzhashchaia v sebe: sobranie drevnostei rossiiskikh, po istorii, geografii i genealogii rossiiskiia kasaiushchikhsia* [Ancient Russian library, which contains a collection of Russian antiquities concerning history, geography, and genealogy]. Moscow, 1788–1791. 20 vols.

Sbornik dogovorov rossii s kitaem, 1689–1881 g.g. [A collection of treaties of Russia with China], a publication of the Ministry of Foreign Affairs. St. Petersburg, 1889.

Sobstvennaia ego imperatorskago velichestva kantseliariia [His Majesty's own office]. *Dvortsovye razriady* [Court registers]. St. Petersburg, 1850–1855. 4 vols.

———. *Knigi razriadnyia* [Register books]. St. Petersburg, 1853–1855. 4 vols.

———. *Pamiatniki diplomaticheskikh snoshenii* [Memorials of diplomatic relations]. St. Petersburg, 1851–1871. 10 vols.

———. *Polnoe sobranie zakonov rossiiskoi imperii s 1649 goda* [Complete collection of laws of the Russian Empire since 1649]. Series I. St. Petersburg, 1830. 44 vols.

Ta Ch'ing Shên-tsu Jên Huang-ti Shêng-hsun [Edicts and Proclamations of the Manchu Emperor, Kang-hsi], A.D. 1662–1721.
Extracts from this collection have been translated under the direction of Professor Robert J. Kerner, and have been used by special permission.
Tung Hua Lu, 26. K'ang Hsi, 28th year, 12th month, 13th day. January 23, 1690 [Report of Chinese negotiations of the Treaty of Nerchinsk, 1689]. Trans. by Chih Pei Sha under the direction of Professor R. J. Kerner; used by special permission of Professor Kerner.
Veselovskii, Nikolai I., comp. *Pamiatniki diplomaticheskikh i torgovykh snoshenii moskovskoi Rusi s Persiei* [Memorials of diplomatic and commercial relations of Muscovite Russia with Persia]. St. Petersburg, 1890–1898. 3 vols.
Viktorov, Aleksei G., ed. *Opisanie zapisnykh knig i bumag starinnykh dvortsovykh prikazov, 1584–1725 g.* [Description of the record books and papers of the old court prikazes, 1584–1725]. Moscow, 1877–1883. 2 vols.

Contemporary Accounts

Aleppo, Archdeacon Paul of. *Puteshestvie antiokhiiskago patriarkha Makariia v Rossiiu v polovine XVII v., opisannoe ego synom arkhidiakonom Pavlom Aleppskim* [Journey of Patriarch Macarius of Antioch in Russia in the middle of the XVII century]. *Chteniia*, no. 3 (1898), pp. 1–208.
Avvakum, the Archpriest. *Zhitie protopopa Avvakuma im samim napisannoe i drugie ego sochineniia* [Life of the Archpriest Avvakum by himself, and other of his writings]. Moscow, 1934.
———. *The Life of the Archpriest Avvakum by Himself.* Translated from the Seventeenth Century Russian by Jane Harrison and Hope Mirrlees, with a Preface by Prince D. S. Mirsky. London, 1924.
Collins, Samuel. "Nyneshnee sostoianie Rossii, izlozhennoe v pis'me k drugu zhivushchemu v Londone" [The present state of Russia, written in a letter to a friend living in London], *Chteniia*, no. 1 (Jan.–Mar., 1846), pt. 3, 1–47.
Fletcher, Giles, and Sir Jerome Horsey. *Russia at the Close of the Sixteenth Century. Comprising the treatise "Of the Russe Common Wealth" by Dr. Giles Fletcher, and the travels of Sir Jerome Horsey, knt....* Edited by Edward A. Bondon. London, 1856.
Gordon, Patrick. *Passages from the Diary of General Patrick Gordon of Auchleuchries.* Aberdeen, 1859.
———. *Tagebuch des Generals Patrick Gordon während seiner kriegsdienste unter den Schwenden und Polen, 1655–1661, und seines aufenthaltes in Russland, 1661–1699.* Moscow, 1849–1852. 3 vols.
Herberstein, Sigmund von, and others. *Notes upon Russia; being a translation of the earliest account of that country, entitled Rerum moscoviticarum commentarii, by the Baron Sigismund von Herberstein....* Translated and edited by R. H. Major. London, 1851–1852.
Jenkinson, Anthony, and others. *Early voyages and Travels to Russia and Persia. With account of the first intercourse of the English with Russia and Central Asia, by way of the Caspian Sea.* Edited by E. Delmar Morgan and C. H. Coote. London, 1886. 2 vols.

Kilburger, Johann P., "Kurzer Unterricht von dem russischen Handel, wie selbiger mit aus- und eingehenden Waaren 1674 durch ganz Russland getrieben worden," *Buschings Magazin für neue Historie und Geographie*, III (1769), 246–386.

Koch, Christopher von. "Pis'ma Khristofora fon Kokhen, shvedskago poslannika pri russkom dvore," in *Russkaia Starina*, vol. 23:3 (1878), 121–130. [Nine letters of Christopher von Koch, Swedish envoy at the Russian court.]

Korb, Johann George. "Dnevnik Ioanna Georga Korba vo vremia posol'stva Imperatora Leopol'da v Moskovskoe gosudarstvo v. 1689 g." [Diary of Johann George Korb at the time of the embassy of the Emperor Leopold to the Muscovite state in the year 1698], *Chteniia*, no. 3 (1867), 207–382.

Kotoshikhin, Grigorii. *O Rossii v tsarstvovanie Aleksiia Mikhailovicha* [Russia in the reign of Aleksei Mikhailovich]. 3d ed. St. Petersburg, 1884.

Krizhanich, Iurii. *Russkoe gosudarstvo v polovine XVII veka. Rukopis' vremen Tsaria Alekseia Mikhailovicha* [The Russian state in the middle of the XVII century]. Moscow, 1859.

Kurakin, F. A., *Arkhiv kniazia F. A. Kurakina, Bumagi kniazia Borisa Ivanovicha Kurakina* [Archives of Prince F. A. Kurakin, Papers of Prince Boris I. Kurakin, 1676–1727]. St. Petersburg, 1890–1902. 10 vols. in 8.

Le Comte, Louis D., *Nouveaux memoire sur l'état present de la Chine*. 2d ed. Paris, 1697. 2 vols.

Matveev, Artemon Sergievich. *Istoriia o nevinnom zatochenii blizhniago boiarina Artemona Sergievicha Matveeva*, ... [History regarding the unjust incarceration of the privy boyar Artemon Sergievich Matveev]. Moscow: Nikolai Novikov, 1785.

Mayerberg, Augustin von. *Puteshestvie v Moskoviiu barona Avgustina Maierberga i Goratsiia Vil'gel'ma Kal'vuchchi, poslov imperatora Leopol'da k tsariu i velikomu kniaziu Alekseiu Mikhailovichu v 1661 godu* [Journey to Muscovy of Baron Augustin Mayerberg and Horace William Kalvuchi, ambassadors of the Emperor Leopold to Tsar and Grand Prince Aleksei Mikhailovich in 1661]. Translated from the German by A. N. Shemiakin. Moscow, 1873. Also in *Chteniia*, no. 3 (July–Sept., 1873), pt. 4, 1–104; no. 4 (Oct.–Dec. 1873), pt. 4, 105–168; no. 1 (Jan.–Mar. 1874), pt. 4, 169–216.

Medvedev, Silvestr. "Sozertsanie kratkoe let 7190, 7191, i 7192, . . ."; other writings, edited by A. Prozorovskii, *Chteniia*, no. 4 (1894), 1–197. [Brief contemplation of the years 1682, 1683, and 1684.]; no. 4 (1896), 379–606.

Neuville, de la (pseudonym for Adrien Baillet, 1649–1706). "Zapiski de-la Nevillia o Moskovii" [Memoirs of de la Neuville about Muscovy], *Russkaia starina*, LXXI (Sept., 1891), 419–450; LXXII (Nov., 1891), 241–281.

Rhodes, Johann de. "Bedenken über den russischen Handel im Jahre 1653," *Beitrage zur kenntniss Russlands und seiner Geschichte*. Edited by G. Ewers and M. von Engelhardt. Dorpat, 1816–1818. Pp. 241–276. [Sammlung russischer Geschichte, X.]

Spafarii, N. G., "Pis'mo Nikolaia Spafariia k boiarinu Artamonu Sergeevichu Matveevu" [Letter of Nikolai Spafarii to boiarin Artemon Sergeevich Matveev], *Russkii Arkhiv*, no. 1 (1881), 52–57.

SECONDARY WORKS

Aleksandrov, A., *Polnyi russko-angliiskii slovar*, 4th ed. Berlin, n.d.

Andreevskii, I. E., *O namestnikakh, voevodakh i gubernatorakh* [About Namestniks, voevodas and governors]. St. Petersburg, 1864.

Aristov, Nikolai. *Moskovskiia smuty v pravlenie tsarevny Sofii Alekseevny* [Moscow rebellions in the regency of the Tsarevna Sophia Alekseevna]. Warsaw: iz Varshavskikh Universitetskikh Izvestii, 1871.

Ashley, M. P. *Financial and Commercial Policy under the Cromwellian Protectorate.* London, 1934.

Baddeley, John F., *Russia, Mongolia, China* ... London and New York, 1919. 2 vols.

Bain, R. Nisbet., *The First Romanovs (1613–1725).* London, 1905.

Bakhrushin, Sergei V., *Kazaki na Amure* [Cossacks on the Amur]. Leningrad, 1925.

———. *Ocherki po istorii kolonizatsii Sibirii v XVI i XVII vv.* Moscow, 1927–1928.

Bantysh-Kamenskii, Nikolai N. *Diplomaticheskoe sobranie del mezhdu rossiiskim i kitaiskim gosudarstvami s 1619 po 1792-i god* [Diplomatic collection of affairs between the Russian and Chinese states from 1619 to 1792]. Edited by B. M. Florinskii. Kazan, 1882.

———. *Illustrations de la Russie, ou galerie des personages les plus remarquables de cet empire sous le règne de Pierre-le-Grand.* Paris, 1829.

———. *Obzor vneshnikh snoshenii Rossii (po 1800 god)* ... [Survey of the foreign relations of Russia up to the year 1800]. Moscow, 1894–1902. 4 vols.

Barbour, Violet. *Capitalism in Amsterdam in the Seventeenth Century*, The Johns Hopkins Studies in Historical and Political Science, Series LXVII, no. 1. Baltimore, 1950.

Beliaev, I. D., "Sluzhilye liudi v moskovskom gosudarstve" [Serving men in the Muscovite state], *Moskovskii sbornik*, I (1852), 357–382.

Berezhkov, Mikhail N., *O torgovle Rusi s Gansoi do kontsa XVII veka* [The trade of Russia with the Hanse up to the end of the XVII century]. St. Petersburg, 1879.

Bergmann, Benjamin F. *Istoriia Petra Velikago.* St. Petersburg. 6 vols.

Bogoslovskii, M. M., *Petr I, Materialy dlia biografii* [Peter I, Materials for a biography], I. Moscow, 1940.

Bol'shaia Sovetskaya Entsiklopediia [Large Soviet Encyclopedia]. Moscow, 1926–1939, 65 vols. A special volume appeared in 1948: *Bol'shaia Sovetskaia Entsiklopediia: SSSR.* Moscow, 1948.

Bol'shakov, A. M. and Rozhkov, N. A., *Istoriia khoziaistva rossii v materialakh i dokumentakh* [A history of the economy of Russia in materials and documents], 3 vols. Leningrad, 1926.

Brückner, Alexander. *Beiträge zur Kulturgeschichte Russlands im XVII Jahrhundert* [Materials for the cultural history of Russia in the XVII century]. Leipzig, 1887.

———. "Das Kupfergeld in Russland, 1656–1663," in *Finanzgeschichtliche Studien.* Dorpat, 1867. Pp. 1–76.

Buxhoeveden, Sophia Baroness. *A Cavalier in Muscovy.* London, 1932. A popular biography of General Patrick Gordon based largely on Russian sources.

Cahen, Gaston. *Histoire des relations de la Russie avec la Chine sous Pierre le grand (1689–1730).* Paris, 1912.

Cambridge History of Poland from the origins to Sobieski (to 1696). Edited by W. F. Reddaway *et al.* Cambridge, England; Cambridge University Press, 1950.

Chulkov, M. *Istoricheskoe opisanie rossiiskoi kommertsii pri vsekh portakh i granitsakh ot drevnikh vremen do nyne nastoiashchego* [Historical description of Russian commerce at all ports and along all boundaries from ancient times to the present]. St. Petersburg and Moscow, 1781–1788. 21 vols.

Clark, G. N. *The Seventeenth Century*. 2d ed. London, 1947.
Conybeare, Frederick C., *Russian Dissenters*. Cambridge, Mass.; Harvard University Press, 1921.
Coxe, William. *Account of the Russian discoveries between Asia and America; to which are added, the conquest of Siberia, and the history of the transactions and commerce between Russia and China*. 2d ed., rev. London, 1780.
D'iakonov, Mikhail A. *Ocherki obshchestvennago i gosudarstevennago stroia drevnei Rusi* [Outlines of the social and political structure of old Russia]. 4th ed., rev. St. Petersburg, 1912.
Diplomaticheskii slovar [Diplomatic dictionary]. Edited by A. Ia. Vyshinskii *et al.* Moscow, 1948, 1950. 2 vols.
Dobrov, L. *Iuzhnoe slaviantsvo, Turtsiia, i sopernichestvo evropeiskikh pravitel'stv na Balkanskom poluostrove* [Southern Slavdom, Turkey, and the rivalry of European powers in the Balkan peninsula]. St. Petersburg, 1879.
Du Halde, Jean B. *Description géographique, historique, chronologique, politique, et physique de l'empire de la Chine et de la Tartarie chinoise*. 2d ed. The Hague, 1736. 4 vols.
Falke, Johannes. *Die Geschichte des deutschen Handels*. 2 vols. in 1. Leipzig, 1859.
Fedotov, G. P. *A Treasury of Russian Spirituality*. New York, 1948.
———. *The Russian Religious Mind*. Cambridge, Mass., 1947.
Fisher, Raymond H. *The Russian Fur Trade 1550–1700*. Berkeley: University of California Press, 1943.
Golder, Frank A. *Russian Expansion on the Pacific, 1641–1850*. . . . Cleveland, 1914.
Golubinskii, E. E., *Istoriia russkoi tserkvi* [History of the Russian Church]. Moscow, 1900–1917. 2 vols. in 4.
———. *O reforme v byte russkoi tserkvi* [Concerning reform in the life of the Russian Church]. Moscow, 1913.
Gradovskii, A. D. *Istoriia mestnago upravleniia v Rossii* [History of local government in Russia]. St. Petersburg, 1868.
Grass, K. K. *Die russischen Sekten*. Leipzig, 1905–1914. 3 vols.
Grekov, B. D., *Istoriia SSSR* (History of the USSR), I. Moscow, 1948.
Grushevskii, M. S. *A History of the Ukraine*. Edited by O. J. Fredericksen. New Haven, 1941.
———. *Ocherk istorii ukrainskago naroda* [Outline of the history of the Ukrainian people]. St. Petersburg, 1904.
Gudzy, N. K., *History of Early Russian Literature*. New York, 1949.
Grekov, B. D., *Krest'iane na rusi s drevneishikh vremen do XVII veka* [The Peasant in Rus from ancient times to the XVII century]. Moscow, 1946.
Hammer, Joseph von. *Histoire de l'empire Ottoman depuis son origine jusqu'à nos jours*. Paris, 1835–1843. 18 vols.
Hans, Nicholas. *History of Russian Educational Policy (1701–1917)*. London, 1931.
Iakovlev, A. *Kholopstvo i kholopy v moskovskom gosudarstve XVII v.* [Bondage and bondsmen in the Muscovite state of the XVII c.], I. Moscow, 1943.
Immich, Max. *Geschichte des Europäischen Staatensystems von 1660 bis 1789*. Munich and Berlin, 1905.
———. *Papst Innocenz XI, 1676–1689*. Berlin, 1900.
Jorga, N. *Geschichte des Osmanischen Reiches*. Gotha, 1908–1913. 5 vols.

Kapterev, N. F. *Kharakter otnoshenii Rossii k pravoslavnomu vostoku v XVI i XVII stoletiiakh* [Character of the relation of Russia to the Orthodox East in the XVI and XVII centuries]. 2d ed. Sergiev Posad, 1914.

———. *Patriarkh Nikon i Tsar' Aleksei Mikhailovich* [Patriarch Nikon and Tsar Aleksei Mikhailovich]. Sergiev Posad, 1909–1912. 2 vols.

Kapustin, M. N. *Diplomaticheskiia snosheniia Rossii s zapadnoiu Evropoiu vo vtoroi polovine XVII veka* [Diplomatic relations of Russia with Western Europe in the second half of the XVII century]. Moscow, 1852.

Karamzin, Nikolai M., *Istoriia gosudarstva rossiiskago* [History of the Russian state]. 2d ed. St. Petersburg, 1818–1829. 12 vols.

Kashin, V. N. *Torgovlia i torgovyi kapital v moskovskom gosudarstve* [Trade and commercial capital in the Muscovite state]. Leningrad, 1925.

Katanaev, G. E. *Zapadno-sibirskoe sluzhiloe kazachestvo i ego rol' v obsledovanii i zaniati russkimi Sibiri i Srednei Azii; Vypusk I, Konets shestnadtsatago i nachalo vos'mnadtsatago stoletii* [West-Siberian serving Cossacks and their role in the Russian exploration and occupation of Siberia and of Central Asia; Issue I, The end of the XVI and the beginning of the XVIII centuries]. St. Petersburg, 1908.

Kerner, Robert J., *The Urge to the Sea: The Course of Russian History* ... Berkeley: University of California Press, 1942.

Kizevetter, Aleksandr A., *Russkii sever* [Russian north]. Vologda, 1919.

Kliuchevskii, Vasilii. *History of Russia*. Translated by C. J. Hogarth. London and New York, 1911–1931. 5 vols.

———. *Kurs russkoi istorii* [Course of Russian history]. Moscow, 1937. 5 vols. American Council of Learned Societies Reprints, 1948.

———. "Russki Rubl'," *Opyty i issledovaniia* [Essays and investigations]. Petrograd, 1918.

———. *Skazaniia inostrantsev o moskovskom gosudarstve* [Foreign accounts about the Muscovite state]. New ed. Petrograd, 1918.

Korsak, Aleksandr K. *Istoriko-statisticheskoe obozrenie torgovykh snoshenii Rossii s Kitaem* [Historical-statistical survey of trade relations of Russia with China]. Kazan, 1857.

Kostomarov, N. I., *Ocherk domashnei zhizni i nravov velikorusskago naroda v XVI i XVII stoletiiakh* [Outline of the domestic life and character of the Great Russian People in the XVI and XVII centuries]. St. Petersburg, 1887.

———. *Ocherki torgovli moskovskago gosudarstva v XVI i XVII v.v.* [Outlines of the trade of the Muscovite state in the XVI and XVII centuries]. St. Petersburg, 1905.

———. *Russkaia istoriia v zhizneopisaniiakh eia glavneishikh deiatelei* [Russian history in the biographies of her foremost figures]. St. Petersburg, 1881.

Kotoshikhin, Gregory. *O Rossii v tsarstvovanie Aleksiia Mikhailovicha* [About Russia in the reign of Alexis Mikhailovich]. 3d ed. St. Petersburg, 1884.

Kulischer, Iosif M., *Istoriia russkogo narodnogo khoziaistva* [History of Russian national economy]. Moscow, 1925. 2 vols.

———. *Istoriia russkoi torgovli do XIX-go veka vkliuchitel'no* [History of Russian trade up to the XIX century]. Petrograd, 1923.

Kulischer, Iosif M., *Russische Wirtschaftsgeschichte*. Jena, 1925. [*Handbuch der Wirtschaftsgeschichte*]. Edited by George Brodnitz.

Kurts, B. G., *Russko-kitaiskie snosheniia v XVI, XVII i XVIII stoletiiakh* [Russo-Chinese relations in the XVI, XVII and XVIII centuries]. Kharkov, 1929. [Vseukrainskaia nauchnaia assotsiatsiia vostokovedeniia.]

Lantzeff, George V., *Siberia in the Seventeenth Century: A Study of the Colonial Administration*. Berkeley: University of California Press, 1943.

Lebedev, D. M., *Geografiia v Rossii XVII veka* [Geography in Russia of the Seventeenth Century]. Moscow, 1949.

Liubomirov, P. T., *Ocherki po istorii russkoi promyshlennosti XVII, XVIII i nachalo XIX veka* [Outlines of the history of Russian industry of the XVII, XVIII, and beginning of the XIX centuries]. Moscow, 1947.

Lodyzhenskii, Konstantin. *Istoriia russkago tamozhennago tarifa* [History of the Russian customs tariff]. St. Petersburg, 1886.

Lubimenko, Inna. *Les Relations commerciales et politiques de l'Angleterre avec la Russie avant Pierre le Grand*. Paris, 1933.

Lyashchenko, P. I., *Istoriia narodnogo khoziaistva SSSR* [History of the national economy of the USSR]. 2d ed. Moscow, 1947–1948.

———. *History of the National Economy of Russia to the 1917 Revolution*. New York, 1949.

Maikov, L. N., *Ocherki iz istorii russkoi literatury XVII i XVIII stoletii* [Outlines from the history of Russian literature of the XVII and XVIII centuries]. St. Petersburg, 1889.

Maslov, P., *Agrarnyi Vopros v Rossii* [The Agrarian Question in Russia]. St. Petersburg, 1905. 2 vols.

Mavor, James, *An Economic History of Russia*. 2d ed. London, 1925. 2 vols.

Mel'gunov, Petr P., *Ocherki po istorii russkoi torgovli IX–XVIII v.v.* [Outlines of the history of Russian trade from the 9th to the 18th centuries]. Moscow, 1905.

Miliukov, P. *Gosudarstvennoe khoziaistvo rossii v pervoi chetverti XVIII stoletiia i reforma Petra Velikago* [National economy of Russia in the first quarter of the XVIII c. and the reform of Peter the Great]. 2d ed. St. Petersburg, 1905.

———. *Ocherki po istorii russkoi kul'tury* [Outlines on the history of Russian culture]. 6th rev. ed. St. Petersburg, 1909–1912.

———. *Outlines of Russian Culture*. Edited by Michael Karpovich [translated by V. Ughet and E. Davis]. Philadelphia: University of Pennsylvania Press, 1942. 3 vols.

Moskva v ee proshlom i nastoiashchem [Moscow in its past and present]. Edited by D. N. Anuchin, M. M. Bogoslovskii, A. A. Kizevetter, P. N. Miliukov, V. V. Nechaev, S. F. Platonov, *et al.* Moscow, n.d. 12 vols.

Müller, Gerhard F. *Istoriia Sibiri*. St. Petersburg, 1750 and 1787; Moscow-Leningrad, 1937.

———. *Opisanie sibirskago tsarstva i vsekh proizshedshikh v nem del ot nachala, a osoblivo ot pokoreniia ego rossiiskoi derzhave po sii vremena* [Description of the Siberian kingdom and all events occurring there from the beginning, especially from its conquest by Russian power, up to these times]. 2d ed. St. Petersburg, 1787.

Ogorodnikov, V. I. *Ocherk istorii Sibiri do nachala XIX veka*. Irkutsk-Vladivostok, 1920–1924. 3 vols. in 2.

Palmer, William. *The Patriarch and the Tsar: Services of the Patriarch Nikon to the church and state of his country* ... London, 1873–1876. 5 vols.

Pavlovsky, Michel N. *Chinese-Russian Relations*. New York, 1949.

Pekarskii, P. *Nauka i literatura v Rossii pri Petre Velikom* [Science and literature in Russia at the time of Peter the Great]. St. Petersburg, 1862.

Platonov, S. F. *Lektsii po russkoi istorii* [Lectures on Russian history]. 5th ed. St. Petersburg, 1907.

——. *Moskva i zapad* [Moscow and the West]. Moscow, 1912.

Pokrovskii, Mikhail N. *History of Russia, from the earliest times to the rise of commercial capitalism*. Translated from Vol. 1 of the Russian edition and edited by J. D. Clarkson and M. R. M. Griffths. New York, 1931.

——. *Ocherk istorii russkoi kultury* [Outline of the history of Russian culture]. 5th ed. Petrograd, 1932. 2 vols.

——. *Russkaia istoriia s drevneishikh vremen* [History of Russia from the earliest times]. 3d ed. Moscow, 1920. 5 vols.

Pokrovskii, S. A. *Vneshniaia torgovlia i vneshniaia torgovaia politika rossii* [Foreign trade and the foreign trade policy of Russia]. Moscow, 1947.

Potemkin, V. O., ed. *Istoriia diplomatii* [History of diplomacy]. Edited by V. P. Potemkin, S. V. Bakhrushin, A. V. Efimov, E. A. Kosminskii, and others. Moscow, 1941.

Rozhkov, N. A. *Russkaia istoriia v sravnitel'no-istoricheskom osveshchenii* [Russian history in a comparative historical light]. Petrograd-Moscow, 1919–1926. 12 vols. in 10.

Schaff, P. *History of the Christian Church*. New York, 1858–1910. 7 vols.

See, Henri. *Modern Capitalism, Its Origin and Evolution*. New York, 1928.

Semenov, Aleksei V. *Izuchenie istoricheskikh svedenii o rossiiskoi vneshnei torgovle i promyshlennosti s poloviny XVII-go stoletiia po 1858 god* [Study of the historical knowledge about Russian foreign trade and industry from the middle of the XVII century to 1858]. St. Petersburg, 1859. 3 vols.

Semevskii, V. I. *Krest'ianskii vopros v Rossii* [The peasant problem in Russia]. St. Petersburg, 1888. 2 vols.

Shchebal'skii, Peter K. *Pravlenie Tsarevny Sofii* [Regency of the Tsarevna Sophia]. Moscow, 1856.

Shebunin, A. N. *Rossiia na blizhnem vostoke* [Russia in the Near East]. Leningrad, 1926.

Shmurlo, E. *Vostok i zapad v russkoi istorii* [East and West in Russian history]. Iur'ev, 1895.

Solov'ev, Sergei M. *Istoriia Rossii s drevneishikh vremen* [History of Russia from the earliest times]. 2d ed. St. Petersburg, 1894–1895. 29 vols. in 7.

Stählin, Karl, *Geschichte Russlands von dem Anfangen bis zur Gegenwart*. Berlin, 1923–1939. 4 vols. in 5.

Storch, Heinrich. *Historisch-statistiche gemälde des russischen Reichs am Ende des XVIII Jahrhunderts*. St. Petersburg and Leipzig, 1799–1803. 8 vols.

Smirnov, P., *Posadskie liudi i ikh klassoviia bor'ba do serediny XVII veka* [The townsmen and their class struggle up to the middle of the XVII c.], I. Moscow, 1947.

Strakhovsky, L. I., ed. *A Handbook of Slavic Studies*. Cambridge, Mass.: Harvard University Press, 1949.

Szujski, Joseph. *Dzieje polski podug ostatnich badań* [History of Poland according to the latest investigations]. Lvov, 1862–1866. 4 vols.

Tikhomirov, M. N., S. S. Dmitriev. *Istoriia SSSR* [History of Russia], I. Moscow, 1948.

Tri Veka [Three Centuries]. Edited by V. V. Kallash, V. N. Bochkarev, V. V. Nechaev, et al. Moscow, 1912–1913. 6 vols.

Trusevich, Kh. *Posol'skiia i torgovyia snosheniia Rossii s Kitaem (do XIX v.)* [Ambassadorial and commercial relations of Russia with China (to the XIX century)]. Moscow, 1882.

Tumanskii, Feodor V. *Sobranie raznykh zapisok i sochinenii . . . o zhizni i deianiiakh . . . Petra Velikago . . .* [Collection of various notes and works regarding the life and acts of Peter the Great]. St. Petersburg, 1787–1788. 4 vols.

Ustrialov, N. *Istoriia tsarstvovaniia Petra Velikago* [History of the reign of Peter the Great]. St. Petersburg, 1858–1863. 6 vols., vol. 5 not published.

Vvedenskii, Andrei A. *Torgovyi dom, XVI–XVII vekov* [A commercial house of the XVI–XVII centuries]. Leningrad, 1924.

Zabelin, I. *Domashnii byt russkikh tsarits v XVI i XVII st.* [Domestic life of the Russian tsaritsas in the XVI and XVII centuries]. Moscow, 1872.

———. *Istoriia goroda Moskvy* [History of the city of Moscow]. Moscow, 1904.

Zaozerskaia, E. I. *Manufaktura pri Petre I* [Manufacturing at the time of Peter I]. Leningrad, 1947.

Zaozerskii, A. I. *Tsar Aleksei Mikhailovich v svoem khoziaistve* [Tsar Alexis Mikhailovich and his economy]. Moscow, 1917.

Zhigarev, Sergei. *Russkaia politika v vostochnom voprose (eia istoriia v XVI–XIX vekakh, kriticheskaia otsenka i budushchiia zadachi)* [Russian policy in the Eastern question (its history in the 16th–19th centuries, a critical evaluation of it, and its future problems)]. Moscow, 1896. 2 vols.

Zinkeisen, Johann W. *Geschichte des Osmanischen Reiches in Europa*. Hamburg, 1840–1863. 7 vols.

Articles and Essays

Avvakum, Archpriest. "Selected Texts from The Book of Discourses." Translated by Henry Lanz in *The Slavonic Review*, VIII (Dec. 1929), 249–258.

Babushkina, G. K., "*Mezhdunarodnoe znachenie krymskikh pokhodov 1687 i 1689 gg.*," in *Istoricheskie zapiski*, no. 33 (1950), Moscow.

Bakhrushin, S. V. "Torgi gostia Nikitina v Sibiri i Kitae" [Trade of the Guest Nikitin in Siberia and China], *Trudy instituta istorii Rossiiskoi assotsiatsii nauchno—issledovatel'-skikh institutov obshchestvennykh nauk*, I (1926), 355–390. Moscow.

Bazilevich, K. V. "Krupnoe torgovoe predpriiatie v moskovskom gosudarstve v pervoi polovine XVII veka" [Great trade enterprises in the Muscovite state in the first half of the 17th century], *Izvestiia Akademii nauk, otdelenie obshchesvennykh nauk*, Series VIIb, no. 9 (1932), 783–811. Leningrad.

———. "K voprosu ob izuchenii tamozhennykh knig XVII v." [Toward the question of the study of the customs books of the 17th century], *Problemy istochnik-*

ovedeniia, II (1936), 71–90. [*Trudy istoriko-arkheograficheskogo instituta Akademii nauk SSSR*, XVII.]

———. "Tamozhennye knigi kak istochnik ekonomicheskoi istorii Rossii" [The customs books as a source of the economic history of Russia], *Problemy istochnikovedeniia*, I (1933), 110–129. [*Trudy istoriko-arkheograficheskogo instituta Akademiia nauk SSSR*, IX.]

Beliaev, I. D. "Zhiteli moskovskago gosudarstva" [Inhabitants of the Muscovite state], *Vremennik*, III (1849), 1–88. Moscow.

Belov, A. Evgenii. "Moskovskiia smuty v kontse XVII veka" [Moscow rebellions at the end of the 17th century], in the *Zh.M.N.P.*, CCXLIX (1887); 99–146; (1887); pt. 2, pp. 319–366). St. Petersburg.

Bogoiavlenskii, S. K. "Khovanshchina" ["The Khovanshchina,"] in *Akademiia Nauk SSSR, Institut Istorii, Istoricheskie Zapiski*, X (1941), 180–221. Moscow.

Bogoroditskii, D. "Ocherk torgovli Nizhniago-Novgoroda za XVI i XVII vv." [Outline of the trade of Nizhnii-Novgorod for the 16th and 17th centuries], *Kievskiia universitetskiia izvestiia*, LII (July, 1912), 1–24.

Brückner, A. G., "Patrick Gordon i ego dnevnik" [Patrick Gordon and his diary], in *Zh.M.N.P.*, vol. 194 (1877), 33–63, 149–173; vol. 197 (1878), 203–246.

Chowaniec, Czesław. "Z dziejow polityki Jana III na Bliskim Wschodzie, 1683–1686" [From the history of the policy of John III in the Orient, 1683–1686], *Kwartalnik historyczny* (1926), pp. 151–160.

Derzhavin, N. S. "Russkii absoliutizm i iuzhnoe slavianstvo" [Russian absolutism and southern slavdom], *Izvestiia Leningradskogo gosudarstvennogo universiteta*, no. 1 (1928), 43–82. Leningrad.

Forsten, G. V. "Datskie diplomaty pri Moskovskom dvore vo vtoroi polovine XVII veka" [Danish diplomats at the Muscovite court in the second half of the 17th century], *Zh.M.N.P.*, CCCLV (Sept. 1904), 110–181; CCCLVI (Nov. 1904), 67–101; CCCLVI (Dec. 1904), 291–374.

Frank V. S. "The Territorial Terms of the Sino-Russian Treaty of Nerchinsk, 1689," *Pacific Historical Review*, XVI (Aug. 1947), 265–270.

Gradovskii, A. D. "Obshchestvennye klassy i administrativnoe delenie Rossii do Petra I" [Classes of society and administrative partition of Russia to Peter I], *Zh.M.N.P.*, CXXXVIII (April, 1868), pt. 2, 1–91; (May), pt. 2, 405–436; (June), pt. 2, 631–698; CXXXIX (July), pt. 2, 72–241. St. Petersburg.

Hsuän-Ming Liu. "Russo-Chinese Relations up to the Treaty of Nerchinsk...," *Chinese Social and Political Science Review*..., 23 (Jan.–March, 1940), no. 4, 391–441.

Ikonnikov, A. "Tsaritsy i tsarevny iz doma Romanovykh" [Tsaritsas and tsarevnas of the Romanov house], *Russkii Arkhiv*, 3 (1913), 345–371.

"Istoricheskaia zapiska o kitaiiskoi granitse, sostavlennaia sovetnikom Troitsko-Savskago pogranichnago pravleniia Sychevskim, v 1846 godu" [Historical notes about the Chinese border, compiled by the counselor Sychevskii of the Troisko-Savskii frontier administration], *Chteniia*, no. 2 (1875), 1–292.

Iziumov, A. "Razmery russkoi torgovli XVII veka cherez Arkhangel'sk v sviazi s neobsledovannymi arkhivnymi istochnikami" [Size of Russian trade of the 17th century through Arkhangelsk in connection with unworked archival sources], *Izvestiia arkhangel'skago obshchestva izucheniia russkago obshchestva izucheniia russkago severa*, 6 (Mar. 15, 1912), 250–258.

Kurts, B. G. "Iz istorii torgovykh snoshenii Rossii s Kitaem v XVII st." [From the history of the commercial relations of Russia with China in the 17th century], *Novyi vostok*, XXIII–XXIV (1928), 331–340. Moscow.

Lappo-Danilevskii, A. A. "Inozemtsy v Rossii v tsarstvovanie Mikhaila Feodorovicha" [Foreigners in Russia in the reign of Mikhail Federovich], *Zh.M.N.P.*, XXLI (Sept. 1885), 66–106. St. Petersburg.

———. "Organizatsiia priamogo oblozheniia v moskovskom gosudarstve so vremen smuty do epokhi preobrazovanii" [Organization of direct taxation in the Muscovite state from the Time of Troubles to the era of reforms], *Zapiski istorikofilologicheskago fakul'teta S.-Peterburgskago universiteta* XXIII (1890), 1–557. St. Petersburg.

Lermontov, E., ed. "Pis'ma malorossiiskikh getmanov Ivana Samoilovicha i Ivana Mazepy" [Letters of the Hetmans of Little Russia, Ivan Samoilovich and Ivan Mazeppa], *Russkii Arkhiv*, 3 (1913), 372–406.

Liubimenko, Inna I. "Letters Illustrating the Relations of England and Russia in the Seventeenth Century," *English Historical Review*, XXXII (Jan., 1917), no. 125, 92–103.

———. "Les Marchands anglais en Russie au XVII-e siècle," *Revue historique*, CXLI (Sept.–Oct. 1922), no. 1, 1–39.

———. "The struggle of the Dutch with the English for the Russian market in the seventeenth century," *Transactions of the Royal Historical Society*, series 4, VII (1924), 27–51.

Malinovskii, A. F. "Bytnost' vo Frantsii u korolia Ludovika XIV polnomochnym poslom kniazia Iakova Fedorovicha Dolgorukogo" [Sojourn in France of Prince Iakov F. Dolgorukii as Plenipotentiary Envoy to the Court of King Louis XIV], *Trudy i Letopisi*, vol. 7 (1837), 86–114.

Melgunov, S. "Les Mouvements religieux et sociaux en Russie aux XVIIe–XVIIIe siècles," *Le Monde Slave*, no. 12 (Dec. 1926), 381–411. Paris.

Nevolin, K. A. "Upravlenie v Rossii ot Ioanna III do Petra Velikago" [Russian government from Ivan III to Peter the Great], *Zh.M.N.P.*, XLI (1844), no. 2, pt. v, 1–149. St. Petersburg.

Ogorodnikov, V. I., "Tuzemnoe i russkoe zemledelie na Amure v XVII v." [Native and Russian agriculture on the Amur in the XVII c.] *Trudy gosudastvennogo dal'nevostochnogo universiteta*, series III (1927), no. 4, 1–91. Vladivostok.

N. N. [Danilov?], "V. V. Golicyn bis zum staatsreich vom Mai 1682," *Jahrbücher für Geschichte Osteuropas*, I (1936), 1–33.

Pogodin, M. P. "Drevniaia russkaia torgovlia" [Early Russian trade], *Zh.M.N.P.*, XLVIII (1845), pt. 2, 81–132.

———. "Streletskie bunty" [Strel'tsy uprisings], in *Zh.M.N.P.*, CLXX (1873), 193–240; CLXXV (1874), 182–210.

Pomialovskii, M. "Sofiia Alekseevna," *Russkii biograficheski slovar'* [Russian Biographical Dictionary], XIX (1909), 126–143. St. Petersburg.

Potanin, Grigorii N. "Privoz i vyvoz tovarov goroda Tomska v polovine XVII stoletiia" [The import and export of goods at Tomsk in the middle of the 17th century], *Vestnik imperatorskago russkago geograficheskago obshchestva*, XXVII (1859), pt. 2, 125–144.

Prozorovskii, Alexander. "Sil'vestr Medvedev: Ego Zhizn' i deiatel'nost'" [Silvester Medvedev: His life and activities], *Chteniia*, nos. 3–4 (1896), 149–378, 379–606.

Rachel, Hugo. "Polnische handels- und zollverhältnisse im 16. bis 18, Jahrhundert," *Jahrbuch für gesetzgebung, verwaltung und volkswirtschaft im deutschen reich*, new series, XXXIII (1909), pt. 2, 41–62 [469–490].

Rowbotham, A. H. "The Jesuits at the Court of Peking," in *The Chinese Social and Political Science Review*, 5 (Dec. 1919), no. 4, 297–326.

Shmurlo, E. F. "From Krizanić to the Slavophils," *The Slavonic Review*, VI (Dec. 1927), 321–335.

———. "O zapiskakh Sil'vestra Medvedeva" [About the notes of Silvester Medvedev], in *Zh.M.N.P.*, CCLXII (1889), 335–369.

———. "Padenie tsarevny Sof'i" [Fall of the Tsarevna Sophia], *Zh.M.N.P.*, CCCIII (Jan. 1896), 38–95. St. Petersburg.

Smirnov, N. A., "Rossiia i Turtsiia v XVI–XVII vv." [Russia and Turkey in the XVI and XVII centuries], *Uchenye zapiski moskovskago universiteta*, no. 1 (1946), 3–159; no. 2 (1946), 3–173.

Spasskii, G. I. "Svedeniia russkikh o reke Amure v XVII stoletii" [Information of the Russians concerning the river Amur in the XVII century], *Vestnik imperatorskago russkago geograficheskago obshchestva*, VII (1853), pt. 2, 15–42. St. Petersburg.

Vernadskii, G. V. "Protiv solntsa" [Against the sun], *Russkaia mysl'*, XXXV (Jan., 1914), 56–79. Moscow, St. Petersburg.

———. "The expansion of Russia," *Transactions of the Connecticut Academy of Sciences*, XXXI (July 1933), 393–425.

Viskovatov, K. A., "Prizyv rossii na bor'bu s turtsiei, 1684 g." [The Calling of Russia into the struggle with Turkey, 1684], *Russkaia starina*, II (1878), 445–447.

Zabelin, I. E., "Russkiia posol'stva v Turtsiiu, v XVII-m stoletii" [Russian embassies in Turkey in the 17th century], *Russkaia Starina* (Sept. 1877), 1–33.

Zamyslovskii, Egor E. "Snosheniia Rossii s Pol'shei v tsarstvovanie Fedora Alekseevicha" [The relations of Russia with Poland in the reign of Feodor Alekseevich], in *Zh.M.N.P.*, CCLV (1888), 1–23, 464–485; CCLVI, 161–197.

———. "Snosheniia Rossii s Shvetsiei i Daniei v tsarstvovanie Fedora Alekseevich" [Russia's relations with Sweden and Denmark in the reign of Feodor Alekseevich], *Russkii vestnik*, no. 1 (Jan., 1889), 1–36.

INDEX

Academy of Moscow, 48, 56, 59–60, 147–148

Agriculture: right to land from tsar, 7; handicaps, 9–10; imperial farms, 9–10, 64; evacuation of labor from land, 9, 13; in late seventeenth century, 63–64; specialized crops, 64; land titles, 80–81

Albazin: established, 105; voevoda anticipates attack on, 107; Chinese attacks, 111–113; siege raised during negotiations, 113; Golovin to arrange settlement, 113 ff.; Treaty of Nerchinsk provides for destruction, 119

Alekseevna, Tsarevna Ekaterina, 27

Alexis Mikhailovich, Tsar, 3; 1648 outbreaks against, 8; reforms, 12; frontiers during reign, 12, 105; marriages, 15–16; son Peter, 15, 17; death, 17; income from estates, 64; reforms in trade, 67 ff.

Amur River: Russian penetrations to, 4, 105; subjugation of Daurians and Duchers along, 106; issue of struggle with China over control of, 106 ff.; Manchu dynasty militarizes, 106; ultimatum to Russians to abandon, 109; position of ostrogs near, 110–111

Andrusovo, Truce of: eastern Ukraine and Smolensk region incorporated into Russia by, 4, 88; renewed periodically, 88; Golitsyn protests violation of, 96; "Treaty of Eternal Peace" establishes terms as permanent, 98

Apraksina, Tsaritsa Martha Matveevna, 17

Arkhangel: trade, 73; port and pilot fees, 78–79, and decree of 1682, 79

Athanasius, Bishop of Kholmogory, 31

Austria: war with Turkey, 89, 94; siege of Vienna, 89, 90; second Crimean campaign, 135–136; secret negotiations with Turks, 136. *See also* Leopold I

Avvakum, Archpriest, 29

Belobodsky, Jan, 56
Bogoiavlenskii Monastery School, 59
Budget, 65, 82; income, 64–66 *passim*, 148

Census, 65, 81

China: issue of boundary between Russia and, 4, 105 ff.; commercial agreement by Treaty of Nerchinsk, 78; Russia's diplomatic relations with, 107; Moscow's interest in trade with, 107; asks Gantimur's extradition, 107; Spafarii as envoy to, 108 ff.; ultimatum to Russians to abandon Amur Valley, 109; Golitsyn seeks solution with, 110; attacks upon Albazin, 111–113; Golovin arranges settlement with, 113 ff.; Treaty of Nerchinsk, 119 ff.

Church, Russian Orthodox: clergy, 5, 44; religious controversy, 11, 13; compromise with government, 11; schism, 11, 30; 1682 conclave, 31–33; intellectual conflict, 43–44; education, 44; national church, 44; cultural tie with Byzantium, 44; Greek influences, 44–45; heretics apprehended, 53–55; debate on transubstantiation, 56, 59; in loan business, 70. *See also* Old Believers

Copper riots, 8, 70

Cossacks: personal freedom, 5; Razin's uprising, 9; question of loyalty, 94; Doroshenko's efforts, 94; Polish intrigues among, 94–96 *passim;* attack Chinese settlements in Amur Valley, 109; in Crimean campaign, 129

Crimean campaigns: Golitsyn consults Gordon about, 93; Russia agrees to siege, 100; preparations, 100, 127–128; Golitsyn commander in chief, 128; first campaign, 129; failure, 130; Sophia's attitude, 130–131; Golitsyn prepares for second campaign, 134–135, 136–137; Moscow's aims in Black Sea, 136; second campaign begins, 137–138; terms for truce, 138; return to Moscow, 138–139; Sophia glorifies, 140–141; results of, 145–146, 150

Customs: payment of dues in rubles, 67; government effort to stamp out corruption in, 74–75; barrier between Ukraine and Russia removed, 75, 148

Daurians and Duchers, 106
Dolgorukii, Prince Ia. F., 101, 102
Dolgorukii, Prince Iurii, 23–26 *passim*, 28

Duma, Boyar, 6; plans for Crimean campaign, 127; Peter attends sessions, 133–134

Economy, national: change from domestic, to trade capitalism, 63; Sophia's efforts to free Russia from dependence on West, 76; land titles, 80–81; Sophia's accomplishments, 81–82. *See also* Industry; Trade
Education: seventeenth-century controversy about, 44; church schools, 44; Greek influence, 45; school curricula, 45; Kievan scholars, 45, 46; Academy of Kiev, 46; Moscow schools, 47–48. *See also* Medvedev, Silvester
Eternal Peace, Treaty of, 98–99
Eurasia, 3

Far Eastern Question, 121, 149
Feodor Alekseevich, Tsar: reforms, 3, 12, 51; marriages, 15; accession, 17; question of successor, 17, 19, 20–21; political groups at court of, 17; Sophia's solicitude for, 19–20; death, 20; tax reforms, 66
Foreign relations: foreign-trade policy, 77; embassies to eleven capitals, 77, 78; 1667 truce with Poland, 85; special missions, 86; peace with Crimean khan reconfirmed in 1682, 86; principal designs with Europe, 87; Golitsyn's charters of amity, 89 ff.; European envoys to Moscow, 90; aid sought against Turks, 90 ff.; Treaty of Eternal Peace, 98–99; diplomatic missions to European countries, 100–104; with China, 105 ff., 121–122; Moscow's interests outlined to Leopold, 136. *See also* Crimean campaigns; Trade
Frontiers, 3–4; territorial ambitions of Moscow, 105

Gerbillon, John, 114, 116–117 *passim*
Golitsyn, Prince Vasilii V., 18; titles, 38; education, 50–51; abolishes mestnichestvo, 51; changes legal procedure, 51; interest in foreigners, 51–52; estimates of, 52; Moscow buildings, 52–53; arranges commercial relations, 77–78; charters of amity, 89; agrees to alliance against Turks, 91 ff.; meeting at Andrusovo, 91; reopens negotiations with Poles, 94; Sandyrev's report to, 95; receives Polish embassy, 96–97; insists on permanent cession of Kiev, 97; sends envoys to European countries, 101–104; seeks solution with China, 110; accepts risks in Polish alliance, 127; Crimean campaigns, 128 ff.; retires, 145; criminal charges against, 145; exiled, 145. *See also* Crimean campaigns
Golovin, Feodor A., 113–115 *passim*, 119; appraisal of, 121, 150
Gordon, Patrick, 51–52; Golitsyn consults about Crimean campaign, 91, 93, 127, 137; supports Peter, 135
Graeco-Latin School, 47; Joachim supports, 55
Graecophilism, 44–45, 48–49; and Medvedev's academy, 57 ff.; Likhudy's school, 59
Guests (*Gosti*), 70

Iazykov, Ivan Maksimovich, 17, 22, 25, 28
Illarion, Metropolitan of Suzdal, 35
Income. *See* Budget
Industry: trade competition from peasants, 8, 13, 74; craft, poorly organized, 63; iron, 76; textile, 76–77; serf, 148
Innocent XI, Pope: Austrians plan to seek help of, 93; aids Poles, 96; appeals to Moscow, 96
Istomin, Karion, 19, 50
Ivan Alekseevich, Tsarevich, 15; Miloslavskiis support, 18; Sophia supports, 21; announcement of death, 24–25; "first tsar," 27

Joachim, Patriarch: supports Naryshkins, 18, 143; summons Sobor, 20; proclaims Peter tsar, 21; Graecophilism, 30, 48–49; friendship with Sophia, 30; debate with Old Believers, 30; Strel'tsy ask intercession of, 35–36; opposes extirpation of Old Believers, 53; deserts Sophia, 143

Khovanskii, Prince Ivan: spokesman for Strel'tsy, 27; leader of schism, 29, 30, 32; opportunism, 29–32 *passim;* position in capital, 32; caters to Strel'tsy, 32; government action against, 33–35; executed, 35; son Andrei, 34, 35; son Ivan, 35

Index

Kiev: influence of, in education, 45–47 *passim*, 147; Academy of, 46; declining popularity, 47; question of loyalty of church, 47; church at, teaches Latin, 60; question of possession of, 97, 98. *See also* Ukraine

Kolomenskoe Village: copper riots, 8; government moves to, 33

Land titles: right to land from tsar, 7; amount assigned to serf, 9; irregularities in, 80; no primogeniture, 80; grants, 80; government investigation, 80–81; surveys under decree of 1683, 81

Law Code of 1649, 8, 51, 79

Leopold I: twenty-year alliance with Venice, 96; assurances to Russian embassy but no formal alliance, 103; war with France, 135–136; Russians fear separate peace with Turks and, 136

Likhachev family, 17, 22, 27; Semion, 17

Likhudy brothers, 58–60; open Graecophile school, 59

Lopukhina, Evdokia, 134, 135

Louis XIV: territorial designs, 86; intrigues in Turkey, 95; fails to achieve anti-Austrian bloc, 100; rebuffs Russian envoys, 100–102

Marcelis, Christian, 76

Maria Il'inishna [Miloslavskaia], Tsaritsa, 15

Matveev, Artemon, 15, 17, 22–26 *passim*

Mazeppa, Ivan, 130

Medvedev, Silvester: teaches Sophia, 19, 50; counsel in education, 38; Kievan scholar, 48; at Zaikonospasskii School, 48; friendship with Feodor and Sophia, 48 ff.; ambition for academy in Moscow, 48, 56 ff.; adherent of Latin trend, 50, 55; editor in Moscow Printing Office, 50; reopens Zaikonospasskii School, 55; refutes Belobodsky, 56; *Khleb Zhivotnyi*, 56; involved in question of transubstantiation, 56, 59; Charter of Privileges, 56–57; dismissed from Printing Office, 59; retires, 59

Merchants, 5, 67; special privileges, 7–8; classes, 70; Guests, 70; Guest and Cloth Hundreds, 70–71; lives of, 71–72. *See also* Trade

Mestnichestvo, 51, 127

Miloslavskii family, 15, 17; Maria Il'inishna, 15; third party at Feodor's court, 18; hope of Ivan's succession, 18; intrigue against Naryshkins, 23 ff.; Ivan, 15, 17, 18, 32–33

Monetary system, 69; counterfeiting, 70; loan business of Church, 70

Moscow: Strel'tsy outbreak, 25; flight from, 33; religious and political capital, 44; schools, 47–48; Academy of, 48, 56, 59–60, 147–148; description, 52; new buildings, 53; trade center, 72; influence in Europe, 104; political tension in, 142

Moscow, Treaty of, 100

Moscow Printing Office, 50; Graecophile school, 55

Naryshkin family: tsar marries Natalia, 15, 17; second party at Feodor's court, 17; candidate for succession, 17; Natalia leader of, 17; support among boyar families, 17–18; in power, 21–23; opposition to, 23; Strel'tsy search for, 26–27; returns to political activity during Crimean campaign, 132–133; accuses Shaklovityi, 139; at Troitsa-Sergeiev Monastery, 143; refuses to receive Sophia, 143; final struggle with Sophia, 144

Natalia Naryshkina, Tsaritsa: marries tsar, 15; son Peter, 15, 17; leader of Naryshkins, 17; departs from service for Feodor, 22; acquiesces to Strel'tsy, 23; on Red Staircase, 25; retires from Moscow with Peter, 37; role in 1689, 139; Sophia complains of enmity of, 142–143

Near Eastern Question, 94, 149, 150

Nikon, Patriarch: controversy over religious reforms, 11; needs support of government, 30; 1682 conclave with Old Believers, 31–32; Greek influence in Church, 44–45; founds Graeco-Latin School, 47

Nerchinsk: trade, 73; Treaty of, 78; negotiations for, 113 ff.; versions, 118; terms, 118–119; criticisms, 120 ff.; actual gains for Russia in, 121–122

Nikita Alekseev, 30–32 *passim*, 89

Old Believers: schism, 11–12, 13; migrations, 12; connections with Strel'tsy,

Old Believers (*Continued*)
29; debate with Church, 30–32; attitude of Sophia's government toward, 53, 60; decrees against, 53–55, 60; in Paleostrovski Monastery, 55

Ordyn-Nashchokin, Afanasii L., 48, 87

ostrog, 109

Ozerov, Lt. Col. Ivan, 24

Paulus, Abraham, 76

Peasants: many become serfs, 5; classifications, 5; 1667–1671 uprising, 9; communal production of goods, 8, 74; mass migrations, 9, 79–80, and Sophia's campaign for return of, 80. *See also* Serfs

Peter: Tsar Feodor's delight in, 15; possible successor to Feodor, 17, 19; popularity, 19, 21; proclaimed tsar, 21; accession, 21; "second tsar," 27; youth, 37 ff.; supporters, 131; demands information about state affairs, 133–134; marriage, 135; Gordon supports, 135; reproaches Golitsyn for military failures, 141, 145; flees to Troitsa-Sergeiev Monastery, 142; own campaign against Turks and Tatars, 145–146

Poland: 1682 peace with, 85; Truce of Andrusovo, 88; Golitsyn's charter of amity to, 89; intrigues with Cossacks, 88, 94–96 *passim;* enters Austria-Turkish struggle, 89, 94; mission to Moscow, 89; 1684 conference at Andrusovo, 91; demands, 91–92; breakdown of negotiations, 92, 93; Golitsyn reopens negotiations, 94; Innocent XI sends aid to, 96; new embassy to Moscow, 96–97; tension between Russia and, 96; question of Kiev, 97–98; Treaty of Eternal Peace, 98–99; principal gain in Treaty, 100; Golitsyn tries to enlarge alliance, 101–104; importance of alliance, 125; opposition to alliance, 127, 129; fear of separate peace between Turkey and, 127; calls for renewed struggle against Tatars, 134

Polotskii, Simeon, teaches Sophia, 19, 49–50; theologian, 46; founds Zaikonospasskii Monastery School, 47; mystery plays, 50

pomesties, 5

prikazes, 6, 7

Raspravnaia Palata, 6

Razin, Stenka, 9

Religion. *See* Church

Romanov family: patriarchal absolutism in seventeenth century, 6; marriages, 14–15; succession, 15; two branches, 15; prestige undermined, 28

Sambulov, Maxim, 21

Samoilovich, Hetman Ivan, 129–130

Sandyrev, Savva, 95, 96

Seniukov, N., 89

Serfs: peasants become, 5; bondage, 8; Law Code legalizes serfdom, 8; tiaglo-paying households become, 8; privately owned, 8–9; land for, 8–9; mass migrations, 9, 13, 79; Office sacked, 29, and serfs liberated, 29; Strel'tsy seek support from, 29; industry, 148

Shaklovityi, Feodor: Strel'tsy chief; 36–37, 38, 96–97; relations with Sophia, 133; suggests crowning Sophia, 133; in struggle with Naryshkins, 139 ff.; indicted and executed, 144

So E Tu, Prince, 114, 116–117

Sobieski, Jan: Russian envoy sent to, 89; letter and aid to Cossacks, 94; refuses peace with Turks, 95; weeps at Treaty of Eternal Peace, 99; defeat near Pruth River, 100; approves Russian plan of campaign, 100; enthusiasm for new drive against Turk, 121

Social structure, 5

Sophia Alekseevna, Tsarevna, 18–19; education, 19, 49–50; solicitude for Feodor, 19–20, 21–22; opposes Peter's accession, 21–22; intrigue to undermine Naryshkins, 23 ff.; assumes active political role, 26; liaison with supporters of Miloslavskiis, 26; regent, 27; interest in theology, 30; at conclave between Church and Old Believers, 32; moves government to Kolomenskoe Village, 33, to Troitsa-Sergeiev Monastery, 34; terms to Strel'tsy, 36; pacifies Strel'tsy, 36–37; appoints officials, 38; attitude toward Old Believers, 53–54, 60; toward other minorities, 54, 60; Medvedev requests academy, 56 ff.; interest in Western innovations, 60–61, 62, 82, 148; reforms: in customs collections, 74–75, in trade with Ukraine, 75, 82, in industry, 76–

Index

77, in foreign trade, 77–79, in peasant migrations, 79–80, in land titles, 80–81, in census, 81; Treaty of Eternal Peace, 98–99; orders preparations against Tatars, 100; strength in clergy and lesser nobles, 110; depicts success of Crimean campaigns, 130–131, 134, 139–144; royal prerogatives, 132; rumors about, 132–133; Shaklovityi's plan to crown, 133; second Crimean campaign, 139–144; political tension, 142; barricades self in Kremlin, 143; journey to Troitsa, 143; final struggle with Naryshkins, 144 ff.; retires to convent, 144; abilities, 147

Spafarii, Nikolai G., 108–109

Strel'tsy: decline in status, 10; morale, 10, 13; demands to Peter, 22–23; Natalia acquiesces, 23; intrigue against Naryshkins, 24; outbreak, 24–26; accept Ivan as tsarevich, 25; Khovanskii leader, 27, 29, 32, 34; ask joint rule, 27; unrest continues, 28 ff.; petition for approval and for pillar in Red Square, 28; called Court Infantry, 28; support from Old Believers, 29; sack Serf Office, 29; continued disorders, 32, 33; petition tsars for forgiveness, 35–36; Sophia's terms, 36; replaced as Kremlin guards, 36; Shaklovityi new commander, 36–37; 1682 threat of revolt, 110; Shaklovityi plot, 133; renewed unrest in 1688, 135; desertions to Peter, 144

Sweden: Ordin-Nashchokin's efforts against, 87; takes Karelia and Ingria from Russia, 87; campaign over, 87; Treaty of Kardis, 87; strained relations continue, 88; anti-Swedish coalition, 88; Golitsyn's charter of amity, 89

Tarbet, Matthew, 76

Tatars, Crimean: truce in 1681, 85, 86; tribute to khan, 86; renew raids into Ukraine, 100; raid Cossack settlements, 100; army against, 125; steppe fires, 129; 1688 raids, 134; Russia demands evacuation from Crimea, 136, and indemnity, 136; attack Kazan regiment, 137–138; negotiations, 138; Turks rely on, 146. *See also* Crimean campaigns

Taxes: seventeenth-century collection of, 7, 13, 65–66; copper riots, 8; on serfs, 9; hearth-money, 9; direct and indirect, 64; state collections, 65–66; reforms under Feodor, 66–67; collections by tax farmers abolished, 67; special, for Crimean campaign, 127

terem, 18

Textiles, 76–77

Timothy (monk), 55

Tolstoi, Peter and Ivan, 18, 21, 24

Trade: seventeenth-century restrictions, 7; controlled by "hundreds," 7; special privileges, 7–8, 63, 67; taxes on, 8; barter-money economy, 63; competition with peasant craftsmen, 8; state income from, 63; government efforts to free restrictions, 63; foreign traders, 63, 67; regional basis until 1650, 67; private prerogatives, 67; 1654 trade statute, 67; government supervision, 67; government monopolies, 68; localized, 68; concept of profit, 68–69; prices, 69; monetary system, 69; trade centers, 72–73; fairs, 73–74; peasant trade, 74; government policy in domestic, 74; abolition of customs barrier with Ukraine, 75; Western imports, 75; objects of Sophia's foreign trade policy, 77; markets, 77; Golitsyn arranges commercial relations, 77–78; Arkhangel abuses corrected, 78; under Treaty of Eternal Peace, 98; Russia's interest in China, 107; Treaty of Nerchinsk, 119, 122. *See also* Merchants

Troitsa-Sergeiev Monastery: leaders, 18; government moves to, 34; Strel'tsy representatives at, 36; Naryshkins at, 143; Sophia tries to see Peter at, 144

Tsars: character of office, 6; advisors, 6; country heritable property of, 7; altered relation with people, 12; tsaritsas, 14, and offices for family of, 15; daughters, 18. *See also* Alexis; Feodor; Ivan

Tsykler, Ivan, 24, 143

Turkey: danger from, 87; war between Austria and, 89; siege of Vienna, 89; crusading spirit against, 90; determination of Austria and Poland, 90; proposed military alliance against, 92 ff.; Sandyrev's report to Golitsyn, 95;

Turkey (*Continued*)
political reversals, 95–96; under Treaty of Eternal Peace, 98–99

Ukraine: under Truce of Andrusovo, 4; conflicts over Russia's control, 4; school system, 44; incorporation into Russia, 46; loyalty to Feodor disappointing, 46–47; customs barrier removed, 75; trade, 75; political gravitation toward Russia, 75; Russia's incorporation of large areas, 85, 88, and political repercussions, 88; Poland demands independent status for, 92; separatism, 94; Tatar raids into, 100. *See also* Kiev

Venetians, friendship with Russia, 104
voevodas, 6
Von Blumberg, Sebastian, 92–94 *passim*, 103
votchinas, 5

Zaikonospasskii Monastery School: Polotskii founds, 47; Feodor closes, 48; reopens under Medvedev, 55; Latin tendencies, 55, 147
Zaporozh'e, 3, 125
Zembotski, Jan, 89, 96
Zemskii Sobor, 20, 27

www.ingramcontent.com/pod-product-compliance
Lightning Source LLC
Chambersburg PA
CBHW021709230426
43668CB00008B/773